Advances in Pattern Recognition

For other titles published in this series, go to
http://www.springer.com/4205

Branislav Kisačanin · Shuvra S. Bhattacharyya
Sek Chai

Editors

Embedded Computer Vision

 Springer

Editors
Branislav Kisačanin, PhD
Texas Instruments
Dallas, TX, USA

Shuvra S. Bhattacharyya, PhD
University of Maryland
College Park, MD, USA

Sek Chai, PhD
Motorola
Schaumburg, IL, USA

Series editor
Professor Sameer Singh, PhD
Research School of Informatics, Loughborough University, Loughborough, UK

Advances in Pattern Recognition Series ISSN 1617-7916
ISBN 978-1-84996-776-1   e-ISBN 978-1-84800-304-0
DOI 10.1007/978-1-84800-304-0

British Library Cataloguing in Publication Data
A catalogue record for this book is available from the British Library

Springer Science+Business Media
springer.com

Foreword

As a graduate student at Ohio State in the mid-1970s, I inherited a unique computer vision laboratory from the doctoral research of previous students. They had designed and built an early frame-grabber to deliver digitized color video from a (very large) electronic video camera on a tripod to a mini-computer (sic) with a (huge!) disk drive—about the size of four washing machines. They had also designed a binary image array processor and programming language, complete with a user's guide, to facilitate designing software for this one-of-a-kind processor. The overall system enabled programmable real-time image processing at video rate for many operations.

I had the whole lab to myself. I designed software that detected an object in the field of view, tracked its movements in real time, and displayed a running description of the events in English. For example: *"An object has appeared in the upper right corner . . . It is moving down and to the left . . . Now the object is getting closer . . . The object moved out of sight to the left"*—about like that. The algorithms were simple, relying on a sufficient image intensity difference to separate the object from the background (a plain wall). From computer vision papers I had read, I knew that vision in general imaging conditions is much more sophisticated. But it worked, it was great fun, and I was hooked.

A lot has changed since! Dissertation after dissertation, the computer vision research community has contributed many new techniques to expand the scope and reliability of real-time computer vision systems. Cameras changed from analog to digital and became incredibly small. At the same time, computers shrank from mini-computers to workstations to personal computers to microprocessors to digital signal processors to programmable digital media systems on a chip. Disk drives became very small and are starting to give way to multi-gigabyte flash memories.

Many computer vision systems are so small and embedded in other systems that we don't even call them "computers" anymore. We call them automotive vision sensors, such as lane departure and blind spot warning sensors. We call them smart cameras and digital video recorders for video surveillance. We call them mobile phones (which happen to have embedded cameras and 5+ million lines of wide-ranging software), and so on.

Today that entire computer vision laboratory of the 1970s is upstaged by a battery-powered camera phone in my pocket.

So we are entering the age of "embedded vision." Like optical character recognition and industrial inspection (machine vision) applications previously became sufficiently useful and cost-effective to be economically important, diverse embedded vision applications are emerging now to make the world a safer and better place to live. We still have a lot of work to do!

In this book we look at some of the latest techniques from universities and companies poking outside the envelope of what we already knew how to build. We see emphasis on tackling important problems for society. We see engineers evaluating many of the trade-offs needed to design cost-effective systems for successful products. Should I use this processor or design my own? How many processors do I need? Which algorithm is sufficient for a given problem? Can I re-design my algorithm to use a fixed-point processor?

I see all of the chapters in this book as marking the embedded vision age. The lessons learned that the authors share will help many of us to build better vision systems, align new research with important needs, and deliver it all in extraordinarily small systems.

May 2008   *Bruce Flinchbaugh*
                                                              Dallas, TX

Preface

Embedded Computer Vision

We are witnessing a major shift in the way computer vision applications are implemented, even developed. The most obvious manifestation of this shift is in the platforms that computer vision algorithms are running on: from powerful workstations to embedded processors. As is often the case, this shift came about at the intersection of enabling technologies and market needs. In turn, a new discipline has emerged within the imaging/vision community to deal with the new challenges: embedded computer vision (ECV).

Building on synergistic advances over the past decades in computer vision algorithms, embedded processing architectures, integrated circuit technology, and electronic system design methodologies, ECV techniques are increasingly being deployed in a wide variety of important applications. They include high volume, cost-centric consumer applications, as well as accuracy- and performance-centric, mission-critical systems. For example, in the multi-billion dollar computer and video gaming industry, the Sony EyeToy^{TM} camera, which includes processing to detect color and motion, is reaching out to gamers to play without any other interfaces. Very soon, new camera-based games will detect body gestures based on movements of the hands, arms, and legs, to enhance the user experience. These games are built upon computer vision research on articulated body pose estimation and other kinds of motion capture analysis. As a prominent example outside of the gaming industry, the rapidly expanding medical imaging industry makes extensive use of ECV techniques to improve the accuracy of medical diagnoses, and to greatly reduce the side effects of surgical and diagnostic procedures.

Furthermore, ECV techniques can help address some of society's basic needs for safety and security. They are well suited for automated surveillance applications, which help to protect against malicious or otherwise unwanted intruders and activities, as well as for automotive safety applications, which aim to assist the driver and improve road safety.

Some well-established products and highly publicized technologies may be seen as early examples of ECV. Two examples are the optical mouse (which uses a hardware implementation of an optical flow algorithm), and NASA's Martian rovers, *Spirit* and *Opportunity* (which used computer vision on a processor of very limited capabilities during the landing, and which have a capability for vision-based self-navigation).

In addition to the rapidly increasing importance and variety of ECV applications, this domain of embedded systems warrants specialized focus because ECV applications have a number of distinguishing requirements compared to general-purpose systems and other embedded domains. For example, in low- to middle-end general-purpose systems, and in domains of embedded computing outside of ECV, performance requirements are often significantly lower than what we encounter in ECV. Cost and power consumption considerations are important for some areas of ECV, as they are in other areas of consumer electronics. However, in some areas of ECV, such as medical imaging and surveillance, considerations of real-time performance and accuracy dominate. Performance in turn is strongly related to considerations of buffering efficiency and memory management due to the large volumes of pixel data that must be processed in ECV systems. This convergence of high-volume, multidimensional data processing; real-time performance requirements; and complex trade-offs between achievable accuracy and performance gives rise to some of the key distinguishing aspects in the design and implementation of ECV systems. These aspects have also helped to influence the evolution of some of the major classes of embedded processing devices and platforms—including field programmable gate arrays (FPGAs), programmable digital signal processors (DSPs), graphics processing units (GPUs), and various kinds of heterogeneous embedded multiprocessor devices—that are relevant to the ECV domain.

Target Audience

This book is written for researchers, practitioners, and managers of innovation in the field of ECV. The researchers are those interested in advancing theory and application conception. For this audience, we present the state of the art of the field today, and provide insight about where major applications may go in the near future. The practitioners are those involved in the implementation, development, and deployment of products. For this audience, we provide the latest approaches and methodologies to designing on the different processing platforms for ECV. Lastly, the managers are those tasked with leading the product innovation in a corporation. For this audience, we provide an understanding of the technology so that necessary resources and competencies can be put in place to effectively develop a product based on computer vision.

For designers starting in this field, we provide in this book a historical perspective on early work in ECV that is a necessary foundation for their work. For those in the midst of development, we have compiled a list of recent research from industry and academia. In either case, we hope to give a well-rounded discussion of future developments in ECV, from implementation methodology to applications.

The book can also be used to provide an integrated collection of readings for specialized graduate courses or professionally oriented short courses on ECV. The book could, for example, help to complement a project-oriented emphasis in such a course with readings that would help to give a broader perspective on both the state of the art and evolution of the field.

Organization of the Book

Each chapter in this book is a stand-alone exposition of a particular topic. The chapters are grouped into three parts:

Part I: Introduction, which comprises three introductory chapters: one on hardware and architectures for ECV, another on design methodologies, and one that introduces the reader to video analytics, possibly the fastest growing area of application of ECV.

Part II: Advances in Embedded Computer Vision, which contains seven chapters on the state-of-the art developments in ECV. These chapters explore advantages of various architectures, develop high-level software frameworks, and develop algorithmic alternatives that are close in performance to standard approaches, yet computationally less expensive. We also learn about issues of implementation on a fixed-point processor, presented on an example of an automotive safety application.

Part III: Looking Ahead, which consists of three forward-looking chapters describing challenges in mobile environments, video analytics, and automotive safety applications.

Overview of Chapters

Each chapter mimics the organization of the book. They all provide introduction, results, and challenges, but to a different degree, depending on whether they were written for Part I, II, or III. Here is a summary of each chapter's contribution:

Part I: Introduction

- Chapter 1: *Hardware Considerations for Embedded Vision Systems* by Mathias Kölsch and Steven Butner. This chapter is a gentle introduction into the complicated world of processing architectures suitable for vision: DSPs, FPGAs, SoCs, ASICs, GPUs, and GPPs. The authors argue that in order to better understand the trade-offs involved in choosing the right architecture for a particular application, one needs to understand the entire *real-time vision pipeline*. Following the pipeline, they discuss all of its parts, tracing the information flow from photons on the front end to the high-level output produced by the system at the back end.

- Chapter 2: *Design Methodology for Embedded Computer Vision Systems* by Sankalita Saha and Shuvra S. Bhattacharyya. In this chapter the authors provide a broad overview of literature regarding design methodologies for embedded computer vision.
- Chapter 3: *We Can Watch It for You Wholesale* by Alan J. Lipton. In this chapter the reader is taken on a tour of one of the fastest growing application areas in embedded computer vision—video analytics. This chapter provides a rare insight into the commercial side of our field.

Part II: Advances in Embedded Computer Vision

- Chapter 4: *Using Robust Local Features on DSP-based Embedded Systems* by Clemens Arth, Christian Leistner, and Horst Bischof. In this chapter the authors present their work on robust local feature detectors and their suitability for embedded implementation. They also describe their embedded implementation on a DSP platform and their evaluation of feature detectors on camera calibration and object detection tasks.
- Chapter 5: *Benchmarks of Low-Level Vision Algorithms for DSP, FPGA, and Mobile PC Processors* by Daniel Baumgartner, Peter Roessler, Wilfried Kubinger, Christian Zinner, and Karina Ambrosch. This chapter provides a comparison of performance of several low-level vision kernels on three fundamentally different processing platforms: DSPs, FPGAs, and GPPs. The authors show the optimization details for each platform and share their experiences and conclusions.
- Chapter 6: *SAD-Based Stereo Matching Using FPGAs* by Karina Ambrosch, Martin Humenberger, Wilfried Kubinger, and Andreas Steininger. In this chapter we see an FPGA implementation of SAD-based stereo matching. The authors describe various trade-offs involved in their design and compare the performance to a desktop PC implementation based on OpenCV.
- Chapter 7: *Motion History Histograms for Human Action Recognition* by Hongying Meng, Nick Pears, Michael Freeman, and Chris Bailey. In this chapter we learn about the authors' work on human action recognition. In order to improve the performance of existing techniques and, at the same time, make these techniques more suitable for embedded implementation, the authors introduce novel features and demonstrate their advantages on a reconfigurable embedded system for gesture recognition.
- Chapter 8: *Embedded Real-Time Surveillance Using Multimodal Mean Background Modeling* by Senyo Apewokin, Brian Valentine, Dana Forsthoefel, Linda Wills, Scott Wills, and Antonio Gentile. In this chapter we learn about a new approach to background subtraction, that approaches the performance of mixture of Gaussians, while being much more suitable for embedded implementation. To complete the picture, the authors provide comparison of two different embedded PC implementations.
- Chapter 9: *Implementation Considerations for Automotive Vision Systems on a Fixed-Point DSP* by Zoran Nikolić. This chapter is an introduction to issues related to floating- to fixed-point conversion process. A practical approach to this

difficult problem is demonstrated on the case of an automotive safety application being implemented on a fixed-point DSP.

- Chapter 10: *Towards OpenVL: Improving Real-Time Performance of Computer Vision Applications* by Changsong Shen, James J. Little, and Sidney Fels. In this chapter the authors present their work on a unified software architecture, OpenVL, which addresses a variety of problems faced by designers of embedded vision systems, such as hardware acceleration, reusability, and scalability.

Part III: Looking Ahead

- Chapter 11: *Mobile Challenges for Embedded Computer Vision* by Sek Chai. In this chapter we learn about the usability and other requirements a new application idea must satisfy in order to become a "killer-app." The author discusses these issues on a particularly resource-constrained case of mobile devices such as camera phones. While being a great introduction into this emerging area, this chapter also provides many insights into the challenges to be solved in the future.
- Chapter 12: *Challenges in Video Analytics* by Nikhil Gagvani. This chapter is another rare insight into the area of video analytics, this one more on the forward looking side. We learn about what challenges lie ahead of this fast growing area, both technical and nontechnical.
- Chapter 13: *Challenges of Embedded Computer Vision in Automotive Safety Systems* by Yan Zhang, Arnab S. Dhua, Stephen J. Kiselewich, and William A. Bauson. This chapter provides a gentle introduction into the numerous techniques that will one day have to be implemented on an embedded platform in order to help improve automotive safety. The system described in this chapter sets the automotive performance standards and provides a number of challenges to all parts of the design process: algorithm developers may be able to find algorithmic alternatives that provide equal performance while being more suitable for embedded platforms; chip-makers may find good pointers on what their future chips will have to deal with; software developers may introduce new techniques for parallelization of multiple automotive applications sharing the same hardware resources.

All in all, this book offers the first comprehensive look into various issues facing developers of embedded vision systems. As Bruce Flinchbaugh declares in the Foreword to this book, "we are entering the age of embedded vision." This book is a very timely resource!

How This Book Came About

As organizers of the 2007 IEEE Workshop on ECV (ECVW 2007), we were acutely aware of the gap in the available literature. While the workshop has established itself as an annual event happening in conjunction with IEEE CVPR conferences, there is very little focused coverage of this topic elsewhere. An occasional short course and tutorial, a few scattered papers in journals and conferences, are certainly not satisfying the need for knowledge sharing in this area. That is why we decided to invite the contributors to the ECVW 2007 to expand their papers and turn them into the stand-alone chapters of Part II, and to invite our esteemed colleagues to share their experiences and visions for the future in Parts I and III.

Outlook

While this book covers a good representative cross section of ECV applications and techniques, there are many more applications that are not covered here, some of which may have significant social and business impact, and some not even conceptually feasible with today's technology.

In the following chapters, readers will find experts in the ECV field encouraging others to find, build, and develop further in this area because there are many application possibilities that have not yet been explored. For example, the recent successes in the DARPA Grand Challenge show the possibilities of autonomous vehicles, albeit the camera is currently supplemented with a myriad of other sensors such as radar and laser. In addition to the applications mentioned above, there are applications areas such as image/video manipulation (i.e., editing and labeling an album collection), and visual search (a search based on image shape and texture). In the near future, these applications may find their way into many camera devices, including the ubiquitous mobile handset. They are poised to make significant impact on how users interact and communicate with one another and with different kinds of electronic devices. The contributions in this book are therefore intended not only to provide in-depth information on the state of the art in specific, existing areas of ECV, but also to help promote the use of ECV techniques in new directions.

May 2008   *Branislav Kisačanin*
                                                                Plano, TX
                                                                Shuvra S. Bhattacharyya
                                                                College Park, MD
                                                                Sek Chai
                                                                Schaumburg, IL

Acknowledgements

The editors are grateful to the authors of the chapters in this book for their well-developed contributions and their dedicated cooperation in meeting the ambitious publishing schedule for the book. We are also grateful to the program committee members for ECVW 2007, who helped to review preliminary versions of some of these chapters, and provided valuable feedback for their further development. We would like also to thank the several other experts who helped to provide a thorough peer-review process, and ensure the quality and relevance of the chapters. The chapter authors themselves contributed significantly to this review process through an organization of cross-reviews among the different contributors.

We are grateful also to our Springer editor, Wayne Wheeler, for his help in launching this book project, and to our Springer editorial assistant, Catherine Brett, for her valuable guidance throughout the production process.

Contents

List of Contributors

Karina Ambrosch
Austrian Research Centers GmbH
Vienna, Austria

Senyo Apewokin
Georgia Institute of Technology
Atlanta, GA, USA
senyo@ece.gatech.edu

Clemens Arth
Graz University of Technology
Graz, Austria
arth@icg.tugraz.at

Chris Bailey
University of York
York, UK
chrisb@cs.york.ac.uk

Daniel Baumgartner
Austrian Research Centers GmbH
Vienna, Austria
daniel.baumgartner@arcs.ac.at

William A. Bauson
Delphi Electronics & Safety
Kokomo, IN, USA
william.a.bauson@delphi.com

Shuvra S. Bhattacharyya
University of Maryland
College Park, MD, USA
ssb@umd.edu

Horst Bischof
Graz University of Technology
Graz, Austria
bischof@icg.tugraz.at

Steven Butner
University of California
Santa Barbara, CA, USA
butner@ece.ucsb.edu

Sek Chai
Motorola
Schaumburg, IL, USA
sek.chai@motorola.com

Arnab S. Dhua
Delphi Electronics & Safety
Kokomo, IN, USA
arnab.s.dhua@delphi.com

Sidney S. Fels
University of British Columbia
Vancouver, BC, Canada
ssfels@ece.ubc.ca

Dana Forsthoefel
Georgia Institute of Technology
Atlanta, GA, USA
gtg771w@mail.gatech.edu

Michael Freeman
University of York
York, UK
mjf@cs.york.ac.uk

Nikhil Gagvani
Cernium Corporation
Reston, VA, USA
ngagvani@cernium.com

Antonio Gentile
University of Palermo
Palermo, Italy
gentile@unipa.it

Martin Humenberger
Austrian Research Centers GmbH
Vienna, Austria
martin.humenberger@arcs.ac.at

Branislav Kisačanin
Texas Instruments
Dallas, TX, USA
b.kisacanin@ti.com

Stephen J. Kiselewich
Delphi Electronics & Safety
Kokomo, IN, USA
stephen.j.kiselewich@delphi.com

Mathias Kölsch
Naval Postgraduate School
Monterey, CA, USA
kolsch@nps.edu

Wilfried Kubinger
Austrian Research Centers GmbH
Vienna, Austria
wilfried.kubinger@arcs.ac.at

Christian Leistner
Graz University of Technology
Graz, Austria
leistner@icg.tugraz.at

Alan J. Lipton
ObjectVideo
Reston, VA, USA
alipton@objectvideo.com

James J. Little
University of British Columbia
Vancouver, BC, Canada
little@cs.ubc.ca

Hongying Meng
University of Lincoln
Lincoln, UK
hmeng@lincoln.ac.uk

Zoran Nikolić
Texas Instruments
Houston, TX, USA
nikolicz@ti.com

Nick Pears
University of York
York, UK
nep@cs.york.ac.uk

Peter Roessler
University of Applied Sciences Technikum Wien
Vienna, Austria
peter.roessler@technikum-wien.at

Sankalita Saha
RIACS/NASA Ames Research Center
Moffett Field, CA, USA
ssaha@riacs.edu

Changsong Shen
University of British Columbia
Vancouver, BC, Canada
csshen@ece.ubc.ca

Andreas Steininger
Vienna University of Technology
Vienna, Austria
steininger@ecs.tuwien.ac.at

Brian Valentine
Georgia Institute of Technology
Atlanta, GA, USA
bvalent@ece.gatech.edu

Linda Wills
Georgia Institute of Technology
Atlanta, GA, USA
linda.wills@ece.gatech.edu

Scott Wills
Georgia Institute of Technology
Atlanta, GA, USA
scott.wills@ece.gatech.edu

Yan Zhang
Delphi Electronics & Safety
Kokomo, IN, USA
yan.zhang@delphi.com

Christian Zinner
Austrian Research Centers GmbH
Vienna, Austria
christian.zinner@arcs.ac.at

Part I
Introduction

Chapter 1
Hardware Considerations for Embedded Vision Systems

Mathias Kölsch and Steven Butner

Abstract Image processing and computer vision do not start with a frame in the frame buffer. Embedded vision systems need to consider the entire real-time vision pipeline from image acquisition to result output, including the operations that are to be performed on the images. This chapter gives an overview of this pipeline and the involved hardware components. It discusses several types of image sensors as well as their readout styles, speeds, and interface styles. Interconnection options for such sensors are presented with low-voltage differential signaling highlighted due to performance and prevalence. Typical image operations are overviewed in the context of an embedded system containing one or more sensors and their interfaces. Several hardware storage and processing components (including DSPs, various system-on-a-chip combinations, FPGAs, GPUs, and memories) are explained as building blocks from which a vision system might be realized. Component-to-component relationships, data and control pathways, and signaling methods between and among these components are discussed, and specific organizational approaches are compared and contrasted.

1.1 The Real-Time Computer Vision Pipeline

You might be faced with the task of building an embedded system that performs one or multiple computer vision tasks. One of your first and hardest questions would probably be what hardware components you should use. There is a bewildering array of available processing architectures, such as digital signal processors (DSPs), field-programmable gate arrays (FPGAs), systems on chip (SoCs), application-specific

Mathias Kölsch
Naval Postgraduate School, Monterey, CA, USA, e-mail: kolsch@nps.edu

Steven Butner
University of California, Santa Barbara, CA, USA, e-mail: butner@ece.ucsb.edu

integrated circuits (ASICs), general-purpose processors (GPPs), and graphic processing units (GPUs), not to mention interconnects and memory blocks. This chapter presents the choices and tradeoffs between these processing units, along with suggestions for interfaces and component layout. To fully appreciate the challenges and potentials for digital vision systems, we present a complete picture of the real-time digital computer vision pipeline, from the photon to the photodiode, from the charge accumulator to the readout circuitry, from the sensor chip over the wire to the processing chip and board, detailing data flow and onboard data storage, and how sensor parameters are controlled.

Only through complete understanding of this pipeline and of the steps involved at every stage can we fully optimize the process, insert processing and storage at optimal places, and cull data before it incurs unnecessary computational cost. The goal is to achieve the best trade-off between several conflicting goals, dependent variables that embedded systems typically are concerned with:

- Application performance
- Speed
- Power dissipation
- System size

We believe that such a complete and integrated view of hardware and software of computer vision has often been overlooked and hence its potential has not been fully achieved due to the traditionally distinct communities of electrical (hardware) engineers and computer scientists.

What is considered an embedded system? An embedded computer comprises one or multiple processors that serve a dedicated purpose in a larger system, for example, video processors in television sets and DVD players. Their advantages lie in their suitability to the task, resulting in greater speed, lower power consumption, reduced cost, and faster startup than general-purpose systems. Embedded systems are particularly well suited to process streams of data at high speeds with fairly small programs. Dedicated buses can be used to avoid competing with other processing needs. Hardware accelerators can process data in a highly parallel fashion, with blazing speeds, and without interfering with other CPU tasks.

The form factors of embedded computers are ever shrinking, with more and more components being integrated on the same chip. A strong indicator for the increasing importance of systems for real-time data analysis are: the integration of multimedia capabilities such as analog-to-digital converters, the integration of signal processing capabilities, and the implementation of instruction sets foreseeing a need for such processing. With the help of these highly optimized processing capabilities, advanced computer vision applications are already finding their way into consumer products.

The layout of this chapter largely mirrors the computer vision pipeline, from photon to embedded computer vision output. First, we take a look at digital image sensors, followed by a description of interfaces between sensors and processing chips in Section 1.3. Next, we briefly discuss typical image operations and their characteristics before covering the various hardware components in the main section. How these components are organized on a processing board is the topic of Section 1.6. In our conclusions we give a brief outlook on the field and summarize the chapter's main points.

1.2 Sensors

Many of the choices for how digital image sensors work and much of the terminology used are historical. Their first applications were to replace analog sensors, that is, image sensors with an analog output signal. To understand today's sensors, a brief look at these historical choices helps.

1.2.1 Sensor History

The history goes back to 1897 when Ferdinand Braun, a German physicist, invented what came to be known as the cathode ray tube (CRT, Braun tube, "Braunsche Röhre"). First used for oscilloscopes, this technology eventually developed into television sets where an electron beam is "scanned" across a light-emissive surface, producing an image.

Various methods for *sensing* video images electronically have been developed since the 1920s. In the 1960s, the vidicon cathode ray tube became the standard in television recording up through the 1990s. This tube is also built on the principle of CRTs, very similar to television sets, only that the electron beam measures the amount of photons that hit the photoconductive layer in the image plane instead of lighting up a phosphorous emissive layer as in a TV set.

The readout order of lines in vidicon tubes is synchronized with the transmission signal (NTSC, PAL, or SECAM) and the display scan order of TV tubes. For example, the NTSC signal has 525 scan lines of which 486 are visible. A frame is split into two fields, the first field containing all even lines and the second field all odd lines. The reasons for interlaced video transmission and display were bandwidth limitations and picture quality, which depended on light-emissive phosphors. Within a line, pixels are transmitted sequentially from left to right. Synchronization pulses (low voltage levels) are inserted after every line and after every field.

Photoelectric detectors in digital image sensors work surprisingly similar. They also exploit the *photoeffect*, which turns a photon into an electric charge. Upon striking a photodetector, a photon excites an electron that then jumps from one semiconductor band to another, making a hole in one and adding a surplus electron to the other. For charge measurement, the hole is filled and the electron is pulled off by a current that can be measured in a voltage differential. Called the photodiode, photodetector, or photoactive region, these components can be implemented in MOS technology or in TFT technology.

1.2.2 The Charge-Coupled Device

The charge-coupled device (CCD) was invented around 1970. As shown in Fig.1.1, a CCD transfers the acquired analog charge (electrons) from one photodetector through other photodetectors across the chip. This operation is called a "shift," making CCDs a type of shift register. A CCD uses a MOS photodetector for photon acquisition and for readout tasks. Note that the charge is transfered without creating a voltage. Only in the readout stage does the charge get converted into a voltage.

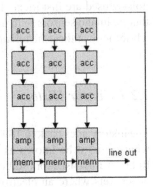

Fig. 1.1 Charge readout from a CCD, a shift register.

There are three types of readout architectures: (1) Full-frame devices consist of large charge accumulators and minimal additional circuitry around every pixel. They require a mechanical shutter because the entire sensor area is exposed to the light and would continue to accumulate charge as the image is transfered out. (2) Frame transfer devices have half the CCD covered with an opaque material. The electronic shutter moves the charge "under cover" and slowly reads it out. Full-frame and frame transfer devices have the disadvantages that the charge needs to be shifted down the entire sensor array. Pixels in the first rows hence incur a larger amount of readout noise. To obtain interlaced output from a frame device, every other row must be discarded before data serialization. This gives these devices different characteristics than vidicon tubes of comparable specs, namely shorter integration time and reduced light sensitivity. (3) Interline transfer devices have storage circuitry at every other line or column, avoiding this large shift noise accumulation and allowing for fast readout. Interline transfer devices can be read out in arbitrary row order, for example, in interlaced order. This makes them particularly well suited for analog output.

The charge accumulators are depleted on readout. Trace remaining charge is considered reset noise for a CCD. In systems without a mechanical shutter, charge accumulates in the photodetectors during the readout stage. To achieve a shorter exposure time, this charge needs to be depleted before exposure starts. This is accomplished by initiating a partial readout that depletes the charge but does not process the measured quantity.

A disadvantage of CCD sensors is that the photonic element can overflow: too bright a light source causes charge to spill into neighboring accumulators which, in turn, causes bright blobs called blooming or, during readout, vertical lines called smear.

Fig. 1.2 shows the pixel flow from photon to digital signal. This is a generalized pipeline, applicable to both CCD and CMOS sensors with the noted differences.

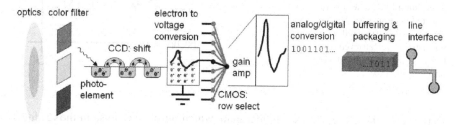

Fig. 1.2 Overview of pixel acquisition in a sensor. Only a CCD performs the electron shift function, whereas a CMOS sensor converts electrons into voltage on a per-pixel basis. Only the CMOS sensor has a row-select function.

1.2.3 CMOS Sensors

The so-called *active pixel sensor* (APS) dedicates circuitry to every pixel to convert the electric charge into voltage. This type of image sensor is typically manufactured with CMOS transistors, hence its more common name "CMOS sensor." Every pixel has its own amplifier, typically three or more transistors (see Fig. 1.3). Therefore, an important issue with CMOS imagers is the pixel fill factor—that is, how much of the space that one pixel takes up is dedicated to photon acquisition and how much is spent on related hardware such as charge conversion, amplification, and readout circuitry. Good fill factors for CMOS sensors are 50% or above, but they can be much lower. A CCD has close to a 100% fill factor. Multilayered sensor arrays, called "stacked dies" or 3D VLSI as opposed to planar VLSI technology, can offset some of these disadvantages and achieve higher fill factors for CMOS sensors.

CMOS sensors typically consume less power than a CCD, have less image lag, and can be manufactured on cheaper and more available semiconductor fabrication lines. Unlike CCDs, CMOS sensors can combine both the image sensor function and image processing functions within the same integrated circuit. CMOS sensors also permit readout in an arbitrary fashion, some even provide for per-pixel access, but most support windowing, meaning readout of an arbitrary rectangular region. This capability can be used to achieve higher frame rates than full-frame readout. Naturally, a frame rate of, for example, 500 Hz reduces the exposure time to 2 ms at best, hence limiting the amount of photons that can be acquired in such a short time.

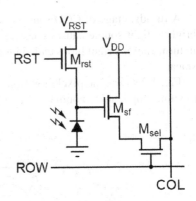

Fig. 1.3 Schematic of one pixel of a CMOS active pixel sensor. The photodetector accumulates the charge that can be measured with the transistor M_{sf}. The measurement is read out on the column line if the row is selected via transistor M_{sel}. A charge reset is triggered with transistor M_{rst}. Retrieved from http://commons.wikimedia.org on 17 April 2008.

Dark scenes therefore require a higher gain, which introduces noise in the readout process.

Similar to a memory chip, there is a criss-cross grid of readout lines running across the image array. The row-select lines select one of the array rows. The column lines transport the pixels' activation down to the readout electronics, typically an amplifier followed by a multiplexer. In contrast to CCDs, the activation in a CMOS is voltage rather than charge, and it is transported to the readout directly, without requiring a shift through all pixels in the same row below the current pixel.

For a more detailed discussion of active pixel sensors see, for example, Eric Fossum's articles [3, 6]. Dave Litwiller at DALSA has some excellent articles comparing CCDs and CMOS sensors [4, 5], accessible via their web site at [11].

1.2.4 Readout and Control

Image sensor control and pixel readout is facilitated with on-chip logic. This circuitry drives the reset signal lines, initiates the charge transfer, chooses one row-select line at a time, sets the gain level, packages the outgoing pixel data and responds to input control commands. These commands are specified in protocols and sent over a control bus to the sensor (see the next section). The sensor reacts by setting control registers accordingly. Its logic reads out the registers regularly, for example, during the reset cycle, so that the next frame that is to be captured conforms to parameters such as exposure, windowing, and gain. Permissible times for the arrival of control packets and their synchronization with frame readout differ between the various manufacturers and from chip to chip.

Many sensors, particularly the newer CMOS sensors, permit extensive readout customization, including selection of a contiguous subset of rows, windowing (select rows and columns) and image flipping (reverse order of rows and/or columns). Note that when reading out a partial image from a sensor with color filters on the photoelements pixels, two or more lines must be read out to accurately reconstruct the color information for one line since (e.g., for a Bayer pattern) the red and blue pixel filters are applied on alternating lines.

The next section discusses the physical connection and the protocol used for communication between the sensor chip and the control and image processing hardware.

1.3 Interconnects to Sensors

When considering the design features associated with the interconnection of an image sensor to a host computer, several issues are critical.

- interface width—should the interface be parallel or serial?
- direction of flow—should the interface be unidirectional or bidirectional?
- power—will it be possible to power the imager through the interconnect?
- distance—what is the maximum cable length?
- connectors, cabling, and signal integrity—what connectors are available and which should be used?

With an imager delivering 10–14 bit pixels at rates in the range of 50 million pixels per second and considering power limitations and signal integrity, it seems most appropriate to choose a *serial* interface that uses low-voltage differential signaling (LVDS). The availability of high-quality LVDS transceivers intended for PCI-Express and other high-speed serial interfaces, particularly those with integrated serializer/deserializer (SERDES) circuits makes this part of the design rather straightforward.

To further leverage the computer industry's developments and standards in the area of high-performance serial interfaces it seems prudent to incorporate pre-built cables and connectors that were designed for the IEEE-1394 (aka FireWire) standard. The FireWire cables and connectors contain six wires: two to supply DC power across the interface and two twisted pairs to support bi-directional differential signaling.

Fig. 1.4 shows the structure of typical link hardware. Note that in addition to the two differential pairs shown in the cabling, there are two power wires as well. This facilitates the delivery of DC power to the imager subsystem. Though the principal flow is from imager to computer, the LVDS transceiver interface is bidirectional so as to provide for control and initialization of the imager. Most imagers have control interfaces such as I^{2}C (Inter-Integrated Circuit bus, pronounced i-squared-c).

The parallel sides of the link interface (i.e., within the imager subsystem and within the processing subsystem) each have 16-bit width. Using an imager with a pixel width close to but less than the parallel link interface width facilitates efficient packetization of image pixel data versus command responses and other control-related data. With a 12-bit imager, a possible packet layout is shown in Fig. 1.5. In this setup a small CPLD located in the image sensor subsystem interacts with

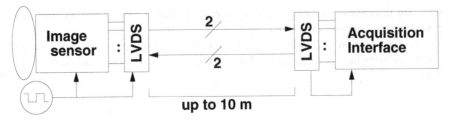

Fig. 1.4 Structure of a typical link. Power connections are not shown.

the LVDS physical layer transceivers to packetize and de-packetize the data flowing
across the link.

Fig. 1.5 shows a candidate packet layout that supports imager pixel widths up to
14 bits. In the given packet layout there would be up to 4 packet types and there
could be different layouts for the incoming vs. outgoing data directions if needed.
The two packet types detailed in Fig. 1.5 would be appropriate for the host-to-imager
direction, providing 16-bit register data to be written into the imager register number
given. Note that the 16-bit data field has been split between two packet types with
14 bits in the (0,1) packet type and the two highest-order bits in the (0,0) packet
type. Such a layout facilitates easy packet decoding and multiplexing in a CPLD or
FPGA located on each end of the cable. In the opposite direction (i.e., imager-to-
host), packets could similarly be defined to support either up to 14-bits of pixel data
per 16-bit packet type or, if needed, a two-type combination with 16 bits of pixel
data together with imager status.

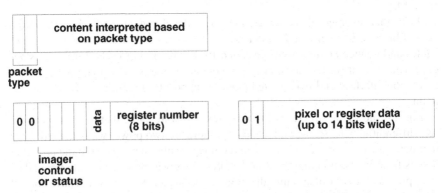

Fig. 1.5 Candidate packet layouts using 2-bit packet type code in every 16-bit packet.

Using readily-available transceivers with LVDS signaling rates of 1.5 Gbps, it
is possible to support image pixel rates in excess of 50 million pixels per second.
As shown in Fig. 1.4, the transceivers utilize a local clock reference for transmitter
timing while deriving all receive timing from the incoming differential data channel.
In order to make clock recovery possible, all link data is encoded using an 8B/10B

line code [10]. This code is used for DC balance; it keeps the running disparity between the number of 1's vs. 0's no greater than two and guarantees no occurrence of five or more consecutive 0's or 1's in the entire frame. Each 8-bit data byte is encoded using 10 bits on the line with the extra code space used to achieve DC balance and with certain reserved code words defined to facilitate link management.

1.4 Image Operations

Before discussing the various types of processing hardware available for embedded vision systems, it helps to keep the objective in mind: processing image data with different operations and algorithms. This section addresses the question of how well certain operations are suited to embedded implementation.

An algorithm's speed performance on a DSP or FPGA often differs vastly from its performance on a general-purpose processor (GPP/CPU). The following algorithm characteristics lend themselves to execution in special hardware:

- data streams and sequential data access, as opposed to random access,
- multiple, largely independent streams of data,
- high data rates with few instructions per datum,
- a fixed data packet size, or a size below a tight bound,
- stream computations that can be broken up into pipeline stages, that is, the same (possible parameterized) set of computations can be applied to lots of data,
- the operations require only fixed-precision values (integer or fixed-point fractions),
- algorithms are parallelizable at instruction and module level, that is, little between-stream communication is necessary.

Desirable operations to be executed on high-performance hardware in the embedded system are typically lower-level functions that pre-process the image for further high-level analysis and might include:

- convolution/cross correlation, 2D and separable filters (Gaussian, wavelets etc.),
- subsampling at regular intervals,
- Canny edge detection,
- sum of absolute differences (SAD) of an image region of interest (ROI) with a stored patch,
- edge orientation and histogram calculation,
- integral image calculation,
- online calculation of global or ROI statistics: min, max, mean, or variance, higher-order moments,
- online Bayer sample pattern conversion into RGB, HSV, GRAY, etc. (depending on camera color pattern this requires a one-line buffer)
- online color space conversion (RGB2GRAY, RGB2HSV).

An "online" algorithm is able to calculate its result even though only a subset of the data is available at any one time, commonly referred to as a window into the data that is slid over the entire data. This is easily possible for simple operations such as the minimum or mean value, but only possible through approximation for median calculation, for example.

Table 1.1 shows common operations and the complexity of their data access patterns. For best speed and memory performance, the algorithm accesses only a single pixel at any one time, and the sequence of pixel accesses is know beforehand. On the opposite end of the spectrum are algorithms that require large amounts of data for the calculation of one result and their data access pattern is not known before hand, for example, when it is dynamically dependent on the result of previous calculations. Hence, the speed and memory complexity of the methods mentioned in Table 1.1 increases from top to bottom. Some algorithms create a data space that is accessed in subsequent passes, rather than accessing the image space multiple times.

1.5 Hardware Components

A perusal of available commercial building blocks yields a rich selection of general- and special-purpose microprocessors, field-programmable arrays, and memories from which the processing unit of an embedded vision system can be realized. Recent experience by the authors with DSPs and FPGAs has yielded some designs that have proven to be very robust, while at the same time flexible and highly adaptive. We briefly describe the main characteristics of hardware components in the following sections, from rather general-purpose to system-specific chips.

1.5.1 Digital Signal Processors

A digital signal processor, or DSP, is similar to a general-purpose processor (GPP) in many aspects. It has fixed logic, that is, the connections between logic gates cannot be changed. It provides a fixed instruction set (ISA) to the programmer, and it expects a program in this ISA that it will then execute in a sequential manner (as opposed to dataflow-driven). Most DSP ISAs exhibit a similar structure as GPP ISAs, complete with arithmetic and logic instructions, memory access, registers, control flow, and so on.

Distinguishing it from general-purpose CPUs, a DSP's instruction set is optimized for matrix operations, particularly multiplication and accumulation (MAC), traditionally in fixed-point arithmetic, but increasingly also for double-precision floating point arithmetic. DSPs exhibit deep pipelining and thus expect a very linear program flow with infrequent conditional jumps. They provide for SIMD (single instruction, multiple data) instructions, assuming a large amount of data that has to be processed by the same, relatively simple, mathematical program. SIMD programs exploit instruction-level parallelism, executing the exact same instruction simultane-

Table 1.1 Data Interdependency in Image Space

Pixel processing: a single pass over the image is sufficient, and a pixel's new value is only determined by exactly one source pixel value.

- lookup-tables (LUT)
- graylevel or color thresholding
- color space conversion
- brightness correction
- arithmetic operations
- logic operations

N-pass: multiple passes over the image and data space are necessary; however, only one source pixel value determines the new pixel value.

- count, min, max, avg, stddev
- histogram equalization or histogram matching
- Hough transforms

Fixed-size block access: the values of pixels in an area of known and fixed size determines the output value.

- morphology
- convolution, filtering
- pyramids
- wavelets
- KLT (Lucas-Kanade) feature tracking

Data-independent, global access: multiple source pixel values from pixels all over the image determine the outcome of the operation. The access pattern is known, however.

- Viola-Jones
- warping or remapping for distortion correction

Data-dependent, random access: multiple source pixel values from pixels all over the image determine the outcome of the operation. The access pattern is determined by the values read from the source pixels.

- naive flood fill
- contour finding

ously on multiple data. VLIW (very long instruction word) relaxes this constraint by allowing different instructions (opcodes) to be packed together in a VLIW, and every instruction therein processes a different datum concurrently. Many DSPs are VLIW architectures. The types of instructions that are allowed together within one VLIW (and thus will be executed in parallel) depend on the function units that can operate in parallel. For example, if a DSP has two fixed-point MAC units and two floating-point MAC units, then at most two fixed-point MAC operations can be placed into the same VLIW. This constraint is relaxed even further in so-called MIMD machines (multiple instruction, multiple data), where multiple identical processors can independently execute arbitrary instructions on non-dependent data.

You might note that modern CPUs and their multiple-dispatch (superscalar) pipelines do exactly that—schedule multiple instructions concurrently. With DSPs, however, there is no such intelligent pipeline. Instead, the burden of scheduling is on the compiler: it has to co-schedule instructions for independent data operations and optimize the packing of instructions in width (e.g., four instructions per word) and in sequence (control flow). DSPs do not perform such complex CPU operations as branch prediction or instruction reordering. Here, too, the compiler has to perform the optimizations.

DSP programs are relatively small programs (tens or hundreds of LOC), with few branch and control instructions, as opposed to entire operating systems running on general-purpose CPUs. Frequently, a single, tight, and heavily optimized loop is executed once for every data element or set thereof. Fig. 1.6 shows how the serialized pixel data is streamed through a DSP with a simple one-dimensional smoothing filter.

Fig. 1.6 One-dimensional filters such as Gaussian smoothing can be implemented in even the simplest DSPs. Here, pixels are fed into a pipeline that calculates a weighted sum on a five-pixel window into the pixel stream. The height of the gray curve depicts the weights.

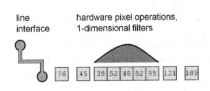

Since DSPs usually execute small programs on huge amounts or endless streams of data, these two pieces of information are stored in separate memory blocks, often accessible through separate buses. This is called a *Harvard architecture*, as opposed to the GPP's *von Neumann architecture*, in which both program and data are stored in the same memory. Because the program does not change (firmware!), many DSPs provide on-chip ROM (typically in the order of 10 kB) for program storage, and a small but efficient RAM hierarchy for data storage. Frequently, an embedded system also includes a separate non-volatile memory chip such as an EEPROM or flash memory.

There are several high-performance DSPs available, including several that have multi-core DSP-with-general-purpose-CPU system on a chip structure. Of particular interest are the DSPs with specialization toward video and image processing, also known as media processors. These tend to include multiple (perhaps as many as 64) enhanced DMA units and multiple dedicated I/O streams adapted toward the movement of pixels onto and off the chip. Media processors are a common choice for video applications owing to characteristics that make them equally attractive for embedded vision systems: programmability, direct memory access (DMA) architectures, some level of parallelism (VLIW or SIMD), low power and low cost.

Example vision systems using DSPs are discussed in Chapters 4 and 9. Manufacturers of DSPs include Agere Systems, Analog Devices, Infineon, Lucent Technologies, Equator Technologies, Freescale Semiconductor (formerly part of Motorola), NXP (formerly part of Philips Electronics), Texas Instruments, and Zilog. Most of these manufacturers also offer DSP development boards specific for image processing and computer vision, complete with the required auxiliary chips, with cameras and software. Those are an ideal starting point for an experimental embedded vision system. Bruno Paillard wrote a good introduction to DSPs that can be found at [12]. A good textbook resource is Lynn and Fuerst's *Introductory Digital Signal Processing with Computer Applications.* The USENET group comp.dsp might also be of interest to the reader.

1.5.2 *Field-Programmable Gate Arrays*

A field-programmable gate array, or FPGA, is a semiconductor in which the actual logic circuit can be modified to the application builder's needs. The chip is a relatively inexpensive, off-the-shelf device that can be programmed in the "field" and not the semiconductor fab. It is important to note the difference between software programming and logic programming, or logic design as it is usually called: a software program always needs to run on some microcontroller with an appropriate instruction set architecture (ISA), whereas a logic program *is* the microcontroller. In fact, this logic program can specify a controller that accepts as input a particular ISA, for example, the ISA of an ARM CPU, effectively turning the FPGA into an ARM CPU.

This is a so-called *soft core*, built from general-purpose logic blocks. These soft cores, or better the right to use the intellectual property, can be purchased from companies such as Xilinx, Inc., and Altera Corporation. They are then "downloaded" to the FPGA where they implement the desired functionality. Some of the modern FPGAs integrate platform- or *hard* multipurpose processors on the logic such as a PowerPC, ARM, or a DSP architecture. Other common hard and soft modules include multipliers, interface logic, and memory blocks.

The *logic design* determines the FPGA's functionality. This configuration is written to the device and is retained until it is erased. To be precise, there are three types of FGPAs: antifuse, SRAM, and FLASH. Antifuse chips are not reprogrammable. FLASH (EPROM) is also nonvolatile, meaning that the logic design stays on the chip through power cycles. It can be erased and reprogrammed many times. SRAM programming on the other hand is volatile; it has to be programmed at power on.

The huge benefit of an FPGA is the great flexibility in logic, offering extreme parallelism in data flow and processing to vision applications. One can, for example, create 320 parallel accumulation buffers and ALUs, summing up an entire 320×240 image in 240 clock cycles. Another example would be to place a region of interest in the FPGA and then perform pixel operations on the entire region simultaneously (see Fig. 1.7). FPGAs can achieve speeds close to DSPs and ASICs, require a bit more power than an ASIC, have much lower non-recurring engineering (NRE) costs, but higher volume prices than ASICs.

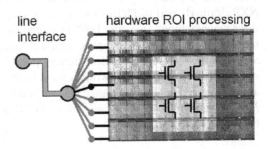

line interface   hardware ROI processing

Fig. 1.7 Region of interest (ROI) processing in hardware (FPGA) after spreading the image over the chip.

Algorithm developers and software engineers are usually trained on a sequential model. That and the flexibility of logic circuitry make parallel designs on FPGAs a challenging task, particularly because the best implementation is often not intuitively apparent. One of the first difficulties is dividing the responsibilities between the FPGA and a GPP, and between the FPGA's core CPU and into possible other chips on the platform. Common "hardware description languages" for logic design are Verilog and VHDL and the topic of many engineering courses and books.

FPGAs are a great resource for parallelism and offer tremendous flexibility in the embedded vision processing system. On the other hand, large FPGAs are quite power hungry and their clock rates are lower than a typical DSPs' clock rate. A wide variety of field-programmable array chips are available on the commercial market today. The optimal choice for an embedded vision system is a combination of a single FPGA with sufficient general-purpose I/O resources to handle the imager's incoming and outgoing interfaces plus a 64-bit interface to/from the DSP. An equally important selection criterion will be the amount of embedded FPGA memory as well as the package. Most FPGAs have an abundance of I/O capability as compared with internal logic so it is probable that an optional 32-bit SDRAM interface may also be possible. Such an interface in an embedded vision system would provide the FPGA with private access to its own storage area at the cost of access time and added FPGA complexity. The plentiful I/O resources are also used to let FPGAs control the input gates of other onboard chips.

Example vision systems using FPGAs are discussed in Chapters 6 and 7. FPGA manufacturers include Achronix Semiconductor, Actel, Altera, AMI Semiconductor, Atmel, Cypress Semiconductor, Lattice Semiconductor, QuickLogic, and Xilinx. Most of these manufacturers also offer FPGA development boards specific for image processing and computer vision, usually with at least one DSP onboard, and complete with cameras and software. Those are an ideal starting point for experimentation. An introduction to FPGAs can be found at [13].

1.5.3 Graphics Processing Units

Interface standardization in the world of computer graphics took a long time to come together. Its need was seen since the 1970s [8], but it wasn't until the 1990s that SGI and Microsoft were successful publishing their respective standards OpenGL and Direct3D. The effect on the graphics hardware and software industries was immense, as billion-dollar-strong markets indicate. The special processors developed for graphics rendering, called graphics processing units, or GPUs, have surpassed transistor integration densities of consumer general-purpose processors (GPPs or CPUs). Many graphics operations lend themselves very well to parallelization due to their mutual independence. This led to the development of parallel processing units in GPUs, called shaders. The most recent GPUs have *hundreds* of shader processing units that can each perform operations on different sets of data, producing independent results. Typically, subgroups of these shaders run in a SIMD mode, executing the same instruction at the same time on different data. In contrast to DSPs and similar to CPUs, the GPU takes care of scheduling and synchronization of the tasks assuming, however, that their executing is largely independent from one another.

The so-called shader programs are short snippets of code that have to conform to certain restrictions. While more recent specifications permit relaxation of some of these, traditionally shader programs may not have dynamic branch instructions, are limited to floating-point operations, and may not exceed 100 or so instructions. Shader programs are intended either for vertices or for fragments. Vertices are points in 3D space, and vertex shaders perform operations such as determining vertex position or vertex color with geometric calculations. Fragment shaders (or pixel shaders), on the other hand, perform operations on pixels in a 2D space, such as texturing or color blending. It is expected that one common type, geometry shaders, will unite the functionality of vertex and fragment shaders.

The programming model for shaders is traditionally data-driven. For this and other reasons, to utilize GPUs and shaders for tasks such as image processing or computer vision, data has to be packaged to act like graphics data, and operations have to be disguised as graphics operations. Higher-level languages that are compiled into shader languages have sprung up, however, making programming vastly easier and program conversion more and more automatic. Examples are Nvidia's Cg, Microsoft's HLSL, and most recently Nvidia's CUDA development environment. CUDA (which stands for computer unified device architecture) clearly shows the trend of GPU utilization for applications other than computer graphics: along with a C-style language definition and compiler, it provides a general matrix calculation library (BLAS) and a fast Fourier transform implementation, code for image convolution and other image processing tasks.

GPUs provide raw horsepower for data-intensive application that require real-time performance. Although these processors have been traditionally designed for graphics rendering, they are essentially parallel multiprocessors that can efficiently handle mathematical computations. Also, GPUs are optimized for floating point calculations in contrast to most integer-optimized DSPs. Hence, there is now a growing research, coined GPGPU which stands for general-purpose computation on GPUs, to use these device as coprocessors for computer vision and other applications beyond graphics. GPGPU is driven with the availability of high performance, low-cost GPUs; they are now standard components in devices such as our portable computers as well as mobile handsets. GPUs are briefly covered in Chapter 11 with respect to mobile phones.

Designers must still consider the tradeoffs between power and performance as higher-end GPUs tend to demand high-power resources. Very often, GPUs are matched with specialized memories (VRAM or video RAM) that offer higher bandwidth at a higher system cost. To realize the full benefits of GPUs, programmers must properly partition their algorithms for the GPUs since there may be setup penalties to initiate tasks on GPUs. GPUs are extremely powerful resources and we are only seeing the beginning of their utilization for vision tasks. It is up to the system designers to consider their match to the characteristics required for many embedded vision systems: low power requirements, low volume cost, and specialization to the task at hand. The following section discusses chips at that end of the spectrum: custom-developed for a specific tasks.

1.5.4 Smart Camera Chips and Boards

An application-specific integrated circuit (ASIC) is a chip that is designed and optimized for one particular application. The logic is customized to include only those components that are necessary to perform its task. Even though modules are reused from ASIC to ASIC just like FPGA modules, a large amount of design and implementation work goes into every ASIC. Their long production cycle, their immensely high one-time cost, and their limited benefits in speed gains put them slightly out of scope of this tutorial. Contributing to the high cost, they need to be respun if the design changes just slightly, costing months and usually hundreds of thousands of dollars. Their benefits lie in potential power savings and a decreasing asymptotic cost (with high unit numbers).

ASICs, processors, SoCs, and chip sets that directly support higher-level computer vision tasks come in various flavors, from CMOS image capture chips that include one or multiple small processors to framegrabber PCI boards with multiple full-scale CPUs. Some examples of devices and companies that manufacture them are:

- OmniVision Technology in Sunnyvale, CA, builds still camera chips (CMOS) with integrated processing power.
- NuCORE Technology in San Jose, CA, offers a digital image processor with an "object detection engine" for real-time face detection.
- Zoran Corp. in Sunnyvale, CA, sells the COACH image processing ASIC for digital cameras, which can perform motion stabilization.
- Alacron of Nashua, NH, manufactures frame grabber boards with various processors on board, for example, FPGAs, DSPs, or PowerPCs.

- Matrox in Dorval, Canada, also manufactures frame grabbers, for example, the Odyssey Xpro+ contains a G4 PowerPC, a Matrox ASIC, and an Altera Stratix II FPGA.
- Anafocus, a spin-off from the Universidad de Sevilla in Spain, builds mixed-signal CMOS chips (ACE4K, ACE16K, Eye-RIS) with an image acquisition array, digitally programmable analog signal processors, and DSP functionality [1, 7].
- Eutecus in Austin, TX, creates the "Bi-i" smart camera from the ACE16k_v2 chip and a Texas Instruments DSP.
- Mobileye in Amstelveen, Netherlands, sells the EyeQ CMOS ASIC which houses two ARMs and four processors that are specialized for image processing tasks.
- Sarnoff of Princeton, NJ, created the Acadia ASIC (see van der Wal et al. [9] and at [14]), a highly specialized image processing chip.
- Pixel Velocity in Ann Arbor, MI, is developing a smart camera that uses 2-6 PowerPC405 (each running at 300MHz) and one Xilinx FPGA to crunch image data faster than a single CPU.
- IQinVision in San Clemente, CA, sells video surveillance systems and software such as face detection that can be uploaded on their IQeye smart cameras.

1.5.5 Memory and Mass Storage

In addition to a processing unit, an embedded vision board will need a reasonably large memory with width and access time commensurate with the required image stream acquisition, processing, and storage needs of the vision application. The detailed selection of a particular type of memory (SRAM, DRAM, SDRAM, flash, etc.) is largely driven by space and capacity concerns and, to a lesser extent, by cost. While a multiported SRAM would be best for creating an easy-to-use shared memory located between a DSP and an FPGA, for example, such a memory would likely be too small in capacity, far too high in cost, and too large in physical size due to the number of I/O pins required. An SDRAM is more appropriate for most vision applications. It is likely to be small enough in physical size while large enough in storage capacity to fit the bill. Such a memory is significantly more difficult to share, however, since its access involves a dedicated SDRAM controller. Luckily, such a controller is usually integrated within a DSP and SoC, and available as soft core for FPGAs. All SDRAM memory accesses need to originate at the SDRAM controller and, thus, the DSP would become the hub (and, unfortunately, also the potential bottleneck) for all memory activities.

Most DSPs suitable to vision applications have a 64-bit wide SDRAM memory interface. Depending on pixel width, accesses across this SDRAM interface will be able to handle 4-8 pixels in a single transfer. Through the use of enhanced DMA units, the DSP does not have to be involved in the lowest-level read or write activities.

Full frame storage in memory (a frame buffer, see Fig. 1.8) permits arbitrary operations on the image with no predetermined pixel access order. Higher-level processing that does not concern pixel data directly often involves higher-dimensional data in a feature space rather than the two- or three-dimensional image data.

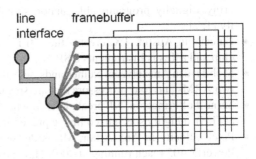

Fig. 1.8 Frame buffer storage of the image, permitting random pixel access.

Mass storage units are available (SATA or PATA disk drives) and would be selected based upon the needs of the main application. Flash-based disk-drive units are attractive from a weight, power, and speed perspective though their capacity is limited and their cost is higher than traditional magnetic disk technology. It is often the case for embedded systems that very little mass storage is required—just enough for booting the O/S and holding a small file system—though for vision systems, particularly those involving video, mass storage needs can be substantial.

1.5.6 System on Chip

A system on chip (SoC) contains all essential components of an embedded system on a single chip. The definition is blurry, as sometimes this only refers to the digital components and sometimes it includes analog components. DSPs have an increasing amount of peripherals included on the die as well, warranting the inclusion in this category. Most SoCs have a GPP such as an ARM, MIPS, PowerPC, or an x86-based core at their heart, supplemented by a DSP. What makes these chips an entire system are the inclusion of a bewildering array of peripherals. In addition to standard microcontroller components (busses, clocks, memory), typical integrated components are:

- Ethernet MAC
- PCMCIA
- USB 1.0 and 2.0 controller
- Bluetooth
- RS232 UART
- IrDA
- IEEE 1394 (FireWire) controller

- display interface
- flash memory interfaces
- ADCs and DACs

Systems on a chip are of particular interest to highly integrated devices such as mobile phones, portable DVD and mp3 players, set-top-boxes and cable modems. Many SoCs have dedicated circuitry for video processing, which usually means hardware support for decoding from (and sometimes for encoding into) the various video formats, including MPEG2, MPEG4, and H.263. An extensive list of SoCs can be found at [15].

1.5.7 CPU and Auxiliary Boards

Many experimental and prototype embedded systems employ a general-purpose host computer at the highest level. This machine can run the overall application. In addition it can stage and boot the attached DSP and FPGA hardware. Volatile FPGAs and the DSPs need their logic and programs loaded. In production systems, this frequently resides in an internal storage such as Flash or a small disk. With a host computer system, the host boots first. Once running, it then initializes and loads the FPGA(s), loads the DSP(s) and starts their programs. After that, software and hardware protocols are used to keep all inter-system transactions orderly. Programs running in the DSP (via the FPGA) can initialize and control the imager. Due to size and power concerns the logical choice for the host is often a PC/104 form factor [2]. Systems with significant capability (e.g., with a dual core x86 CPU, 2Gb main memory, and all of the traditional PC peripheral interfaces) are available in this form factor; Fig. 1.9 shows such a system. With an on-board compact PCI bus connector, it becomes feasible to attach a custom processing unit for vision processing, making development and debugging much easier. The power needs of such a system are a concern, however, particularly for embedded systems that run from battery power. The power budget for the overall system described here (i.e., host plus processing board and imager) is 50W.

1.5.8 Component Interconnects

Any designer of a custom high-performance embedded system must pay careful attention to the interconnections between and among components and to connectors. Fortunately, the computer industry, via its international standards committees, has been extremely helpful in this regard. It is precisely because of bus and point-to-point signaling standards like PCI, compact-PCI, FireWire, USB, I^{2}C, and others (together with the set of connectors and fixtures that supports these standards) that subsystems made by a diverse set of companies can interconnect and reliably work together. The add-on custom processing board envisioned here would use

Fig. 1.9 PC/104 host computer (used by permission of Adlogic, Inc.).

compact-PCI connectors and the PCI protocol to attach the DSP/FPGA resources to the host system. The connection between the imager subsystem and the DSP/FPGA board would be made from LVDS transceivers and would use FireWire connectors and cables (but would not implement any of the IEEE 1394 FireWire protocols).

1.6 Processing Board Organization

The previous section discussed the building blocks and architectural issues surrounding an embedded vision system. Some recommendations for prototype embedded computer vision systems have emerged from that section, namely: PC/104 form factor host, compact PCI bus signaling to/from an attached PC/104 processing board with DSP/FPGA and memory, attachment to an imager subsystem via custom LVDS interface. Given these recommendations, several DSP-FPGA-memory organizations are possible. The optimal one for a vision system depends on the computational needs of the application and are discussed in this section.

The key organizational issue is the location and number of memories on the board. Clearly the highest speed on-chip RAMs, used for caching code and/or temporary data will normally be quite limited in size with no possibility for expansion. Today's DSPs often contain an integrated SDRAM controller. A large system memory is available via such an external interface. There can also be memory resources within the FPGA and these will typically be used to stage and support the data for highly parallel computations within the FPGA. Such FPGA memories are quite limited in size.

Additional FPGA-specific memory can be added by incorporating an SDRAM controller within the FPGA. This method can provide for a significant amount of storage but any such memory would remain private to the FPGA rather than shared with the DSP. More ideal would be a multiported SRAM located between and shared by the DSP and FPGA. Except for a very small one, such a setup would be prohibitively large, expensive, and cumbersome due to the number of pins and traces involved with the address and data buses. Yet another choice might be an SRAM connected to a bus that was shared between the DSP and FPGA. This might be workable though the complexities arising from reserving and releasing bus mastership would take away from overall utility and the cost and size for an SRAM in the megabyte size range would start to be prohibitive. Making this approach work effectively and efficiently would be difficult to achieve with available DSP and FPGA resources.

The chosen memory organization is depicted in Fig. 1.10. This approach uses a large SDRAM attached to the DSP via its integrated SDRAM controller with a wide bus-style attachment to the FPGA via a separate external memory space of the DSP. If a DSP with multiple DMA controllers is used then a few of the DMA units can be allocated to the task of moving pixel rows or columns or other chunks of related data between the DSP and FPGA over the external memory bus.

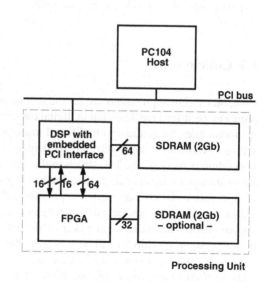

Fig. 1.10 Organization of memories and datapaths on the processing board.

The chosen organization has the imager directly connecting to the FPGA. One could instead connect the LVDS transceiver (with a bit of glue logic help from the FPGA) directly to an incoming pixel port of the DSP but such an organization precludes any early front-end processing happening within the FPGA. By running the pixel stream first to the FPGA, such front-end steps are possible but, if not needed, there is a nearly zero latency overhead incurred by implementing a pass-through to the DSP.

The FPGA has a wide, high-performance path to the DSP but no directly attached memory. A limited amount of memory is embedded within FPGAs and the logic can be configured to act as memory, as well. If additional memory is needed, a private SDRAM could be added when board space allows. Parallelized computations with highly fixed or predictable memory accesses belong in FPGAs. Computations that require on-the-fly flexibility or that are highly variable belong more appropriately in the DSP. The overall approach is to avoid moving large amounts of pixel data back and forth between FPGA and DSP. Many choices must be made as to whether a given processing step should be performed in the DSP or in the FPGA. Some highly parallelized computations need to happen in the FPGA but it is essential that the flow of pixel data through the system be carefully orchestrated so as to maintain efficiency and avoid needless and non-productive data movement between processing sites.

The approach discussed in this section is very high in flexibility. The FPGA gets the first look at pixels from the imager. It can manage the physical signaling to/from the imager as well as perform Bayer filtering, separation into rows and columns, image subsampling, and a variety of other tasks. The DSP plays a central role. Because it manages the main memory, overall supervision and control of the embedded vision computations resides within the DSP.

1.7 Conclusions

Computer vision applications are for the first time making their way into consumer products, be it for face detection in digital cameras or for driver assistance systems in automobiles. In contrast to traditional machine vision applications in industrial settings, consumer systems have higher demands on cost, power consumption, and integration density (size). This drives embedded systems development from both a hardware and a software perspective. Indicators are, for example, that manufacturers of high-volume GPUs have started to provide tools for vision applications. Also, the industry is currently experiencing a strong market pull for video analytics and automotive vision, influencing chip makers to design vision-friendly DSPs. The same is true for systems on chip for cell phones and other handheld consumer products with increasing image and video capabilities. In other words: these are exciting times for embedded computer vision and we might even see a boom similar to the graphics explosion of the 1990s!

This chapter tried to shed light on the hardware components available for embedded vision systems. It presented several types of image sensors as well as their readout styles, speeds, and interface styles. The CMOS active pixel image array sensor, because of its region of interest readout and its flexibility and controllability was identified as a leading candidate for use in an embedded vision system, but CCDs have their place for systems with the highest demands on sensor sensitivity.

Interconnection options for such sensors were also presented with low-voltage differential signaling highlighted due to its excellent performance, range, and bidirectionality properties for embedded projects. A set of image operations was overviewed in the context of an embedded system containing one or more sensors and their interfaces.

Several hardware storage and processing components (including DSPs, various system-on-a-chip combinations, FPGAs, GPUs, and memories) have been considered as building blocks from which a vision system might be realized. Component-to-component relationships, data and control pathways, and signaling methods between and among these components are discussed and specific organizational approaches have been compared and contrasted. In the end, the best overall hardware for a given embedded vision system is the one that can fulfill the processing needs of the vision application with a minimum of back and forth pixel movement between memory and processing units.

By no means is this a complete list or an introduction of sufficient depth to build your own system. But we hope you now have a more complete picture of the real-time, embedded computer vision pipeline that will help you get started.

References

1. L. Carranza, F. Jiménez-Garrido, G. Liñán Cembrano, E. Roca, S. E. Meana, and A. Rodríguez-Vázquez. ACE16k based stand-alone system for real-time pre-processing tasks. In *Proc. Microelectronics for the New Millenium Symposium*, 2005.
2. P. E. Consortium. *PC/104 Specification, Version 2.5*, November 2003.
3. E. R. Fossum. Active Pixel Sensors: Are CCD's Dinosaurs? *Proc. SPIE*, 1900(3), 1993.
4. D. Litwiller. CCD vs. CMOS: Facts and Faction. *Photonics Spectra*, January 2001.
5. D. Litwiller. CMOS vs. CCD: Maturing Technology, Maturing Markets. *Photonics Spectra*, August 2005.
6. S. Mendis, S. E. Kemeny, and E. R. Fossum. CMOS Active Pixel Image Sensor. *IEEE Trans. on Electron Devices*, 41(3), March 1994.
7. G. Liñán, S. Espejo, R. Domínguez-Castro, and A. Rodríguez-Vázquez. ACE4k: An analog I/O 64 64 visual microprocessor chip with 7-bit accuracy. In *Intl. Journal of Circuit Theory and Applications*, volume 30, pages 89–116, March 2002.
8. W. M. Newman and A. van Dam. Recent Efforts Towards Graphics Standardization. *ACM Computing Surveys*, 10, December 1978.
9. G. van der Wal, M. Hansen, and M. Piacentino. The Acadia Vision Processor. In *Proc. IEEE Intl. Workshop on Computer Architectures for Machine Perception*, 2000.
10. A. X. Widmer and P. A. Franaszek. A DC-Balanced, Partitioned Block 8B/10B Transmission Code. *IBM Journal of Research and Development*, 27(5):440, 1983.
11. http://www.dalsa.com/markets/ccd_vs_cmos.asp (accessed May 2008)
12. http://www.softdb.com/media/DSP_Introduction_en.pdf (accessed May 2008)

13. http://www.tutorial-reports.com/computer-science/fpga/tutorial.php (accessed May 2008)
14. http://www.pyramidvision.com/products/acadia/index.asp (accessed May 2008)
15. http://www.linuxdevices.com/articles/AT4313418436.html (accessed May 2008)

Chapter 2
Design Methodology for Embedded Computer Vision Systems

Sankalita Saha and Shuvra S. Bhattacharyya

Abstract Computer vision has emerged as one of the most popular domains of embedded applications. The applications in this domain are characterized by complex, intensive computations along with very large memory requirements. Parallelization and multiprocessor implementations have become increasingly important for this domain, and various powerful new embedded platforms to support these applications have emerged in recent years. However, the problem of efficient design methodology for optimized implementation of such systems remains vastly unexplored. In this chapter, we look into the main research problems faced in this area and how they vary from other embedded design methodologies in light of key application characteristics in the embedded computer vision domain. We also provide discussion on emerging solutions to these various problems.

2.1 Introduction

Embedded systems that deploy computer vision applications are becoming common in our day-to-day consumer lives with the advent of cell-phones, PDAs, cameras, portable game systems, smart cameras, and so on. The complexity of such embedded systems is expected to rise even further as consumers demand more functionality and performance out of such devices. To support such complex systems, new heterogeneous multiprocessor system on chip (SoC) platforms have already emerged in the market. These platforms demonstrate the wide range of architectures available to designers today for such applications, varying from dedicated and programmable to configurable processors, such as programmable DSP, ASIC, FPGA subsystems, and their combinations. They not only consist of hardware components, but also

Sankalita Saha
RIACS/NASA Ames Research Center, Moffett Field, CA, USA, e-mail: ssaha@riacs.edu

Shuvra S. Bhattacharyya
University of Maryland, College Park, MD, USA, e-mail: ssb@umd.edu

integrate embedded software modules. Such heterogeneous systems pose new and difficult challenges in the design process, because now the designer not only has to take care of the effectiveness of hardware but also has to ensure the correctness and efficiency of software along multiple dimensions, such as response time, memory footprint, and power consumption.

In addition, newer, more sophisticated algorithms and product features emerge continually to keep up with the demands of consumers, and to help differentiate products in highly competitive markets. Balancing these specifications and their large computational and communication demands with the stringent size, power, and memory resource constraints of embedded platforms have created formidable new research challenges in design methodology for embedded systems—that is, in the step-by-step process of starting from a given application specification, and deriving from it a streamlined hardware/software implementation. In this chapter, we present an overview of these various challenges, along with existing techniques and ongoing research directions to address the challenges.

To cope with the tight constraints on performance and cost that are typical of embedded systems, most designers use low-level programming languages such as C or assembly language for embedded software, and hardware description languages such as Verilog or VHDL for hardware. Although there are a number of tools emerging for creating and debugging such designs from higher levels of abstraction, they are generally not sophisticated enough to handle such complex systems and often designers have no choice but to manually design, implement and verify the systems. These are very time-consuming tasks because they not only involve embedded software and/or hardware design, but also interfacing of the various heterogeneous components. Aggravating this problem is the lack of standards for such interfaces. For example, in the case of embedded software, because of performance and memory requirements, typically designers use application-dependent, proprietary operating systems, which vary from platform to platform.

Many design groups have enhanced their design methodologies to increase productivity and product quality by adopting object-oriented approaches, and other syntactically-driven methods. Although such methods aid in clarifying system structure and improving documentation, they are not sufficient to handle the details of diverse implementation platforms while ensuring quality and time to market. In some applications, the need to capture specifications at high abstraction levels has led to the use of modeling tools such as The MathWorks' MATLAB and Simulink tools. These tools let designers quickly assemble algorithms and simulate behavior. However, these tools do not cover the full embedded-system design spectrum, and hence do not generally lead to highly optimized final implementations.

Before we look into the details of the design process for embedded computer vision systems, it is important to have an understanding of the unique characteristics of this application domain, and the associated implementation constraints. Computer vision applications involve very high levels of computational complexity. Typically, these applications require complex math operations, including intensive floating point operations, as well as high volumes of memory transactions, because large amounts of data need to be processed. These operations must be carried out and the outputs transmitted in a continuous manner while satisfying stringent timing constraints to ensure that the results are meaningful to the end-user. Therefore, computation time, and in particular, the processing throughput is of significant importance.

Two other important considerations are reduction of energy consumption to maximize battery life, and reduction of area requirements to minimize cost and size. These considerations limit the computational capabilities of the underlying processing platforms. Besides these important constraints, other performance metrics such as latency, jitter (unwanted variation of one or more characteristics of a periodic signal such as the interval between successive pulses, or the amplitude, frequency, or phase of successive cycles), and overall cost are used to evaluate a design as well. Although all of these metrics collectively may come across as common to many domains of embedded system design, what distinguishes computer vision systems is the relative importance of each of them. For example, due to the large volumes of data that need to be processed, computer vision applications require consistently high throughput, but can tolerate reasonable levels of jitter and packet errors. In contrast, consider audio applications, which typically manipulate much smaller volumes of data and hence do not require such a high bandwidth, but place tighter constraints on jitter and error rates. Motivated by the needs of embedded computer vision systems, the discussions in the remainder of this chapter focus mainly on implementation considerations and constraints associated with computational performance, area requirements, and energy consumption.

The lack of effective high-level design methodologies and tools for embedded computer vision systems is a significant impediment to high-productivity product development, and to exploiting the full potential of embedded processing platforms for such systems. However, other aspects of the design and implementation process, such as algorithm selection/development and architecture design are also important problems. Thus, in this chapter, we categorize design and implementation for embedded computer systems into the following different subtasks:

- *Algorithms:* Due to the special characteristics of the targeted embedded platforms, various efforts have been spent on devising computer vision algorithms that are especially streamlined for this domain. Most such algorithms attempt to provide solutions in general to the high computational and memory requirements of the applications, while some also attempt to provide energy-efficient alternatives.
- *Architectures:* Innovative architectures for hardware subsystems already exist and continue to emerge to facilitate optimized implementation of embedded computer vision systems. These approaches range from hardware solutions—involving both system- and circuit-level optimizations—to efficient software methods.
- *Interfaces:* Interfaces can be viewed as "glue subsystems" that hold together a complete system implementation, and ensure the proper interoperability of its distinct components. Interfaces can consist of software as well as hardware components. The diverse, heterogeneous nature of state-of-the-art embedded

platforms makes the job of designing interfaces complex and necessitates new approaches.

- *Design methodology:* Design methodology deals with the actual job of developing a complete implementation given an algorithm (or a collection of algorithms that needs to be supported) and the targeted implementation platform. The task of design methodology is the main focus of this chapter. As we shall see, design methodology comprises various important subproblems, each of which is complex and multifaceted in itself. As a result, the subproblems associated with design methodology are often considered independent research problems, and a main aspect of design methodology is therefore how to relate, integrate, and develop better synergies across different solutions and methods that are geared towards these subproblems.

2.2 Algorithms

Because of resource constraints for the target platforms, algorithms for embedded computer vision and for embedded signal processing in general require special design efforts. Thus, optimized versions of various often-used subsystems or low-level functions have been designed over the years, and packaged in ways to promote reuse in many implementations. Examples of such optimized signal processing library modules involve Gaussian noise generators, trigonometric functions such as *sin* or *cos* and computationally expensive functions such as fast Fourier transform computations. In general, certain characteristics make some computer vision algorithms better suited for embedded implementation. Such algorithm characteristics include sequential data access (as opposed to random access); multiple, independent or mostly independent streams of data; and fixed or tightly bounded sizes for data packets. However, all these features are not necessarily present in a given algorithm and hence various trade-offs need to be considered. In [80], requirements for embedded vision systems and issues involved in software optimization to meet these requirements are analyzed. The authors proceed by first replacing optimized algorithms for various functions whenever they exist, followed by analyzing the bottleneck portions in the code, which are then appropriately rewritten after careful selection of data structures. Such an approach is a viable option for a large and complex system though it does not necessarily ensure a globally optimized design system.

Until now, most computer vision algorithms have been developed without considering in depth the target platform, and hence, aspects related to parallelization and distribution across hardware resources have conventionally been applied as a separate, later stage of design. However, in recent years, researchers have started exploring design of algorithms while considering the final implementation platforms, for example, distributed algorithms for networks of smart cameras. Such algorithms take into account the distributed nature of image capture and processing that is enabled by environments where multiple cameras observe a scene from different viewpoints. In [14], the authors present an approach for motion detection and analysis for gesture recognition for a two-camera system. The authors use MPI (message passing interface) for communication between the cameras. To ensure efficient communication, it is imperative to minimize message length. This is done in several ways; one important approach being replacement of irregular shapes (to represent hands and face for gesture recognition) by regular geometric models such as ellipses so that only parameters for the model can be communicated instead of a large set of pixels. For distributed camera systems, one needs to develop vision algorithms using a different premise that considers the fact that a lot of redundant information may be present. Such a design space is considered in [57], which presents a multi-camera tracking system that uses several omnidirectional sensors and [26] where scene reconstruction using several uncalibrated cameras is presented. The trend shown by these works is encouraging. However, more effort in this direction involving more platform considerations is required. For example, memory size and requirements often pose major design bottlenecks for computer vision systems. Thus, memory architecture of the target platform need to be taken into account while designing the algorithms.

2.3 Architectures

Architectural exploration for embedded computer vision systems ranges from high-level system architecture to analog and circuit-level design. The architectural design space should not only include architectures for the main functional components, but should also encompass network architecture, because parallelization and spatial distribution are used increasingly for such systems. Software architectures are important as well, because in current hardware/software platforms, optimized embedded software architecture is essential for efficient implementation and high-productivity code development. Because new approaches in this area are numerous, the following discussion is by no means exhaustive, and is limited to a small, representative subset of approaches to help illustrate the variety of techniques that have been explored in this area.

New architectures initially were proposed for low-level functions such as edge-detection and smoothing. However, in recent years, new designs for complete embedded computer visions systems—made possible largely by the development of powerful new SoC platforms—have emerged. In general, the computational engines for these architectures can be classified as fast, customized single processors; networks of parallel processing units; and more recently, heterogeneous multiprocessor-on-chip (MPSoCs) devices that employ special accelerators.

Trimedia and Texas Instruments' DaVinci VLIW are well-known commercial DSPs used in video processing. In the noncommercial domain, representative examples include *Imagine* a programmable stream processor by Kapasi et al. [35], the MOLEN reconfigurable microcoded processor developed at Delft University [44] and the HiBRID-SoC architecture for video and image processing by Berkovic et al.

[5]. *Imagine* was designed and prototyped at Stanford University and is the first programmable streaming-media processor that implements a stream instruction set. It can operate at 288 MHz at controlled voltage and temperature at which the peak performance is 11.8 billion 32-bit floating-point operations per second, or 23.0 billion 16-bit fixed point operations per second. The *Imagine* processor architecture has been commercialized resulting in STORM-1 from Stream Processors, Inc. The *Imagine* architecture inspired other designs such as the *Cell* processor (jointly developed by Sony, IBM, and Toshiba). However, unlike *Imagine*, which can be programmed in C, the *Cell* processor cannot be programmed efficiently using standard sequential languages. The MOLEN reconfigurable processor utilizes microcode and custom-configured hardware to improve performance and caters to the application market that requires fast reconfigurability. It allows dynamic and static adaptation of the microarchitectures to fit application design requirements. The HiBRID-SoC integrates three fully programmable processor cores and various interfaces on a single chip. It operates at 145 MHz, and consumes 3.5 Watts. The processor cores are individually optimized to the particular computational characteristics of different application fields.

With the advent of powerful new FPGA platforms comprising of both hardware and software components, embedded computer vision architectures for FPGAs are becoming increasingly popular. In [69], a hardware/software implementation on a Xilinx FPGA platform is presented for a 3D facial pose tracking application; the most-computation intensive part was implemented in hardware while the remaining were implemented on the soft-core processors. A similar implementation of an optical-flow based object tracking algorithm is explored in [73] where matrix multiplication and matrix inversion operations where parallelized. Various architectures employ programmable DSPs with additional resources, such as special graphics controllers and reconfigurable logic devices, as shown in [41] and [53].

Because most computer vision systems employ intensive memory operations, an efficient memory architecture is required to prevent the memory system from becoming a major bottleneck in an implementation. A novel technique to reduce the on-chip memory size required for stream processing on MPSoC architectures is presented in [66]. This technique involves redistributing playout delay associated with the display device in a multimedia embedded system to processing elements on-chip connected in pipeline to the output device. Playout delay in this case is the artificial initial delay introduced before playing of received packet to ensure continuous output. The delay is introduced to make sure that all packets for a certain length of time (corresponding to the length of the playout buffer from which the output device reads) are received before starting their playout. In [18], the authors present a methodology to evaluate different memory architectures for a video signal processor. They show how variations in circuit sizes and configurations can help in determining the variations in the delay of both the memory system and the network; the associated delay curves can be used to design, compare, and choose from different memory system architectures. In [60], a comprehensive survey of memory optimizations for embedded systems is presented, where starting from architecture-independent optimizations such as transformations, direct optimization techniques ranging from register files to on-chip memory, data caches, and dynamic memory (DRAM) are covered. Such a list of possible optimizations are important to consider in the design of vision systems, especially because of the extraordinary memory requirements involved.

Architectures for low-level computer vision algorithms mainly consist of arrangements of linear 1D arrays, 2D meshes of processing elements [25], systolic arrays of processing elements (PEs) (e.g., [13], [43]) and networks of transputers [75]. New analog as well as mixed-signal circuit designs have also been explored. In [75] and [77] analog implementation of particle-filter based tracking is explored, where non-linear functions such as exponential and arctangent computations are implemented using multiple-input, translinear element (MITE) networks. The use of mixed-signal circuits present an interesting option for computer vision systems since they can provide significant optimizations not achievable using digital circuits. However, they need to be explored judiciously for complex systems comprising of multiple subsystems since they add further challenges to the already complex design process.

2.4 Interfaces

In our context, interfaces in general refer to the "glue" subsystems that connect the various components of an embedded computer system. Such interfaces include drivers, communication interfaces, I/O components, and middleware. An interface can be a software-based component or a hardware component. Middleware refers to the software layer that lies between the operating system and the applications at each "terminal" of a networked computing system. Many designers refer to any software in an embedded system as embedded software. However, in our discussions in this chapter, embedded software refers only to the application software and the associated APIs used to access various functions from within the application software. Thus, we exclude middleware from the notion of "embedded software" and instead, we consider middleware as part of the platform-based, interface infrastructure.

In a hardware/software platform, the role of the interface on the software side is to hide the CPU from the application developer under a low-level software layer ranging from basic drivers and I/O functionality to sophisticated operating systems and middleware. On the hardware side, the interface hides CPU bus details through a hardware adaptation layer besides making applications more portable among different hardware platforms. This layer can range from simple registers to sophisticated I/O peripherals, including direct memory access queues and complex data conversion and buffering systems. On a heterogeneous platform, interfaces also hide the varying characteristics of the computing elements, such as differences in operating frequencies (hidden through appropriate buffering), data widths, and instruction widths. The need to comprehensively handle such mismatches further complicates the design of the interfaces and makes the design process time-consuming because it requires knowledge of all the hardware and software components and their interactions. In [33] the authors provide detailed insight into the interface between hardware and software components in MPSoC (multi-processor system on chip) architectures.

For computer vision systems, memory interfaces are of great importance because of the large memory requirements. Also, since almost all system architectures use data-parallelization, communication between the different parallel components—mostly involving streams of data—has to be carefully designed to enable maximum use of parallelization. In [83], the authors report a case study of multiprocessor SoC (MPSoC) design for a complex video encoder. The initial specification was provided in sequential C code that was parallelized to execute on four different processors. MPI was used for inter-task communication; but it required the design of an additional hardware-dependent software layer to refine the abstract programming model. The design was compiled by three types of designers—application software, hardware-dependent software and hardware platform designers—signifying the complexity of the interface design problem.

Various innovative interface designs have been explored in the multimedia domain. These interface designs generally extend to vision applications as well. For example, in [4], the problem of data storage and access optimizations for dynamic data types is addressed by using a component-based abstract data type library that can handle efficiently the dynamic data access and storage requirements of complex multimedia applications. For advanced DSP chips with multiple co-processors, networks on chips (NoCs) are emerging as a scalable interconnect. Integration of co-processors with NoCs requires load/store packetizing wrappers on the network interfaces. Communication in such NoCs using a task transaction level high-level hardware interface is presented in [27].

Considering the popularity as well as the importance of parallelization in embedded computer vision systems to meet throughput requirements, efficient inter-processor communication is extremely important. A flexible and efficient queue-based communication library for MPSoCs called MP-queue is presented in [76]. Although, there are many powerful parallel hardware platforms available in the market, such as the *Cell* processor [64], Intel's quad-core processors, Stream Processor, Inc.'s Storm-1 family [86], and so on, there is a distinct lack of a standard communication interface that takes care of the associated heterogeneity while catering to the special needs of signal processing applications.

In [69] and [72], an effort is described to create such a standard interface by merging two important existing paradigms—synchronous dataflow (see Section 2.5.1) and MPI—to formulate a new optimized communication interface for signal processing systems called the signal passing interface (SPI). Software- as well as FPGA-based hardware communication libraries are created for SPI and tested on image processing applications as well as on other signal processing applications. Although pure synchronous dataflow semantics can model applications with *static* inter-module communication behaviors only, capability in SPI is provided to handle significant amounts of dynamic behavior through structured use of variable token sizes (called "virtual token sizes or VTS" in SPI terminology) [72]. Such interfaces are of significant importance, because they can be easily integrated to an existing design environments—in this case dataflow-based design flow—seamlessly. However, standards for most of the interfaces utilized are still lacking and more focussed attention on interface development and their optimization is required.

2.5 Design Methodology

As mentioned earlier, design methodology for embedded computer vision system implementation is a critical and challenging problem due to the increasing complexity in both the applications and targeted platforms. The problem can be decomposed into several, inter-related subproblems: (1) modeling, specification and transformation; (2) partitioning and mapping; (3) scheduling; (4) design space exploration; and (5) code generation and verification. This is neither a rigid nor standard decomposition for the design and implementation process, but it highlights considerations that are of key importance in most design flows. Due to their strong inter-relationships, in many cases there is significant overlap between these subtasks. Similarly, various alternative categorizations into different subtasks exist. However, for the remainder of this chapter, we restrict ourselves to the specific decomposition above for concreteness and clarity. Note also that the overall design and implementation problem is typically addressed out through an iterative process—that is, if at a given subtask level, performance constraints are not met or the design is deemed to be otherwise unfeasible or undesirable, then redesign and subsequent reassessment is carried out based on the findings of the previous iterations.

2.5.1 Modeling and Specification

A suitable model to specify an application is an extremely important first step towards an efficient implementation. The most popular approach for modeling and specification of embedded systems continues to be in terms of procedural programming languages, especially C. However, various formal models and formally rooted specification languages exist for this purpose and such approaches are finding increasing use in certain domains, such as signal processing and control systems. Design using a well-suited, high-level formal model aids in a better understanding of the system behavior, as well as of the interaction between the various subsystems. Hence, formal models can be extremely useful in detecting problems early in the design stage. Also, when aided by an automatic code generation framework, such a design process can eliminate human errors, especially for complex systems such as computer vision systems.

A design (at all levels of the abstraction hierarchy) is generally represented as a set of components, which can be considered as isolated monolithic blocks, interacting with one another and with an environment that is not part of the design. A formal *model* defines the behavior and interaction of these blocks. Various formal models in use for embedded system design include finite state machines, dataflow, Petri nets, and statecharts. Amongst these, dataflow is of significant importance because it is widely considered—due for example, to its correspondence with signal flow graph formulations—as one of the most natural and intuitive modeling paradigms for DSP applications. A formal *language*, on the other hand, allows the designer to specify intercomponent interactions as well as sets of system constraints through a formal set of symbols and language grammar. To ensure a robust design, a language should have strong formal properties. Examples of such languages include ML [51], dataflow languages (e.g., Lucid [79], Haskell [15], DIF [29], CAL [20]) and synchronous languages (e.g., Luster, Signal, Esterel [24]).

Dataflow graphs provide one of the most natural and intuitive modeling paradigms for DSP systems. In the dataflow modeling paradigm, the computational behavior of a system is represented as a directed graph. A vertex or node in this graph represents a computational module or a hierarchically nested subgraph and is called an *actor*. A directed *edge* represents a FIFO buffer from a source actor to its sink actor. An edge can have a non-negative integer *delay* associated with it, which specifies the number of initial data values (*tokens*) on the edge before execution of the graph.

Dataflow graphs use a data-driven execution model. Thus, an actor can execute (*fire*) whenever it has sufficient numbers of data values (tokens) on all of its input edges to perform a meaningful computation. On firing, an actor consumes certain numbers of tokens from its input edges and executes based on its functionality to produce certain numbers of tokens on its output edges. Of all the dataflow models, synchronous dataflow (SDF), proposed by Lee and Messerschmitt [48], has emerged as the most popular model for DSP system design, mainly due to its compile-time predictability, and intuitive simplicity from a modeling viewpoint. However, SDF lacks significantly in terms of expressive power and is often not sufficient for modeling computer vision systems. Alternative DSP-oriented dataflow models, such as cyclo-static dataflow (CSDF) [11], parameterized dataflow [6], blocked dataflow (BLDF) [38], multidimensional dataflow [54] and windowed SDF [37] are considered more suitable for modeling computer-vision applications. These models try to extend the expressive power of SDF while maintaining as much compile-time predictability as possible.

Associated with the modeling step are transformations, which can be extremely beneficial for deriving optimized implementations. High-level transformations provide an effective technique for steering lower level steps in the design flow towards solutions that are streamlined in terms of given implementation constraints and objectives. These techniques involve transforming a given description of the system to another description that is more desirable in terms of the relevant implementation criteria. Although traditional focus has been on optimizing code-generation techniques and hence relevant compiler technology, high-level transformations, such as those operating at the formal dataflow graph level, have been gaining importance because of their inherent portability and resultant boost in performance when applied appropriately (e.g., [21], [50]).

Dataflow graph transformations can be of various kinds, such as algorithmic, architectural [61], and source-to-source [22]. These methods comprise optimizations such as loop transformations [67], clustering [65], block processing optimization [40, 68] and so on. All of these techniques are important techniques to consider based on their relevance to the system under design.

However, most of these existing techniques are applicable to applications with static data rates. Transformation techniques that are more streamlined towards dynamically structured (in a dataflow sense) computer vision systems have also come up in recent years, such as dynamic stream processing by Geilen and Basten in [23]. In [19], the authors present a new approach to express and analyze implementation-specific aspects in CSDF graphs for computer vision applications with concentration only on the channel/edge implementation. A new transformation technique for CSDF graphs is demonstrated in [71] where the approach was based on transforming a given CSDF model to an intermediate SDF model using clustering, thereby allowing SDF-based optimizations while retaining a significant amount of the expressive power and useful modeling details of CSDF. CSDF is gradually gaining importance as a powerful model for computer vision applications, and thus optimization techniques for this model are of significant value.

2.5.2 Partitioning and Mapping

After an initial model of the system and specification of the implementation platform are obtained, the next step involves partitioning the computational tasks and mapping them onto the various processing units of the platform. Most partitioning algorithms involve computing the system's critical performance paths and hence require information about the performance constraints of the system. Partitioning and mapping can be applied at a macro as well as micro level. High-level coarse partitioning of the tasks can be identified early on and suitably mapped and scheduled, while pipelining within a macro task can be performed with detailed considerations of the system architecture. However, the initial macro partitioning may be changed later on in order to achieve a more optimized solution. The partitioning step is of course trivial for a single-processor system. However, for a system comprising multiple integrated circuits or heterogeneous processing units (CPUs, ASICs, etc.), this is generally a complex, multivariable and multiobjective optimization problem.

Most computer vision algorithms involve significant amounts of data-parallelism and hence parallelization is frequently used to improve the throughput performance. However, parallelizing tasks across different processing resources does not in general guarantee optimal throughput performance for the whole system, nor does it ensure benefit towards other performance criteria such as area and power. This is because of the overheads associated with parallelization such as interprocessor communication, synchronization, optimal scheduling of tasks and memory management associated with parallelization. Because intensive memory operations are another major concern, optimized memory architecture and associated data partitioning is of great importance as well. In video processing, it is often required to partition the image into blocks/tiles and then process or transmit these blocks—for example, in convolution or motion estimation. Such a partitioning problem has been investigated in [1]; the work is based on the concept that if the blocks used in images are close to squares then there is less data overhead. In [32], the authors look into dynamic data partitioning methods where processing of the basic video frames is delegated to multiple microcontrollers in a coordinated fashion; three regular ways to partition a full video frame which allows an entire frame can be divided into several *regions* (or slices), each region being mapped to one available processor of the platform for real-time processing. This allows higher frame rate with low energy consumption because different regions of a frame can be processed in parallel. Also, the frame partitioning scheme is decided adaptively to meet the changing characteristics of the incoming scenes. In [47], the authors address automatic partitioning and scheduling methods for distributed memory systems by using a compile-time processor assignment and data partitioning scheme. This approach aims to optimize the average run-time by partitioning of task chains with nested loops in a way that carefully considers data redistribution overheads and possible run-time parameter variations.

In terms of task-based partitioning, the partitioning algorithms depend on the underlying model being used for the system. For the case of dataflow graphs, various partitioning algorithms have been developed over the years in particular for synchronous dataflow graphs [34, 74]. However, as mentioned in Section 2.5.1, other dataflow graphs allowing dynamic data interaction are of more significance. In [2], the authors investigate the system partitioning problem based on a constructive design space exploration heuristic for applications described by a control-data-flow specification.

2.5.3 Scheduling

Scheduling refers to the task of determining the execution order of the various functions on subsystems in a design such that the required performance constraints are met. For a distributed or multiprocessor system, scheduling involves not only scheduling the execution order of the various processing units but also tasks on individual units. A schedule can be static, dynamic or a combination of both. In general, a statically determined schedule is the most preferred for the case of embedded systems because it avoids the run-time overhead associated with dynamic scheduling, and it also evolves in a more predictable way. However, for many systems it may not be possible to generate a static schedule because certain scheduling decisions may have to be dependent on the input or on some intermediate result of the system that cannot be predicted ahead of time. Thus, often a combination of static and dynamic schedules is used, where part of the schedule structure is fixed before execution of the system, and the rest is determined at run-time. The term *quasi-static scheduling* is used to describe scenarios in which a combination of static and dynamic scheduling is used, and a relatively large portion of the overall schedule structure is subsumed by the static component.

Scheduling for embedded system implementation have been studied in great details. However, the focus in this section is mainly on representative developments in the embedded computer vision domain. As mentioned earlier in Section 2.5.1, dataflow graphs, in particular, new variants of SDF graphs have showed immense potential for modeling computer vision systems. Therefore, in this section we focus considerably on scheduling algorithms for these graphs. We start by first defining the problem of scheduling of dataflow graphs.

In the area of DSP-oriented dataflow-graph models, especially SDF graphs, a graph is said to have a *valid schedule* if it is free from deadlock and is sample rate consistent—that is, it has a periodic schedule that fires each actor at least once and produces no net change in the number of tokens on each edge [48]. To provide for more memory-efficient storage of schedules, actor firing sequences can be represented through looping constructs [9]. For this purpose, a schedule loop, $L = (mT_1T_2...T_n)$, is defined as the successive repetition m times of the invocation sequence $T_1T_2...T_n$, where each T_i is either an actor firing or a (nested) schedule loop. A looped schedule $S = (T_1T_2...T_n)$, is an SDF schedule that is expressed in terms of the schedule loop notation define above. If every actor appears only once in S, then S is called a *single appearance schedule*, otherwise, is called a *multiple appearance schedule* [9].

The first scheduling strategy for CSDF graphs—a uniprocessor scheduling approach—was proposed by Bilsen et al. [10]. The same authors formulated computation of the minimum repetition count for each actor in a CSDF graph. Their scheduling strategy is based on a greedy heuristic that proceeds by adding one node at a time to the existing schedule; the node selected adds the minimum cost to the existing cost of the schedule. Another possible method is by decomposing a CSDF graph into an SDF graph [62]. However, it is not always possible to transform a CSDF graph into a deadlock-free SDF graph, and such an approach cannot in general exploit the versatility of CSDF to produce more efficient schedules. In [81], the authors provide an algorithm based on a min-cost network flow formulation that obtains close to minimal buffer capacities for CSDF graphs. These capacities satisfy both the time constraints of the system as well as any buffer capacity constraints that are, for instance, caused by finite memory sizes. An efficient scheduling approach for parameterized dataflow graphs is the quasi-static scheduling method presented in [7]. As described earlier, in a quasi-static schedule some actor firing decisions are made at run-time, but only where absolutely necessary.

Task graphs have also been used extensively in general embedded systems modeling and hence are of considerable importance for computer vision system. Scheduling strategies for task-graph models is explored by Lee et al. in [46] by decomposing the task graphs into simpler subchains, each of which is a linear sequence of tasks without loops. An energy-aware method to schedule multiple real-time tasks in multiprocessor systems that support dynamic voltage scaling (DVS) is explored in [82]. The authors used probabilistic distributions of the tasks' execution time to partition the workload for better energy reduction while using applications typical in a computer vision system for experiments.

In [39], a novel data structure called the pipeline decomposition tree (PDT), and an associated scheduling framework, PDT scheduling, is presented that exploits both heterogeneous data parallelism and task-level parallelism for scheduling image processing applications. PDT scheduling considers various scheduling constraints, such as number of available processors, and the amounts of on-chip and off-chip memory, as well as performance-related constraints (i.e., constraints involving latency and throughput) and generates schedules with different latency/throughput trade-offs.

2.5.4 Design Space Exploration

Design space exploration involves evaluation of the current system design and examination of alternative designs in relation to performance requirements and other relevant implementation criteria. In most cases, the process involves examining multiple designs and choosing the one that is considered to provide the best overall combination of trade-offs. In some situations, especially when one or more of the constraints is particularly stringent, none of the designs may meet all of the relevant constraints. In such a case, the designer may need to iterate over major segments of the design process to steer the solution space in a different direction. The number of platforms, along with their multifaceted functionalities, together with a multidimensional design evaluation space result in an immense and complex design space. Within such a design space, one is typically able to evaluate only a small subset of solutions, and therefore it is important to employ methods that form this subset strategically. An efficient design space exploration tool can dramatically impact the area, performance, and power consumption of the resulting systems by focusing the designer's attention on promising regions of the overall design space. Such tools may also be used in conjunction with the individual design tasks themselves.

Although most of the existing techniques for design space exploration are based on simulations, some recent studies have started using formal models of computation (e.g., [36, 85]). Formal model based methods may be preferable in many design cases, in particular in the design of safety-critical systems, because they can provide frameworks for verification of system properties as well. For other applications, methods that can save on time—leading to better time-to-market—may be of more importance and hence simulation-based methods can be used. A methodology for system-level design space exploration is presented in [3], where the focus is on partitioning and deriving system specifications from functional descriptions of the application. Peixoto et al. give a comprehensive framework for algorithmic and design space exploration along with definitions for several system-level metrics [63]. A design exploration framework that make estimations about performance and cost based on instruction set simulation of architectures is presented in [45]. A simple, yet intuitive approach to an architectural level design exploration is proposed in [70], which provides models for performance estimation along with means for comprehensive design space exploration. It exploits the concept of synchronization between processors, a function that is essential when mapping to parallel hardware. Such an exploration tool is quite useful, because it eliminates the task of building a separate formal method and instead uses a core form of functionality.

In [84], stochastic automata networks (SANs) have been used as an effective application-architecture formal modeling tool in system-level average-case analysis for a family of heterogeneous architectures that satisfy a set of architectural constraints imposed to allow reuse of hardware and software components. They demonstrate that SANs can be used early in the design cycle to identify the best performance/power trade-offs among several application–architecture combinations. This helps in avoiding lengthy simulations for predicting power and performance figures, as well as in promoting efficient mapping of different applications onto a chosen platform. A new technique based on probabilistically estimating the performance of concurrently executing applications that share resources is presented in [42]. The applications are modeled using SDF graphs while system throughput is estimated by modeling delay as the probability of a resource being blocked by actors. The use of such stochastic and probability-based methods shows an interesting and promising direction for design space exploration.

2.5.5 Code Generation and Verification

After all design steps involving formulation of application tasks and their mapping onto hardware resources, the remaining step of code generation for hardware and software implementation can proceed separately to a certain extent. Code generation for hardware typically goes through several steps: a description of behavior; a register-transfer level design, which provides combinational logic functions among registers, but not the details of logic design; the logic design itself; and the physical design of an integrated circuit, along with placement and routing. Development of embedded software often starts with a set of communicating processes, because embedded systems are effectively expressed as concurrent systems based on decomposition of the overall functionality into modules. For many modular design processes, such as those based on dataflow and other formal models of computation, this step can be performed from early on in the design flow, as described in Section 2.5. As the functional modules in the system decomposition are determined, they are coded in some combination of assembly languages and platform-oriented, high-level languages (e.g., C), or their associated code is obtained from a library of pre-existing intellectual property.

Various researchers have developed code generation tools for automatically translating high-level dataflow representations of DSP applications into monolithic software, and to a lesser extent, hardware implementations. Given the intuitive match between such dataflow representations and computer vision applications, these kinds of code generation methods are promising for integration into design methodologies for embedded computer vision systems. For this form of code generation, the higher level application is described as a dataflow graph, in terms of a formal, DSP-oriented model of computation, such as SDF or CSDF. Code for the individual dataflow blocks (written by the designer or obtained from a library) is written in a platform-oriented language, such as C, assembly language, or a hardware description language. The code generation tool then processes the high-level dataflow graph along with with the intra-block code to generate a stand-alone implementation in terms of the targeted platform-oriented language. This generated implementation can then be mapped into the given processing resources using the associated platform-specific tools for compilation or synthesis.

An early effort on code generation from DSP-oriented dataflow graphs is presented in [28]. A survey on this form of code generation as well as C compiler technology for programmable DSPs is presented in [8]. Code generation techniques to automatically specialize generic descriptions of dataflow actors are developed in [55]. These methods provide for a high degree of automation and simulation-implementation consistency as dataflow blocks are refined from simulation-oriented form into implementation-oriented form. In [59], an approach to dataflow graph code generation geared especially for multimedia applications is presented. In this work, a novel fractional rate dataflow (FRDF) model [58] and buffer sharing based on strategic local and global buffer separation are used to streamline memory management. A code generation framework for exploring trade-offs among dataflow-based scheduling and buffer management techniques is presented in [30].

The final step before release of a product is extensive testing, verification and validation to ensure that the product meets all the design specifications. Verification and validation in particular are very important steps for safety-critical systems. There are many different verification techniques but they all basically fall into two major categories—dynamic testing and static testing. Dynamic testing involves execution of a system or component using numerous test cases. Dynamic testing can be further divided into three categories—functional testing, structural testing, and random testing. Functional testing involves identifying and testing all the functions of the system defined by the system requirements. Structural testing uses the information from the internal structure of a system to devise tests to check the operation of individual components. Both functional and structural testing both choose test cases that investigate a particular characteristic of the system. Random testing randomly chooses test cases among the set of all possible test cases in order to detect faults that go undetected by other systematic testing techniques. Exhaustive testing, where the input test cases consists of every possible set of input values, is a form of random testing. Although exhaustive testing performed at every stage in the life cycle results in a complete verification of the system, it is realistically impossible to accomplish. Static testing does not involve the operation of the system or component. Some of these techniques are performed manually while others are automated.

Validation techniques include formal methods, fault injection and dependability analysis. Formal methods involve use of mathematical and logical techniques to express, investigate and analyze the specification, design, documentation and behavior of both hardware and software. Formal methods mainly comprise two approaches—model checking [12], which consists of a systematically exhaustive exploration of the mathematical model of the system, and theorem proving [16], which consists of logical inference using a formal version of mathematical reasoning about the system. Fault injection uses intentional activation of faults by either hardware or software to observe the system operation under fault conditions. Dependability analysis involves identifying hazards and then proposing methods that reduce the risk of the hazard occurring.

2.6 Conclusions

In this chapter, we have explored challenges in the design and implementation of embedded computer vision systems in light of the distinguishing characteristics of these systems. We have also reviewed various existing and emerging solutions to address these challenges. We have studied these solutions by following a standard design flow that takes into account the characteristics of the targeted processing platforms along with application characteristics and performance constraints. Although new and innovative solutions for many key problems have been proposed by various researchers, numerous unsolved problems still remain, and at the same time, the complexity of the relevant platforms and applications continues to increase. With rising consumer demand for more sophisticated embedded computer vision (ECV) systems, the importance of ECV design methodology, and the challenging nature of this area are expected to continue and escalate, providing ongoing opportunities for an exciting research area.

References

1. Altilar D, Paker Y (2001) Minimum overhead data partitioning algorithms for parallel video processing. In: *Proc. of 12th Intl. Conf. on Domain Decomposition Methods*, 2001.
2. Auguin M, Bianco L, Capella L, Gresset E (2000) Partitioning conditional data flow graphs for embedded system design. In: *IEEE Intl. Conf. on Application-Specific Systems, Architectures, and Processors*, 2000, pp. 339-348.
3. Auguin M, Capella L, Cuesta F, Gresset E (2001) CODEF: a system level design space exploration tool. In: *Proc. of IEEE Intl. Conf. on Acoustics, Speech, and Signal Processing*, May 7-11, 2001, vol. 2, pp. 1145-1148.
4. Baloukas C, Papadopoulos L, Mamagkakis S, Soudris D (2007) Component based library implementation of abstract data types for resource management customization of embedded systems. In: *Proc. of IEEE/ACM/IFIP Workshop on Embedded Systems for Real-Time Multimedia*, Oct. 2007, pp. 99-104.
5. Berekovic M, Flugel S, Stolberg H.-J, Friebe L, Moch S, Kulaczewski M.B, Pirsch P (2003) HiBRID-SoC: a multi-core architecture for image and video applications. In: *Proc. of 2003 Intl. Conf. on Image Processing*, Sept. 14-17, 2003.
6. Bhattacharya B, Bhattacharyya S S (2000) Parameterized dataflow modeling of DSP systems. In *Proc. of the Intl. Conf. on Acoustics, Speech, and Signal Processing, Istanbul*, Turkey, Jun. 2000, pp. 1948-1951.

7. Bhattacharya B, Bhattacharyya S S (2000) Quasi-static scheduling of reconfigurable dataflow graphs for DSP systems. In: *Proc. of the Intl. Wkshp. on Rapid System Prototyping*, Paris, France, Jun. 2000, pp. 84-89.
8. Bhattacharyya S S, Leupers R, Marwedel P (2000) Software synthesis and code generation for signal processing systems. *IEEE Trans. on Circuits and Systems II: Analog and Digital Signal Processing*, Sept. 2000, vol. 47, issue 9, pp. 849-875.
9. Bhattacharyya S S, Murthy P K, Lee E A (1996) *Software Synthesis from Dataflow Graphs*, Boston, MA, Kluwer.
10. Bilsen G, Engels M, Lauwereins R, Peperstraete J (1994) Static scheduling of multi-rate and cyclostatic DSP applications. In: *Wkshp. on VLSI Signal Processing*, 1994, pp. 137-146.
11. Bilsen G, Engels M, Lauwereins R, Peperstraete J (1996) Cyclo-static dataflow. *IEEE Trans. on Signal Processing*, Feb. 1996, vol. 44, no. 2, pp. 397-408.
12. Clarke E M, Grumberg O, Peled D (1999) *Model Checking*, MIT Press, Cambridge, MA.
13. Crisman J.D, Webb J.A (1991) The warp machine on Navlab. *IEEE Trans. Pattern Analysis and Machine Intelligence*, May 1991, vol. 13, no. 5, pp. 451-465.
14. Daniels M, Muldawert K, Schlessman J, Ozert B, Wolf W (2007) Real-time human motion detection with distributed smart cameras. In: *First ACM/IEEE Intl. Conf. on Distributed Smart Cameras*, Sept. 25-28, 2007.
15. Davie A (1992) *An Introduction to Functional Programming Systems Using Haskell*, Cambridge University Press, New York, NY.
16. Duffy D A (1991) *Principles of Automated Theorem Proving*, John Wiley and Sons, New York, NY.
17. Dutta S, Connor K.J, Wolf W, Wolfe A (1998) A design study of a 0.25-μm video signal processor. *IEEE Trans. on Circuits and Systems for Video Technology*, vol. 8, Aug. 1998, issue 4, pp. 501-519.
18. Dutta S, Wolf W, Wolfe A (1998) A methodology to evaluate memory architecture design tradeoffs forvideo signal processors. *IEEE Trans. on Circuits and Systems for Video Technology*, Feb. 1998, vol. 8, issue 1, pp. 36-53.
19. Denolf K, Bekooji M, Cockx J, Verkest D, Corporaal H(2007) Exploiting the expressiveness of cyclo-static dataflow to model multimedia implementations. *EURASIP Journal on Advances in Signal Processing*, doi:10.1155/2007/84078.
20. Eker J, Janneck J W (2003) CAL Language Report: Specification of the CAL Actor Language. Technical Memorandum No. UCB/ERL M03/48, University of California, Berkeley, CA, 94720, USA, Dec. 1, 2003.
21. Franke B, Boyle M. O(2001) An empirical evaluation of high level transformations for embedded processors. In: *Proc. of Intl. Conf. on Compilers, Architecture and Synthesis for Embedded Systems*, Nov. 2001.
22. Franke B, Boyle M. O(2003) Array recovery and high-level transformations for DSP applications. *ACM TECS*, vol. 2, May 2003, pp. 132-162.
23. Geilen M, Basten T(2004) Reactive process networks. In: *Proc. of the Intl. Wkshp on Embedded Software*, Sept. 2004, pp. 137-146.
24. Halbwachs N (1993) *Synchronous Programming of Reactive Systems*, Kluwer Academic Publishers, Norwell, MA.
25. Hammerstrom D.W, Lulich D.P (1996) Image processing using one-dimensional processor arrays. *Proc. of the IEEE*, July 1996, vol. 84, no. 7, pp. 1005-1018.
26. Han M, Kanade T (2001) Multiple motion scene reconstruction from uncalibrated views. In: *Proc. 8th IEEE Intl. Conf. on Computer Vision*, vol. 1, 2001, pp. 163-170.
27. Henriksson T, Wolf P. V. D (2006) TTL hardware interface: a high-level interface for streaming multiprocessor architectures. In: *Proc. of IEEE/ACM/IFIP Wkshp. on Embedded Systems for Real Time Multimedia*, Oct. 2006, pp. 107-112.
28. Ho W. H, Lee E. A, Messerschmitt D G (1988) High level data flow programming for digital signal processing. In: *Proc. of the Intl. Wkshp. on VLSI Signal Processing*, 1988.
29. Hsu C, Bhattacharyya S S (2005) Porting DSP applications across design tools using the dataflow interchange format. In: *Proc. of the Intl. Wkshp. on Rapid System Prototyping*, Montreal, Canada, Jun. 2005, pp. 40-46.

30. Hsu D, Ko M, Bhattacharyya S S (2005), Software Synthesis from the Dataflow Interchange Format. In: *Proc. of the Intl. Wkshp. on Software and Compilers for Embedded Systems*, Dallas, Texas, Sept. 2005, pp. 37-49.
31. Hu X, Greenwood G W, Ravichandran S, Quan G (1999) A framwork for user assisted design space exploration. In: *Proc. of 36th Design Automation Conf.*, New Orleans, Jun. 21-25, 1999.
32. Hu X, Marculescu R (2004) Adaptive data partitioning for ambient multimedia. In: *Proc. of Design Automation Conf.*, June 7-11, 2004, San Diego, California, USA.
33. Jerraya A A, Wolf W (2005) Hardware/Software interface codesign for embedded systems. *Computer*, Feb. 2005, vol. 38, issue 2, pp. 63-69.
34. Kalavade A, Lee E (1995) The extended partitioning problem: hardware/software mapping and implementation-bin selection. In: *Proc. of Intl. Wkshp. on Rapid System Prototyping*, Jun. 7-9, Chapel Hill, NC, 1995.
35. Kapasi U J, Rixner S, Dally W J, Khailany B, Ahn J H, Mattson P, Owens J D (2003) Programmable stream processors. *Computer*, vol. 35, no. 8, Aug. 2003, pp. 54-62.
36. Karkowski I, Corporaal H (1998) Design space sxploration slgorithm for heterogeneous multi-processor embedded system design. In: *Proc. of 35th Design Automation Conf.*, San Francisco, Jun. 15-18, 1998.
37. Keinert J, Haubelt C, Teich J (2006) Modeling and analysis of windowed synchronous algorithms. In: *Proc. of the Intl. Conf. on Acoustics, Speech, and Signal Processing*, May 2006.
38. Ko D, Bhattacharyya S S (2005) Modeling of block-based DSP systems. *Journal of VLSI Signal Processing Systems for Signal, Image, and Video Technology*, Jul. 2005, vol. 40(3), pp. 289-299.
39. Ko D, Bhattacharyya S S (2006). The pipeline decomposition tree: An analysis tool for multiprocessor implementation of image processing applications. In: *Proc. of the Intl. Conf. on Hardware/Software Codesign and System Synthesis*, Seoul, Korea, Oct. 2006, pp. 52-57.
40. Ko M-Y, Shen C-C, Bhattacharyya S S (2006). Memory-constrained block processing for DSP software optimization. In: *Proc. of Embedded Computer Systems: Architectures, Modeling and Simulation*, Jul. 2006, pp. 137-143.
41. Kshirsagar S P, Harvey D M, Hartley D A, Hobson C. A (1994) Design and application of parallel TMS320C40-based image processing system. In: *Proc. of IEE Colloquium on Parallel Architectures for Image Processing*, 1994.
42. Kumar A, Mesman B, Corporaal H, Theelen B, Ha Y (2007) A probabilistic approach to model resource contention for performance estimation of multifeatured media devices. In: *Proc. of Design Automation Conf.*, Jun. 4-8, San Diego, USA.
43. Kung S Y (1988) *VLSI Array Processors*, Prentice Hall, NJ.
44. Kuzmanov G K, Gaydadjiev G N, Vassiliadis S (2005) The Molen media processor: design and evaluation. In: *Proc. of the Intl. Wkshp. on Application Specific Processors*, 2005, New York Metropolitan Area, USA, Sept. 2005, pp. 26-33.
45. Kwon S, Lee C, Kim S, Yi Y, Ha S (2004) Fast design space exploration framework with an efficient performance estimation technique. In: *Proc. of 2nd Workshop on Embedded Systems for Real-Time Multimedia*, 2004, pp. 27-32.
46. Lee C, Wang Y, Yang T (1994) Static global scheduling for optimal computer vision and image processing operations on distributed-memory multiprocessors. Tech. Report: TRCS94-23, University of California at Santa Barbara, Santa Barbara, CA, USA.
47. Lee C, Yang T, Wang Y (1995) Partitioning and scheduling for parallel image processing operations. In: *Proc. of the 7th IEEE Symp. on Parallel and Distributeed Processing*, 1995.
48. Lee E A, Messerschmitt D G (1987) Static scheduling of synchronous dataflow programs for digital signal processing. *IEEE Transactions on Computers*, vol. C-36, no. 2, Feb. 1987.
49. Lee H G, Ogras U Y, Marculescu R, Chang N (2006) Design space exploration and prototyping for on-chip multimedia applications. In: *Proc. of Design Automation Conf.*, Jul. 24-28, 2006, San Francisco, USA,
50. Marwedel P (2002) Embedded software: how to make it efficient. In: *Proc. of the Euromico Symp. on Digital System Design*, Sept. 2002, pp. 201-207.
51. Milner R, Tofte M, Harper R (1990) *The Definition of Standard ML*, MIT Press, Cambridge, MA.

52. Miramond B, Delosme J (2005) Design space exploration for dynamically reconfigurable architectures. In: *Proc. of Design Automation and Test in Europe*, 2005, pp. 366-371.
53. Murphy C W, Harvey D M, Nicholson L J (1999) Low cost TMS320C40/XC6200 based reconfigurable parallel image processing architecture. In: *Proc.of IEEE Colloquium on Reconfigurable Systems*, Mar. 10, 1999.
54. Murthy P K, Lee E A (2002) Multidimensional synchronous dataflow. *IEEE Trans. on Signal Processing*, Aug. 2002, vol. 50, no. 8, pp. 2064-2079.
55. Neuendorffer S (2002) Automatic Specialization of Actor-Oriented Models in Ptolemy II. Master's Thesis, Dec. 2002, Department of Electrical Engineering and Computer Sciences, University of California at Berkeley.
56. Niemann R, Marwedel P(1997) An algorithm for hardware/hoftware partitioning using mixed integer linear programming. *Design Automation for Embedded Systems*, vol. 2, no. 2, Kluwer, Mar. 1997.
57. Ng K, Ishigurob H, Trivedic M, Sogo T (2004) An integrated surveillance system – human tracking and view synthesis using multiple omni-directional vision sensors. *Image and Vision Computing Journal*, Jul. 2004, vol. 22, no. 7, pp. 551-561.
58. Oh H, Ha S (2004), Fractional rate dataflow model for efficient code synthesis. *Journal of VLSI Signal Processing Systems for Signal, Image, and Video Technology*, May 2004, vol. 37, pp. 41-51.
59. Oh H, Ha S (2002) Efficient code synthesis from extended dataflow graphs for multimedia applications. In: *Proc. of 39th Design Automation Conference*, 2002, pp. 275-280.
60. Panda P R, Catthoor F, Dutt N D, Danckaert K, Brockmeyer E, Kulkarni C, Vandercappelle A, Kjeldsberg P G (2001) Data and memory optimization techniques for embedded systems. *ACM Trans. on Design Automation of Electronic Systems*, Apr. 2001, vol. 6, no. 2, pp. 149-206.
61. Parhi K K (1995) High-level algorithm and architecture transformations for DSP synthesis. *Journal of VLSI Signal Processing*, vol. 9(1), pp. 121-143, Jan. 1995.
62. Parks T M, Pino J L, Lee E A (1995) A comparison of synchronous and cyclo-static dataflow. In *Proc. of IEEE Asilomar Conf. on Signals, Systems, and Computers*, Pacific Grove, CA, Oct. 29-Nov. 1, 1995.
63. Peixoto H. P, Jacome M. F(1997) Algorithm and architecture-level design space exploration using hierarchical data flows. In: *Proc. of IEEE Intl. Conference on Application-Specific Systems, Architectures and Processors*, Jul. 14-16, 1997, pp. 272-282.
64. Pham D C, Aipperspach T, Boerstler D, Bolliger M, Chaudhry R, Cox D, Harvey P, Harvey P M, Hofstee H P, Johns C, Kahle J, Kameyama A, Keaty J, Masubuchi Y, Pham M, Pille J, Posluszny S, Riley M, Stasiak D L, Suzuoki M, Takahashi O, Warnock J, Weitzel S, Wendel D, Yazawa K, (2006) Overview of the architecture, circuit design, and physical implementation of a first-generation cell processor. *Journal of solid-state circuits*, Jan. 2006, vol. 41, issue 1, pp. 179-196.
65. Pino J L, Bhattacharyya S S, Lee E A (1995) A hierarchical multiprocessor scheduling system for DSP applications. In: *Proc. of the IEEE Asilomar Conf. on Signals, Systems, and Computers*, Nov. 1995, vol.1, pp. 122-126.
66. Raman B, Chakraborty S, Ooi W T, Dutta S (2007) Reducing data-memory footprint of multimedia applications by delay redistribution. In: *Proc. of 44th ACM/IEEE Design Automation Conference*, Jun. 4-8, 2007, San Diego, CA, USA, pp. 738-743.
67. Rim M, Jain R (1996) Valid transformations: a new class of loop transformations for high-level synthesis and pipelined scheduling applications. *IEEE Trans. on Parallel and Distributed Systems*, Apr. 1996, vol. 7, pp. 399-410.
68. Ritz S, Pankert M, Zivojnovic V, Meyr H (1993) Optimum vectorization of scalable synchronous dataflow graphs. In: *Proc. of Intl. Conf. on Application-Specific Army Processors*, 1993, pp. 285-296.
69. Saha S (2007) Design Methodology for Embedded Computer Vision Systems. PhD Thesis, University of Maryland, College Park, Dec. 2007.

70. Saha S, Kianzad V, Schessman J, Aggarwal G, Bhattacharyya S S, Wolf W, Chellappa R. An architectural level design methodology for smart camera applications. *Intl. Journal of Embedded Systems, Special Issue on Optimizations for DSP and Embedded Systems,* (To appear).
71. Saha S, Puthenpurayil S, Bhattacharyya S S (2006) Dataflow transformations in high-level DSP system design. In: *Proc. of the Intl. Symp. on System-on-Chip,* Tampere, Finland, Nov. 2006, pp. 131-136.
72. Saha S, Puthenpurayil S, Schlessman J, Bhattacharyya S S, Wolf W (2007) An optimized message passing framework for parallel implementation of signal processing applications. In: *Proc. of the Design, Automation and Test in Europe,* Munich, Germany, Mar. 2008.
73. Schlessman J, Chen C-Y, Wolf W, Ozer B, Fujino K, Itoh K (2006) Hardware/Software co-Design of an FPGA-based embedded tracking system. In: *Proc. of 2006 Conf. on Computer Vision and Pattern Recognition Wkshp.,* Jun. 17-22, 2006.
74. Sriram S, Bhattacharyya S S (2000) *Embedded Multiprocessors: Scheduling and Synchronization.* Marcel Dekker Inc, New York, NY.
75. Teoh E K, Mital D P (1993) Real-time image processing using transputers. In: *Proc. of Intl. Conf. on Systems, Man and Cybernetics,* Oct. 17-20, 1993, pp. 505-510.
76. Torre A. D, Ruggiero M, Benini L, Acquaviva A (2007) MP-Queue: an efficient communication library for embedded streaming multimedia platforms. In: *Proc. of IEEE/ACM/IFIP Wkshp. on Embedded Systems for Real-Time Multimedia,* Oct. 4-5, 2007, pp. 105-110.
77. Velmurugan R, Subramanian S, Cevher V, Abramson D, Odame K. M, Gray J D, Lo H-J, McClellan J H, Anderson D V (2006) On low-power analog implementation of particle filters for target tracking. In: *Proc. 14th European Signal Processing Conf.,* Sep. 2006.
78. Velmurugan R, Subramanian S, Cevher V, McClellan J H, Anderson D V (2007) Mixed-mode implementation of particle filters. In: *Proc. of IEEE PACRIM Conf.,* Aug. 2007.
79. Wadge W, Ashcroft E. A (1985) *Lucid, The Dataflow Programming Language,* Academic Press, San Diego, CA.
80. Wardhani A W, Pham B L, (2002) Progamming optimisation for embedded vision. In: *Proc. of DICTA2002: Digital Image Computing Techniques and Applications, Melbourne,* Australia, Jan. 21-22, 2002.
81. Wiggers M H, Bekooji M J G, Smit G J M (2007) Efficient computation of buffer capacities for cyclo-static dataflow graphs. In: *Proc. of Design Automation Conf.,* Jun. 4-8, San Diego, USA.
82. Xian C, Lu Y, Li Z (2007) Energy-aware scheduling for real-time multiprocessor systems with uncertain task execution time. In: *Proc. of Design Automation Conf.,* Jun. 4-8, San Diego, USA.
83. Youssef M, Sungjoo Y, Sasongko A, Paviot Y, Jerraya A A (2004) Debugging HW/SW interface for MPSoC: video encoder system design case study. In: *Proc. of 41st Design Automation Conf.,* 2004, pp. 908- 913.
84. Zamora N H, Hu X, Marculescu R (2007) System-level performance/power analysis for platform-based design of multimedia applications. *ACM Trans. on Design Automation of Electronic Systems,* Jan. 2007, vol. 12, no. 1, article 2.
85. Ziegenbein D, Ernest R, Richter K, Teich J, Thiele L(1998) Combining multiple models of computation for scheduling and allocation. In: *Proc. of Codes/CASHE 1998,* pp. 9-13.
86. Wong W (2007) Architecture Maps DSP Flow To Parallel Processing Platform. In: *Electronic Design,* May 10, 2007.

Chapter 3
We Can Watch It for You Wholesale

Alan J. Lipton

Apologies to Philip K. Dick

Abstract This chapter provides an introduction to video analytics—a branch of computer vision technology that deals with automatic detection of activities and events in surveillance video feeds. Initial applications focused on the security and surveillance space, but as the technology improves it is rapidly finding a home in many other application areas. This chapter looks at some of those spaces, the requirements they impose on video analytics systems, and provides an example architecture and set of technology components to meet those requirements. This exemplary system is put through its paces to see how it stacks up in an embedded environment. Finally, we explore the future of video analytics and examine some of the market requirements that are driving breakthroughs in both video analytics and processor platform technology alike.

3.1 Introduction to Embedded Video Analytics

In our modern, security-focused world, closed-circuit television (CCTV) systems have become commonplace. In fact, the numbers of cameras watching public spaces has been proliferating wildly. By 2007, the number of public CCTV cameras in the United Kingdom, for example, had reached a level where there was a camera for every three citizens. Clearly, this represents not only a significant cultural shift but also a dramatic technology challenge. Millions of CCTV cameras require millions of kilometers of cables, Petabits of IP bandwidth, thousands of video monitoring stations, a vast video storage capacity, and a monumental human workforce to monitor, manage, and mine video data. This situation is even more prevalent in other market

Alan J. Lipton
ObjectVideo, Reston, VA, USA, e-mail: alipton@objectvideo.com

49

sectors such as retail, banking, and gaming. These sectors require different applications for their video systems, and are consuming even more CCTV equipment than security customers [11].

We have engineered a situation in which we have literally millions of eyeballs everywhere—but no brains behind them. Clearly there is a need for technology to help realize the potential of these CCTV systems. Enter computer vision. Computer vision involves the processing of digital imagery for the purpose of either: manipulating the imagery for human or machine consumption; or extracting useful semantic or symbolic information from it.

The result is a set of algorithms and techniques that are capable of automatically teasing apart a complex image or video scene and extracting useful information about activities in the scene. This technology can detect and track people and vehicles, determine where they are, what they are doing, and can report these activities to people in ways that are valuable to their particular missions. A security-focused example is shown in Fig. 3.1. And as we shall see, the technology can *only* be really practical in an embedded format. Simple market forces demand that it must exist as a valuable component or ingredient of video infrastructure.

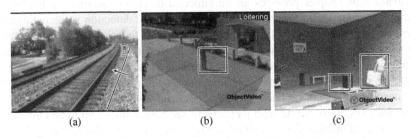

(a)   (b)   (c)

Fig. 3.1 Video analytics—automatic detection of events and activities in video. Sample security applications for video analytics. (a) Perimeter intrusion detection with a tripwire. (b) Suspicious loitering in a public area. (c) Theft of an item from a loading dock.

A short history of video analytics

Early artificial intelligence (AI) researchers needed computer vision results to act as "inputs" for more sophisticated artificial cognition systems. There was a feeling that teaching machines to *think* was the hard part. It should be no problem to get machines to *see*. Researchers in the early AI programs in the 1960s even thought that computer vision could be "solved" as part of a summer research project [19]. That was over 40 years ago. In the intervening time, computer vision has come a long way. Machine vision (mostly for applications such as industrial inspection) has become a multibillion-dollar worldwide industry [3].

However, it is still worth reflecting that even after 40 years, vision is still one of the most complex, and least well developed branches of AI. It is possible to create a very simple vision-based Turing test [24] that almost any 5-year-old human can pass, but that will completely baffle even the most advanced computer vision systems. One such technique is called a *CAPTCHA* (completely automated public Turing test to tell computers and humans apart) [4].

As video capture devices and computer power became cheaper and more ubiquitous in the mid 1990s, it became possible to apply computer vision techniques to video sequences as well as single images. Research organizations in the 1990s were quick to seize upon opportunities to fund video processing research programs. Early funding came from government agencies, so naturally early technology was geared toward government and security types of applications. Video surveillance and monitoring (VSAM [7]) was sponsored by the U.S. Defense Department (DARPA); cooperative distributed vision (CDV [2]) was sponsored by the Japanese Department of Energy; and CHROMATICA [25] was a European academic-industrial consortium sponsored by various European departments of transportation.

The result of these research programs was the commercialization, in the early 2000s, of sophisticated video analytics capabilities geared toward military and governmental critical infrastructure security applications. More complex algorithms were created capable of robustly detecting a broad suite of relevant events in real-world operational environments. Video analytics systems (as they came to be known) could detect activities such as: perimeter breaches; suspicious package deposits; asset theft; suspicious parking or loitering; and many others (see Fig. 3.1 for a few examples). Furthermore, these systems were largely robust to real-world environmental challenges such as diurnal and seasonal scene changes, lighting changes, and environmental clutter (blowing trees, rippling water, and so on). In terms of the technology, with some challenging real-world problems handled for exacting critical infrastructure customers, there was a host of less-challenging applications for video analytics becoming apparent.

3.2 Video Analytics Goes Down-Market

There is a growing need for information to support business intelligence applications. In a retail environment, this may be as simple as counting people going in and out of a store, thus providing store occupancy data over time. Other retail applications include such things as monitoring queue lengths to optimize staffing levels, observing consumer behavior to determine shopping habits, and automated process auditing to determine that corporate policies are being adhered to across the enterprise. Going beyond even these applications, there are uses for video analytics to control automated building management systems. Imagine an image-based sensor installed on the ceiling of a space and did nothing but spit out accurate occupancy information: how many people are currently in the space. This low-cost device would have immediate application to building management systems as a means to control lighting, heating ventilation and cooling (HVAC) systems, and provide useful data for space optimization applications. Fig. 3.2 illustrates a few of these applications.

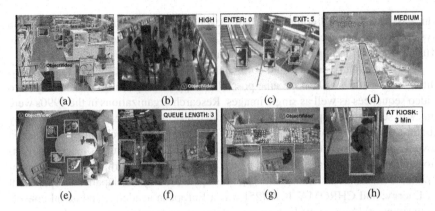

Fig. 3.2 Nonsecurity applications for video analytics. (a) Risk management: slip and fall detection. (b) Risk management: crowd density monitoring. (c) Business intelligence: people counting. (d) Business intelligence: traffic lane density monitoring. (e) Energy or space management: space occupancy monitoring. (f) Retail business intelligence: queue length monitoring. (g) Retail business intelligence: customer shopping habits (which items are being taken). (h) Business intelligence: information kiosk usage.

3.2.1 What Does Analytics Need to Do?

To bring an effective video analytics system to market, it is important to understand the requirements on two separate fronts. Firstly, what is the functionality that the system needs to be able to perform in its given environment; and secondly, what is the infrastructure environment that it must fit into? The benefits that can be derived from video analytics go beyond simply extracting information from video imagery; beyond "catching the bad guy" or "people counting." Video analytics provides a useful set of tools that can help an enterprise optimize its infrastructure and improve processes to gain efficiencies for human resources.

Human efficiency optimization

People are not even very good at monitoring CCTV video. Research indicates that they become ineffective after only 20 minutes. It is clear that there are efficiencies in getting people out from behind monitors. They can concentrate on other tasks and they can be more mobile which means that they are faster to respond to events, and they are more visible to act as a deterrent.

Prior to analytics, video systems were used, as a rule, exclusively for forensic purposes; for after-the-fact analysis of events that had already occurred. Typically, this type of analysis is very manually intensive. At best, a human operator can monitor events in a video feed played at about $3\times$ real-time. At this rate, searching through a day of video data from a single camera will take about 8 hours to accomplish. As a by-product of event detection, a video analytics system can generate a stream of meta-data that consists of a logical description of the activities of every object within a video stream: what they are; their physical properties (color, shape, size, and so forth); where they are; how they move through the scene; and how they physically interact with each other and the scene. Typically, this meta-data is very low-bandwidth compared to video information. And it can be analyzed after the fact to determine if a particular event has taken place. For example, the system could be asked to find any instances, in the last month, of a white van parked outside the perimeter of an airport for more than 20 minutes. The information required to determine these events is typically captured by meta-data, and thus this request can be fulfilled simply by applying some logical rules to the meta-data stream without performing any more image processing at all.

Infrastructure optimization

Video is a very rich medium, and as such, requires a large amount of bandwidth and storage; both of which are expensive. Raw, 24-bit (RGB) mega-pixel imagery consumes bandwidth B of about 720 Mbps, and remember that the market is continually demanding larger pixel resolutions and high-quality imagery. Of course, raw imagery is not a realistic option and there has been a lot of work done over the last few decades on video compression and video encoding. Today there are several standard video coder/decoder (codec) algorithms that have a number of useful properties depending on the application. However, compression technology is reaching a diminishing returns point. Analytics provides the next evolution in bandwidth management. The system only needs to transmit or record video information when something of interest occurs: when some activity is occurring around the perimeter or, indeed, there is a perimeter breach. There are camera and encoder systems on the market today that can throttle back the quality, frame rate, and transmission bandwidth of IP video depending on the level of activity in the scene.

The same kind of argument can be made for video storage. Not only can video analytics help with indexing and retrieval of vast amounts of stored video, but it can also be used to help with storage optimization, and storage degradation policies as well. Typical video storage policies for security and business intelligence applications require video from some or all cameras in a CCTV system to be stored for a period of time, usually between 3 days and 4 weeks, although in some extreme cases it can be several years. After this time, video is to be overwritten. There are three challenges with this. Firstly, it is very manually intensive to retrieve any useful information from these archives. Secondly, the storage costs are very high. Consider that a stream of compressed video at very high quality is about 10 Mbps. This translates to 3.4×10^{12} bytes or about 3.2 TB per month per camera. For an enterprise such as a retailer with thousands of stores, each with hundreds of cameras, this represents a significant investment in storage infrastructure. Finally, some enterprises suffer from their storage policies, when they become publicly known. People start to exploit them. For example, there are retailers with 14-day video storage policies that seem to receive a large number of "slip and fall" complaints after 15 days—just as soon as the corroborating (or contradictory) video evidence has been irretrievably lost. Clearly a large amount of storage space (and therefore cost) can be saved if the storage system need only store video associated with activities of interest.

3.2.2 The Video Ecosystem: Use-Cases for Video Analytics

It is interesting to note that many of the different applications for video analytics technology have very different integration requirements. If we start with the security applications, video analytics represents a tool to aid a human decision maker. Furthermore, information derived from the system is often required for evidentiary purposes. So, the system must be able to produce and store at least imagery if not full-motion video of events. Another common use case in security applications is after-the-fact forensic analysis. And video analytics is often used to create meta-data tagging to enable high-speed searching [17, 18]. Putting these requirements together, security applications for analytics require that the system is able to feed video streams into the analytics algorithms which create two separate types of output: "events" when activities of interest are detected (*including* video or imagery data); and meta-data with which to tag stored video.

There are other classes of applications—such as business intelligence—that tend to have different data output requirements for the analytics systems. In these cases, there is often a human decision-maker in the loop, but typically, the decision-maker doesn't need to view the imagery to make a decision. Retail operations specialists do not need images of all the people that enter their stores; they just need to know *how many* entered on a particular day, and how that compared with store occupancy at other times on other days. So in these cases, video analytics systems generally do not need to create "alerts" that include imagery, but rather, only need to provide a very thin meta-data stream containing specific "events" such as ``Person entered store'' or ``line length: 6 people''. In fact, there are some applications where it is actually *undesirable* to produce imagery—particularly where there are privacy concerns around the monitoring application.

Fig. 3.3 shows a modern network-centric IP-based video ecosystem. At the front edge of the system are information capture devices such as IP video cameras and IP video encoders that capture analog video, compress it, and stream it in an IP video format. There are also other sensing devices, systems and data sources that integrate with the enterprise infrastructure. In a security environment, for example, these may include access control systems, perimeter intrusion detection systems, employee databases, and other data sources. In a retail environment, these may include point-of-sale (POS) systems, inventory management systems, and marketing databases. At the back edge of the system are a set of data exploitation systems and applications. There are video management and visualization systems; video indexing, storage, and retrieval systems; data analysis and reporting tools; and mobile responder support systems.

There has been some debate in the media concerning the right location for video analytics applications within the context of this type of infrastructure [21]. Some

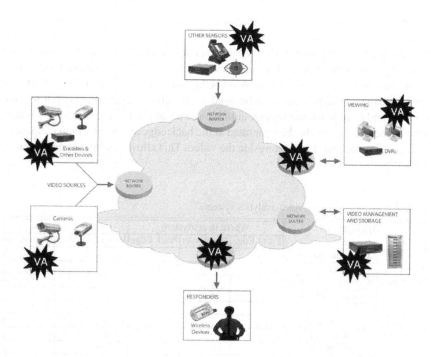

Fig. 3.3 An IP-centric video ecosystem showing possible locations for video analytics (VA) applications or components.

people believe that the best location for analytics is at the front edge: in cameras, encoders, and stand-alone video analytics devices. Others think that the best place for analytics is at the back edge: embedded in video management systems and storage devices. In fact, there are very good arguments for providing analytics at any node of the infrastructure—and there are customers that want to purchase analytics-capable devices in a wide variety of form factors for a variety of applications.

It is very useful to put video analytics at the front edge to help modulate bandwidth over the network as well as all of the other benefits analytics can provide. In its ultimate front-edge incarnation, video analytics can even be part of a pure sensing device: one that captures video but *only* delivers meta-data or event data.

However, there are good reasons to put analytics in other places: such as inside the network itself. One of the "holy grails" of networking is the creation of a data-aware network. The advantage of an intelligent network that understands the traffic flowing through it is obvious. It can optimize quality of service (QoS) and determine routing paths to get the most out of the network. Video analytics provides a means for network infrastructure to peer into any video data flowing through it. With this ability, the network can automatically determine which packets are important, and to whom, and therefore figure out an optimal routing strategy.

Of course, another obvious location for analytics is at the back edge, where video comes to be stored, monitored, visualized, and distributed. Putting video analytics in a storage solution, for example, enables a number of advantages over and above detecting important events. Video analytics can be used to modulate storage so that video only need-be stored (or only need be high quality) when activities of interest are occurring. Analytics can also be used to visualize information within storage systems and to manage intelligent, automatic data degradation policies. Analytics-derived meta-data can also be generated at the back edge as part of a management or storage solution, and stored alongside the video. This allows for high-speed forensic analysis.

Table 3.1 Requirements for video analytics systems

Application		Where in ecosystem			Output data type		
		Front Edge	Net. Layer	Back Edge	Imagery	Events	Meta-data
Real-time	"Catch the bad guy"	◊	◊	◊	◊	◊	
	Business intel.	◊	◊	◊		◊	
	Building automation	◊				◊	◊
	Bandwidth opt.	◊				◊	◊
	Net. QoS opt.		◊			◊	◊
Off-line	Indexing	◊	◊	◊			◊
	Retrieval			◊	◊	◊	
	Storage opt.			◊	◊	◊	
	Storage vis./degrad.			◊	◊	◊	

Table 3.1 puts all of this together. Given what the customer wants to achieve out of their video analytics, the table shows where in the network it can be effective, and what type of data needs to be produced. One thing is clear, though; no matter where in the video ecosystem analytics needs to be, the only way to effectively deliver it—without breaking the cost or footprint budget—is as an embedded *ingredient* in an existing component or device within the system.

3.3 How Does Video Analytics Work?

Video analytics solutions have to be capable of providing a broad range of functionality. And in addition, they have to be flexible in terms of what types of information they provide for downstream processing and analysis. And, perhaps most importantly, analytics has to seamlessly integrate with existing infrastructure. Analytics must be an *ingredient* within some device or application, rather than a stand-alone application. To achieve this, analytics software must be capable of being embedded within the firmware of other devices, and must be flexible enough in its architecture to enable multiple different types of information in different formats to be extracted from video streams.

3.3.1 An Embedded Analytics Architecture

A very powerful architectural model uses the notion that analytics processing is divided into two fundamental components: a video content analysis engine (CA Engine); and an activity inference engine (see Fig. 3.4). The CA engine models the background environment of a video scene and detects environmental conditions such as meteorological phenomena (rain, snow, wind in the trees, and so on); and scene changes such as lights turning on/off, camera motion, and slow lighting changes. The CA engine can then suppress these effects and detect any independently moving foreground objects such as people, vehicles, watercraft, aircraft, and animals. These objects are tracked and classified as they move through the scene. After this, all of the environmental phenomena and detected objects are described in a lightweight symbolic stream of meta-data. This meta-data contains records for each detected object at each frame in the video stream. For each object, such data as object ID, object type, velocity, location, trajectory, shape, and size are encoded in the meta-data. This meta-data stream runs parallel to any video streaming and typically consumes between 50 Kbps and 100 Kbps for most operational video scenes.

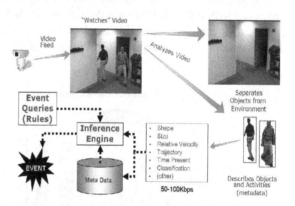

Fig. 3.4 Video analytics processing steps. Content analysis extracts legitimate objects and tracks and classifies them. Then it creates a stream of meta-data describing the activities of everything in the video stream. An inference engine determines if any prescribed events can be detected from the meta-data stream (either in real-time or from a meta-data archive).

The inference engine ingests all of the meta-data from the CA engine and any other meta-data from other systems such as retail POS systems, access control systems, or radio frequency identification (RFID) systems. The inference engine then determines if any user-defined activities (behaviors) have occurred. When these prescribed activities are detected, an event is generated in any required format (typically, an XML packet or SMTP email message) and transmitted to any back-end system. The meta-data can be analyzed in real-time or streamed and archived for future analysis. There are three major advantages to this architectural approach:

1. *Multiple detection rules.* By splitting the meta-data generation from the activity detection, the same low-level processing can be used to detect many different types of activities or behaviors in the scene. So, a single instance of the analytics

software can simultaneously be detecting multiple different types of suspicious activities in a single video stream.

2. *After-the-fact meta-data analysis.* Meta-data, created by the CA engine attached to any video stream, can be archived using minimal storage compared to video. Any supported activity or behavior can be detected after the fact by running the archived meta-data through the inference engine.

3. *Distributed processing.* Meta-data can be streamed from a video device to multiple software applications on a network that house inference engines. The idea is that, for a minimal bandwidth penalty, meta-data can be broadcast to back-end applications running different instances of an inference engine monitoring for different behaviors.

A typical instantiation of a digital signal processor (DSP) library solution may be a video device such as an IP camera, encoder, or DVR where raw video is captured and converted to an IP stream. The raw video is typically split between a third-party compression engine and the analytics engine. The analytics engine performs video processing and produces events when rule conditions are met, and outputs meta-data if desired. The DSP-based device typically communicates through a network via a DSP-based TCP/IP stack to some back-end management system (see Fig. 3.5). Note that, even within the DSP library, the CA engine is separated from the inference engine. It is completely possible to place these two components within different devices or applications within a CCTV infrastructure as desired.

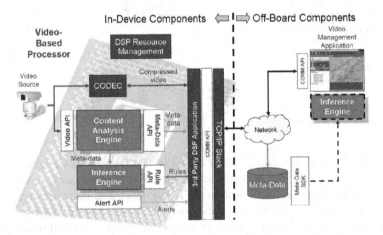

Fig. 3.5 An architecture for embedded video analytics (an IP camera/encoder example is shown here). The content analysis and inference engine components are separated, each with appropriate APIs to allow application programmers to embed the functionality into their third-party applications. The architecture also provides a communication API so that back-end devices and applications can talk to the analytics-enabled device. And there should also be a mechanism for handling meta-data for storage and after-the-fact analysis.

Integrating a library into an existing (or new) device must be as easy as possible, so an analytics library will have to support appropriate public application programming interfaces (APIs). These serve as the integration points between the analytics library and the DSP application layer. In a system such as the one described above, there are four basic integration interfaces required:

1. The video frame API allows third parties to write DSP applications that feed video frames into the analytics libraries.
2. The rule API allows third parties to apply rules, parameters, and other configuration information to the DSP libraries.
3. The alert API allows third parties to write DSP applications that read alert data from the libraries.
4. The meta-data API allows third-party applications to extract real-time meta-data from the CA engine.

Device manufacturers need to write their own DSP application layer to support desired functionality that is native to the device. An important question here is how to control the device from a remote, back-end device or application. Most IP-based video devices have some type of web-based or XML-based back-end interface. For IP cameras and encoders, these interfaces allow users and applications to view video streams, store them, manage video quality, and so forth. There also needs to be an interface of some kind for analytics functions. It must be possible for a back-end user or application to set rules and configuration, receive events or alerts, and stream and manage meta-data. For that purpose, a fifth API is also available to which device manufacturers can conform thus allowing applications to plug-and-play with the analytics components embedded in the device.

3.3.2 Video Analytics Algorithmic Components

Almost all of the computer vision technologies that comprise the aforementioned video analytics applications are made up of several relatively standard functional building blocks. A good tutorial on computer vision techniques and applications can be found in [16]. Fig. 3.6 shows these building blocks. They are generally organized into three areas: physical interaction; low-level vision; and semantic vision.

Physical Interaction

Physical interaction components deal with vision algorithms that are important to describe or control the interaction of the vision system (the camera) with the physical world. These algorithms can be broken into four basic groups:

Calibration Techniques: This set of technologies is used to determine the physical properties of an imaging system or tie the imaging system to another coordinate system: another camera, a real-world map, a geodetic model, or another object's local coordinate system. These techniques are required for a number of common

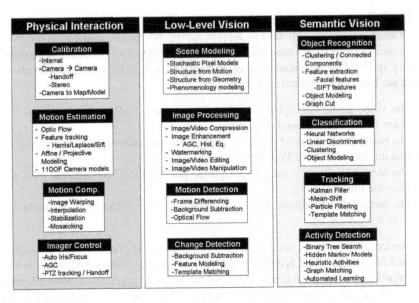

Fig. 3.6 Components of computer vision / video analytics systems.

computer vision functions such as: 3D reconstruction via stereo or other techniques; accurate image-based mensuration; absolute object size/speed determination; target geolocation; camera-to-camera target hand-off; and stereo disparity estimation.

Motion Estimation: These technologies involve processing the imagery from a moving camera to determine the quality and quantity of camera motion. Camera motion typically falls into one of four basic categories. The first is static, meaning the camera is not moving. This is typical in many machine inspection and surveillance applications. Then, there is translational, meaning the camera is "sliding by" the scene. The camera motion model typically consists of two parameters: $(\Delta x, \Delta y)$. This is a good model for many machine inspection applications. It can also work in some electronic stabilization and pan/tilt surveillance camera applications, as well as some stereo machine applications. The third is the affine/projective model, meaning a 6- or 8- parameter linear warping model between frames. The transform is discussed in [12] and has the form:

$$x' = \begin{bmatrix} a & b & c \\ d & e & f \\ (g) & (h) & 1 \end{bmatrix} x$$

This is a good model for most pan/tilt/zoom (PTZ) camera applications and a good approximation for some high-altitude airborne camera applications as well, as long as there a no significant nonlinear lens distortion effects. It is often modified with lens distortion parameters to build a more realistic model. Finally, there is general camera motion, meaning the camera can experience motion in any of the six physical degrees of freedom. This is the type of motion that is typically experienced by hand-held and vehicle-mounted cameras.

Motion Compensation: Motion compensation typically goes hand-in-hand with motion estimation. Motion compensation is about removing the effects of motion from camera images to enable static camera processing techniques to be effective. Examples of applications for motion compensation techniques are image stabilization to remove the effects of camera "jitter;" image deblurring to remove the blur effects caused by camera motion; detection of legitimately moving foreground objects in the presence of background elements that appear to be moving because of camera motion; 3D (or other scene) modeling by detecting disparity or parallax between camera views; mosaic generation by "stitching together" frames from a moving camera. A good discussion of the geometry of motion compensation techniques can be found in [12].

Imager Control: Imager control technologies concern the adjustment of physical properties of the imaging system. Most imaging systems (still and video cameras) have some form of at least rudimentary imager control capabilities. These types of applications include: auto gain correction (AGC) designed to achieve an optimal dynamic range in the image; auto iris control designed to physically control the amount of light that enters the imager; auto focus designed to adjust lens parameters of the imaging system to maintain focus on the targets of interest; and automatic pan, tilt, zoom (PTZ) control which in some, more sophisticated imaging systems, can be made to track objects or maintain a particular view from a moving platform. Computer vision systems are sometimes used in robotic manipulator control. This is a robotic form of "hand-eye" coordination. There is also autonomous vehicle control; a more sophisticated version of PTZ control. Here, a vision system is used to control more than just the camera mount but rather a vehicle such as an autonomous car or unmanned air vehicle (UAV). Here the vision system may be physically mounted on the vehicle, or even be viewing the vehicle remotely.

Low-level vision

The realm of low-level vision is pixels. Low-level vision algorithms take a digitized image as an input, and through measurement and manipulation are able to extract useful information or modify the imagery. Typically such algorithms are employed as pre-processing steps for more complex applications for both human and machine consumption. There are four basic groups:

Scene Modeling: Scene modeling involves techniques for mathematically describing the scene being viewed by a camera system. These models may take the form of relatively simple pixel-based models of a static scene all the way to 3D representation. Typically, scene models are used as a backdrop for more advanced algorithms to obtain some context about the area being viewed. Some typical techniques include: simple, static background images for background subtraction; complex, stochastic pixel models that model both the appearance and the dynamic nature of the scene; context-based semantic models that attempt to model specific elements within a scene; and all of these types of scene models can be further extended to moving cameras through techniques such as mosaicking and optical flow. Scene models are often used to determine various phenomena occurring in the scene such as lighting changes or meteorological phenomenology (rain, snow, water and so on).

Image Processing: Image processing algorithms are used to enhance the quality of an image for human or machine consumption or to manipulate imagery for security or other purposes. Some typical techniques include: image analysis for video or image compression; image enhancement or restoration, automatic gain control (AGC), histogram equalization and so on for creating higher-quality imagery; image manipulation to include watermarks for digital security and digital rights management; image manipulation for visual effects such as special effects, background replacement, foreground replacement, advertisement insertion, and more.

Motion Detection: Motion detection algorithms involve determining the motion of objects within video streams. This process is often called motion segmentation. These approaches are typically precursor algorithms to more sophisticated processes for object tracking and event recognition; although, in its simplest form, video motion detection (VMD) is a feature of many surveillance systems. Examples of motion detection techniques are: frame differencing [7] in which a video frame is compared with a recent frame (or several recent frames) to determine if any pixels in the frame are different and therefore moving; background subtraction in which a video frame is compared to a reference background image to determine if any pixels are different and therefore moving (see Fig. 3.7); optical flow [6] which involves determining how each section of an image is moving from one frame to another and building a "flow field" of motion which can be used to estimate camera motion, independently moving objects in the scene or potentially both.

Change Detection: Change detection is a low-level process designed to determine which pixels in a scene have changed (foreground) between a reference image (background model) and the current frame (see Fig. 3.7). Of course, to be really effective, the background model must be able to adapt to slow changes in the scene caused by lighting and shadow effects and other meteorological conditions such as rain, snow, and wind in foliage. There are a number of good approaches to this type of algorithm such as [7, 10, 22]. The algorithm has two components: pixel classification in which pixels in a frame are labeled as either background or foreground pixels; and model updating in which the background statistical pixel model is updated for dynamic changes.

Semantic Vision

Semantic vision is where computer vision starts to create human-meaningful data from imagery. It is about machines understanding the contents of video imagery in a semantic fashion and being able to describe, symbolically, things that are occurring in those scenes. An easy way to think about this is to use the analogy of speech recognition. Being able to use signal processing techniques to analyze sound waves is a good start, but semantic understanding comes when those sound waves can be recognized as speech. Individual phonemes and words can be recognized, put into context, and expressed as symbolic text.

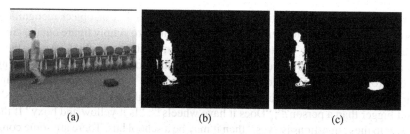

(a)   (b)   (c)

Fig. 3.7 Motion and change detection. Part (a) is the original image. (b) Motion detection. Two or three frame differencing detects pixels that are exhibiting frame-to-frame motion. Notice that the bag, whilst an object of interest in the scene, is not moving and is therefore not detected. (c) Change detection. Comparing each frame to a background model detects all the pixels that are part of the foreground. Sophisticated statistical background models can even adapt to slow lighting changes in the scene.

Object/Scene Recognition: Object or scene recognition is about detecting the presence in a scene of a particular object, feature, or condition. There are a number of low-level techniques to do this, but the goal is to recognize, for example, that if there is a car in the scene, it is "Fred's car"; or that if there is a person in a scene, that the person is "Fred." At the lowest level, clustering pixels into "blobs" (a process called "blobization" reasonably enough) provides a clue that there is a semantic object present in the scene. Simple versions of clustering algorithms use a standard connected components technique [5]. More advanced techniques such as [23] use a multiscale version to improve computational efficiency (see Fig. 3.8).

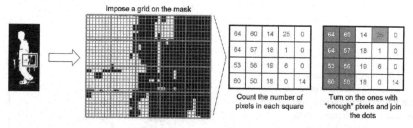

Fig. 3.8 Example blobization algorithm (quasi-connected components [23]). Impose a grid on a foreground mask and count the number of "on" pixels in each grid square. threshold this number and perform a connected components labeling in the lower resolution grid space.

Algorithms such as face detection, facial recognition, and license plate recognition are designed specifically to recognize features in an image and assign unique identification to those features. A more generic form of object recognition involves specific object modeling; if you know the 2D or 3D appearance of an object, there are a number of useful techniques for trying to establish its presence in a video image.

Classification: Classification is a more generic version of object recognition. Here, it is not necessary to identify an object, but rather to simply figure out the characteristics of that object—is it a vehicle or a person? Is it red or yellow? Again, there are a number of ways to achieve this. Most classification schemes involve building models (often statistical models) of features of objects and using rule-based grammar to figure out what a particular object is. It is often like the game "20 questions": "Is it bigger than a person?"; "Does it have wheels?"; "Is it yellow and boxy" If the answer to these questions is "yes," then it may be a school bus. There are some common techniques to achieve this. Artificial neural networks [9] use "rules" that are learned (semi-)automatically and encoded in a network of synthetic nodes (called neurons) trained by showing the system many examples of whatever you want to classify. The network evolves to figure out what features are important and how to combine them to come up with a good classifier. Linear discriminant analysis (LDA) [7, 9] or other clustering approaches involve having human beings deciding what features are important (such as object aspect ratio, dispersedness, and others) and representing a series of training examples in n-dimensional feature space. Algorithms LDA are then used to partition the feature space to optimize the clusters of similar objects (see Fig. 3.9). These partitions in feature space are used as discriminators for the classification process. As with object recognition, object models can also be used for classification. Canonical models of particular object types can be matched to objects detected in video. If the objects match the models well enough, a classification can be made. Another popular recent trend in classification is the use of cascaded boosted classifiers [28].

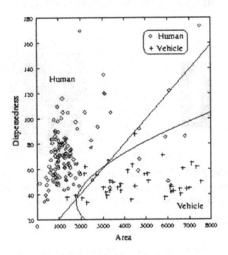

Fig. 3.9 Object classification techniques typically involve creating clusters in some feature space using training data and using them to determine the classes of objects in an operational scene. This case shows an LDA approach in a 2D space where a Mahalanobis distance is used to create the clusters.

Tracking: Tracking algorithms are used to create spatio-temporal descriptions of objects in video scenes (see Fig. 3.10). This is a useful component when trying to detect activities, behaviors, and interactions of objects with each other and the scene. Tracking is typically done by associating visible objects across spans of time. That is, determining that an object at a particular time is the same object at a different time. This is called the *association problem*. This is difficult, in practice, because objects in video streams change their appearance and trajectories rapidly based on their own actions, and interactions with other objects and parts of the scene. For example, an object may turn around and look completely different from the other side. Or a person may walk behind an occluding object and suddenly appear to be half the size.

In computer vision literature, there are a number of popular techniques for tracking video objects and features. A very traditional approach is template matching in which an image of the target is used at a particular time (a template) to match between frames. Kalman filtering [15] (or other trajectory filtering) is a common technique in which an object model goes through a cycle of prediction, matching, and updating from frame to frame in an effort to maintain a description of the target's true trajectory. Particle filtering [13] applies many different target models that are hypothesized and are matched to the image data; the trajectory is taken as a statistical mixture of all of the models. And mean-shift tracking [8] uses feature data essentially to pull an object model to an optimal position in the current image and thus determine where an object is. More advanced target tracking schemas use combinations of these approaches. Basic target tracking may be performed using Kalman filtering. More complex feature tracking (to track specific body parts) may also done with particle filters to help track objects through occlusions. One example target tracking algorithm is further divided into four separate modules with business logic for handling: single visible targets; occluded targets; disappearing targets; and stationary targets.

Fig. 3.10 Tracking turns blobs into spatio-temporal target descriptions. Frame-to-frame tracking of simple targets is straightforward using a number of tracking approaches. The trick is handling different object states.

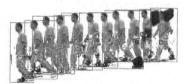

Spatio-Temporal Object Description

Activity Detection: At the highest level of computer vision is the notion of activity detection. These techniques determine events in a video stream at a semantic level and describe those events symbolically. This is where the technology can determine that "a person is climbing a tree." Most practical activity recognition algorithms are also, in some sense, model-based. A user must describe in one form or another what constitutes a particular activity and the algorithms can then figure out if those things are occurring. The difficult part of this is building enough flexibility into the activity description to account for variations in how activities are performed. No two people perform every action exactly the same way.

There are, however, some newer learning-based techniques that can determine activities based purely on observations of a scene. In effect, these techniques learn to build activity models themselves. The catch is that they do not know exactly what those activities are; and still require human intervention to translate a discovered activity model into a semantic description. They also have no idea how "important" a particular activity is—again, this requires human intervention.

Heuristic models such as binary tree models [18, 26, 27] are like "20 questions." An activity can be described in a series of linked logical "ANDs" and "ORs." An example would be: "object type = vehicle" AND "object behavior = stationary" AND "duration > 5 minutes" AND "location = tow-away zone" AND "9:00am < time < 5:00pm." This is an illegal parking rule (see Fig. 3.11 for another example). Hidden Markov models (HMMs) [20] are effectively probabilistic state transition models of activities that include some dynamic notions of time to account for variations in how different people perform the same activity. Automated activity recognition techniques involve self-organizing clusters of object characteristics over time to determine what patterns emerge. This is called *normalcy modeling*. For example, these techniques can learn that vehicles tend to move on roads; then the algorithm can automatically flag an event where a vehicle is somewhere else.

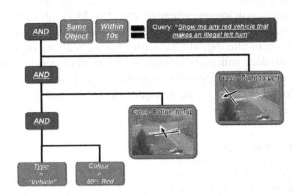

Fig. 3.11 An activity inference rule. A binary tree structure with a couple of modifications: (a) graphical activity elements (such as tripwire crossings) can be included; and (b) binary operators are modified by conditional concepts such as "the same object" and "within 10 seconds."

3.4 An Embedded Video Analytics System: by the Numbers

Now we can explore an exemplary video analytics system from the 2006 time frame. This is an end-to-end system that employs the architecture discussed in Section 3.3.1. We are going to look at how the computer vision components are put together and how they perform in an embedded environment. But before we drill down into the details, we need to determine our requirements: what processing platform are we targeting; how much CPU and RAM are we allowed to consume; what features and functions do we need to support; and so on.

For this particular example, our customer is building an analytics-capable IP video encoder designed for the security market. The analytics needs to be able to detect people or vehicles engaged in perimeter incursion (crossing tripwires), suspicious activity (loitering in secure areas), removing assets, and leaving behind suspicious packages. The analytics requires 320×240 pixels (qVGA resolution) for processing. They would like to be able to process two video channels per device. They need to perform compression as well as video analytics on each channel. They are using an MPEG4 video codec that will consume about 20% of their CPU for each D1 resolution (720×480 pixels) user-viewable video stream; and they have an overhead of about 10% for the communications stack, real-time operating system (RTOS) and DSP application layer. Also, they have a bill of materials budget that allows about 30 MB of RAM for each channel of video analytics.

For our example video analytics system, our customer has chosen an industry standard DSP: The Texas Instruments TMS320DM642-720 digital media DSP [1]. This is a very capable video processing DSP running a 720 MHz DM64x core with appropriate peripherals to ingest video, process video, handle DMA memory access, and manage communication to other devices. Such a device is very common in video encoders, low-end DVRs, and other video devices. It is also code-compatible with other TI DSPs that are common in other types of video devices ranging from image-based sensors to IP video cameras to large scale video management systems. Putting this all together, we get a set of requirements (Table 3.2).

Table 3.2 Real-world embedded video analytics requirements

Processor	TI: TMS320DM642 / 720 MHz
Image dimensions	320×240 (qVGA)
Image format	YCrCb444 or YCrCb420
Frame rate (analytics)	10 fps
CPU budget (per channel)	20% (144 MHz)
RAM budget (per channel)	30 MB
Functionality	Tripwire, loitering, theft, left item

3.4.1 Putting It All Together

Fig. 3.12 illustrates the processing pipeline of our embedded analytics DSP library. It shows the various algorithmic blocks that make up the system. The library is divided into those two major components: the CA engine and the activity inference engine. The CA engine performs generic video processing. That is, it extracts all of the significant objects in the video scene, tracks them, classifies them, and creates a stream of meta-data that describes everything that is going on in the scene. It also monitors the scene itself and determines whether the scene is changing—or even if it can no longer recognize the scene. The inference engine adds higher-level logic to determine if any user-defined activities or behaviors have occurred. It comes with a library of business logic rules that can be combined using a binary-tree-like language to create complex rule definitions. Table 3.3 describes the components in a little more detail.

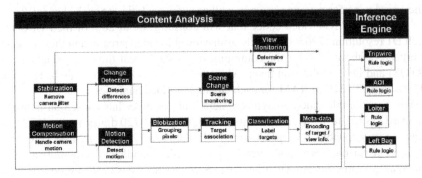

Fig. 3.12 Algorithmic blocks for a sample embedded video analytics system.

Data Types

There are a number of important data types that are useful in the context of this video analytics processing pipeline. Without drilling down in too much detail, here is a description of some of the data that may be necessary:

- *Image frames:* typically, $320 \times 240 \times 8$-bit planar data structure used for storing the Y component and chroma components (C_r, C_b) of an input image or a labeled bit-mask
- *Blob:* a collection of data describing a group of pixels that may represent an object in an individual frame. This data type may contain information such as: bounding box width, height, and location; number of pixels (changed or moving); centroid and "footprint" locations; shape parameters; color histograms (if color is available); and skin tone pixels (if color is available)
- *Target:* a collection of data representing a spatio-temporal object (an object tracked over time). The target data type may contain information such as: target ID; target life-span (when created, how many times seen, and so on); target state (currently visible, occluded, disappeared, or stationary); inter-target relationships (such as the fact that this target split from some other target); classification information; and a list of blob data for each instance of target

3.4.2 Analysis of Embedded Video Analytics System

To determine if we have a viable solution to our customer's requirements, we have to put the system together and measure the overall timing and CPU/RAM

Table 3.3 Description of example analytics system components

Component	Description	Subcomponents (if applicable)
Stabilization and motion compensation	Remove camera motion and camera jitter by matching incoming frames to a reference image and warping them to a common coordinate system [12].	
Motion detection	Create a binary mask of pixels that are "moving." Uses a 3-frame difference technique [7].	
Change detection	Create a binary mask of pixels that are different from a stochastic scene model. Uses a technique similar to [7].	**Classify** determines which pixels are foreground and which are background. **Update** adds new image information to the background model.
Blobization	Creates "blobs" from the motion and change detection masks. Using a technique similar to quasi-connected components [23].	**Subsample** scales the imagery. **Connected components** joins connected pixels into blobs. **Label** assigns unique labels to blobs. **Generate blobs** extracts blob information into data structures. **Refine** filters the blobs to make sure they are legitimate.
Target tracking	Combines blobs into spatio-temporal target descriptions. Basic tracking uses Kalman filtering [15], but specific feature tracking (such as human head tracking) uses particle filters [13].	**VTM** (visual target manager) uses simple Kalman filtering to track unoccluded targets. **OTM** (occluded target manager) tracks targets that are currently occluded. **STM** (stationary target manager) tracks targets that have stopped moving (like parked vehicles). **DTM** (disappeared target manager) tracks targets that are not currently in the view.
Classification	Classifies targets into "Humans," "Vehicles," or "Other" classes. Uses LDA [7] with features such as aspect ratio and dispersedness.	**Classify** performs the LDA target classification algorithm. **Salience** determines if the target looks like a legitimate object or some video noise (such as a car headlight).
Scene change detection	Determines if there is a significant change in the scene. Either through global lighting changes (lights on / off) or through camera motion.	
View monitoring	Handles multiple views if the system is being used with PTZ camera on a guard tour. A number of samples of each of a number of pre-set views is maintained. These views are matched to the camera image to determine which view is being monitored.	
Meta-data generation	Takes all of the view and target meta-data and wraps it into standard format data structures and packets for the Inference Engine.	**Scene Change** is data describing changes to the view. **Target Data** describes all the targets in the scene each frame. **Heartbeat** is a time-based datum used for synchronization when there is no other meta-data from the scene.
Inference engine	Logic to mine the meta-data (in real-time or after the fact) to determine if events such as tripwire crossings, loitering, left items, or stolen items have occurred.	

utilization. To determine the processing requirements of each of these algorithmic modules, timing tests were performed. The base platform was a DM642 / 720 MHz TI evaluation module (EVM). The code-base was ObjectVideo's commercial product, ObjectVideo OnBoard™ version 4.0 (released in June of 2006). The timing of each of the algorithmic modules was determined on a per-frame basis for each of 12 representative video clips. Timing numbers represent the total processing time for the function including CPU time and memory access time. The video clips were all several minutes long, processed at 10 fps, and qVGA resolution (320×240). Average times for each module per frame were obtained and converted into an approximate potential CPU utilization number measured in MHz. Note that the analysis did not include image stabilization (which is not a standard feature of this particular code-base) or any of the inference engine components.

The results of the analysis are shown in Table 3.4. There are a number of low-level components that take up significant processing time. But it looks like the CPU budget of 144 MHz has been met. There is variability in the processor utilization as a function of scenario, particularly for the components that depend on the number of targets. It is clear that there is no overwhelming "hot spot" in the code. This means that the system is well optimized. Table 3.5 illustrates the memory usage for each components. The system consumes a modest 23 MB which can be lowered by reducing the number of views or targets that the system can support. This easily fits into the 30 MB budget allowed.

Table 3.4 Average processing load per frame for algorithmic components

Component	Proc. time (ms)	Component	Proc. time (ms)
Change Detection	**5.81 ± 6%**	**Target Tracking**	**4.66 ± 70%**
Classify	1.52	VTM	3.14
Update	4.29	OTM	0.31
Motion Detection	**0.76 ± 1%**	STM	0.48
Blobization	**4.55 ± 44%**	DTM	0.73
Subsample	0.06	**Classification**	**1.15 ± 12%**
Connected components	0.04	Classify targets	0.45
Label	0.26	Salience	0.7
Generate blobs	2.25	**Meta-Data Generation**	**0.53**
Refine	1.94	Scene change	0.001
Scene Change Detection	**0.03 ± 300%**	Target data	0.53
View Monitoring	**0.07 ± 500%**	Heartbeat	0.002
Total for Content Analysis		**17.55 (126.4 MHz) ± 35%**	

3.5 Future Directions for Embedded Video Analytics

Video analytics technology is complex and is becoming sought after to perform many useful functions in a number of different application areas. As the technology becomes more capable, there will be higher requirements placed on processors to accommodate new algorithms. Let's examine a few areas where market drivers will create new requirements for algorithms and processors. Chapter 12 will provide a more detailed discussion of future challenges faced by video analytics.

Table 3.5 Average memory usage for algorithmic components

Component	Memory Requirements	Approx. mem. usage
Stabilization	A reference image	0.1 MB
Change detection	Stochastic background / foreground model(s)	1 MB
Motion detection	Several partial change masks	1 MB
Blobization	Up to 50 "blobs" (10 KB)	0.5 MB
Scene change detection	A reference image	0.1 MB
Target tracking	Up to 40 "targets" (115 KB)	4.5 MB
View monitoring	Background models of up to 6 "views" (1.8 MB)	10.8 MB
Classification	No internal state	0 MB
Meta-data generation	No internal state	0 MB
Inference	About 0.2 MB per rule up to about 5 rules	1 MB
System state	Video buffer of about 3 seconds	3 MB
Program size	1 MB of Flash	
TOTAL	**23 MB**	

3.5.1 Surveillance and Monitoring Applications

As of 2005, approximately 25 million CCTV cameras shipped annually [11]. As surveillance and monitoring applications become more advanced and IP-centric, there is a strong push to reject the old CCTV standards (PAL, NTSC, and SECAM) in favor of higher resolution IP-cameras based upon new digital transmission and storage standards. Currently, cheap CMOS imagers support up to 10's of megapixels. In fact, it is difficult to purchase a CMOS imager with fewer than 1 Mpix. This extra resolution is driving two different types of applications in the market. Firstly, people are using higher resolution to cover more area. More pixels means a wider or longer field of view. Secondly, more pixels means better target identification. According to the much-cited Johnson criteria [14], identification of individual targets (via facial recognition, license plate reading, or simply human-based identification) requires significantly higher resolution than mere detection or classification.

There are two limitations preventing the proliferation of higher and higher resolution CCTV systems. The first is bandwidth, as high resolution demands correspondingly higher bandwidth for transmission and storage. The second is analysis, as more data makes it more manually intensive (and therefore costly) to derive benefit. For example, one true customer application requires 50 pixels on target at 100 m distance with a 180-degree field of view. This translates to a requirement for 1600×1200 pixel resolution. Another real identification requirement needs 25,000 pixels on target at 100 m with a 2.5-degree field of view. This means the system needs 2000×1600 pixels.

3.5.2 Moving Camera Applications

When camera systems move, many of the basic assumptions behind video analytics algorithms are violated. Different technology must be applied in these cases. In some moving camera applications such as video stabilization, PTZ camera motion, and high-altitude airborne camera motion, traditional technology can be applied after the camera motion has been compensated. In other applications, such as vehicle-mounted cameras and micro-UAVs (low altitude), different technology is required.

Scanning camera example

As an example application involving a moving camera, the U.S. Department of Homeland Security (DHS) has created a requirement to develop an analytics capability for a scanning PTZ camera. Fig. 3.13 illustrates the concept. A PTZ camera on a continuous scan path detects an object in the scene. When such an object is detected, the camera automatically zooms in to interrogate it. This type of technology is particularly targeted for border protection applications in which it is prohibitive to place too many cameras along long stretches of border. This is a way to leverage PTZ capabilities and analytics to get maximal value from minimal infrastructure.

The scanning camera concept involves applying standard analytics technology (detecting, tracking, classifying objects) to a moving camera video feed. Consequently, camera motion must be estimated and compensated before object detection and tracking can occur. Fortunately, the camera motion, in this case, can be modeled by a projective transformation. This is done by building a mosaic of the background scene and registering each frame to the mosaic.

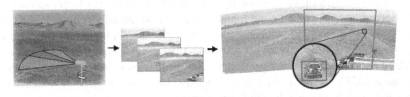

Fig. 3.13 A scanning camera system for border protection. A single PTZ camera scans back and forth looking for activity. When an object is detected, it automatically zooms in and interrogates the object.

3.5.3 Imagery-Based Sensor Solutions

Video is a very rich medium. There is a large amount of useful data that can be extracted from a video feed. Now that video analytics allows that process to be automated, there are many applications for video as a sensor that do not require a human decision-maker in the loop, or at least do not require the use of imagery. These applications use video as a data source to provide useful information to an automated control system in the form of symbolic data.

Imagery-based sensing for occupancy detection

Buildings in the United States today account for over 40% of our nations carbon dioxide emissions. Most of these emissions come from combustion of fossil fuels to power building systems—HVAC (heating, ventilation air conditioning) and lighting—and to run electrical equipment and appliances. Over the past 20 years, energy efficiency has been improved by the deployment of building automation systems. Most of these systems, however, do not incorporate the latest technological developments in processors, embedded software applications and networking. It is estimated that the United States could cut energy usage by up to 6% by adopting advanced building controls.

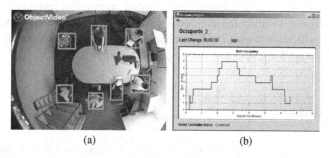

(a)   (b)

Fig. 3.14 A video-based sensor application. (a) An occupancy application: the analytics detects the occupancy within the space. (b) The output from the system is raw numerical occupancy data as a function of time.

One vital piece of input data currently absent from building automation systems is detailed information on actual space occupancy. Video-based sensing technology (see Fig. 3.14) is potentially game-changing in that it provides a range of highly reliable yet cost-effective occupancy intelligence. This implementation is a radical departure from existing passive infrared or ultrasonic technology, providing improved performance not only for replacement applications, but also for a broader array of data not previously available. Person or vehicle occupancy information can be transmitted over wired or wireless infrastructures and can cover anything from a single area to an entire enterprise. With this information, building automation systems can provide significant improvements in efficiency by applying lighting and HVAC not only where people are present, but also in proportion to the actual count of people.

Human verification sensor (HVS) for intrusion detection

Typical security monitoring systems for residential and light commercial properties consist of a series of low-cost sensors that detect such things as motion, smoke/fire, glass breaking, door/window opening, and so on. One such application is monitoring of residential and light commercial properties. The main application of these systems is intrusion detection—"Is someone where they shouldn't be?" Alarms from these sensors are collected at a central control panel, usually located on the premises, which reports the alarms to a central monitoring location via a phone line (or other communication channel). Recently, there have been a number of "do it yourself" solutions for monitoring where sensors (including video sensors) provide alarms directly to the end-customer via the Internet or a wireless mobile device. The primary problem with these systems is false alarms; and the cost of false alarms is quite high. Typically, an alarm is handled by local law enforcement personnel or a guard service. Dispatching human responders when there is no real security breach is costing monitoring services and the general public significant amounts of money.

A solution to this problem is a low-cost image-based sensor that can automatically verify the presence of a human and transmit appropriate imagery back to the central monitoring location for additional verification by human responders. There are human verification sensor (HVS) technologies that have an extremely high detection rate (over 95%), with an extremely low false alarm rate.

3.6 Conclusion

We have looked at what video analytics is, how it works, and how it needs to be deployed in the real world. We have examined an example of an embedded video analytics system and found that it works within the constraints of true customer requirements. And we have looked at the future and seen that, to be frank, no one in the embedded computer vision space need be worried about finding a job for a long time to come.

Video analytics has come out of the lab. There are a large number of very compelling applications for this technology in many existing and nascent markets. The available features and functions match very closely with real commercial needs. Initial security applications such as perimeter protection and suspicious behavior detection are giving way to more high-volume commodity applications such as business intelligence in retail and financial sectors. Ultimately, analytics technology will find a home in many different application spaces. However, to make a good case for analytics in a real-world market, we need more than mere technology. The capabilities have to be available at a price point and in a form factor that are compelling for the end customer. If ever there was a technology destined for firmware it is video analytics. With more capable, low-cost processors being employed in video-based devices it seems the stars are aligning for video analytics.

References

1. www.ti.com.
2. *Proceedings of Third International Workshop on Cooperative Distributed Vision*, Kyoto, Japan, Novemberr 1999.
3. *Automated Imaging Association (AIA) Business Conference*, Orlando, Fl, February 2007.
4. L. von Ahn, M. Blum, N. J. Hopper, and J. Langford. Captcha: Telling humans and computers apart. *Advances in Cryptology, Eurocrypt '03 and Lecture Note in Computer Science*, 2656: 294–311, 2003.
5. Dana H. Ballard and C. M. Brown. *Computer Vision*. Prentice-Hall, 1982.
6. S.S. Beauchemin and J.L. Barron. The computation of optical flow. *ACM Computing Surveys*, 27(3): 433–467, 1995.
7. Robert T. Collins, Alan J. Lipton, Hiro Fujiyoshi, and Takeo Kanade. Algorithms for cooperative multi-sensor surveillance. In G. Goresti, V. Ramesh, and C. Regazzoni, eds., *Proceedings of the IEEE, Special Issue on Video Communications, Processing and Understanding for Third Generation Surveillance Systems*, 89: 1456–1477, October 2001.
8. Dorin Comanesciu, V. Ramesh, and Peter Meer. Real-time tracking of non-rigid objects using mean shift. In *IEEE Conference on Computer Vision and Pattern Recognition*, Hilton Head, SC, 2000.
9. R. Duda, P. Hart, and D. G. Stork. *Pattern Classification* (2nd edition). Wiley, New York, 2001.
10. Ahmed Elgammal, David Harwood, and Larry Davis. Non-parametric model for background subtraction. In *6th European Conference on Computer Vision*, Dublin, Ireland, June 2000.
11. Simon Harris. World market for CCTV and video surveillance equipment. Technical report, IMS Research, 2006.
12. R. Hartley and A. Zisserman. *Multiple View Geometry in Computer Vision*. Cambridge University Press, 2000.
13. Michael Isard and Andrew Blake. Condensation – conditional density propagation for visual tracking. *Int. J. Computer Vision*, 29(1): 5–28, January 1998.
14. John Johnson. Analysis of image forming systems. In *Image Intensifier Symposium, AD 220160*, pp. 244–273, Ft Belvoir, VA, 1958. Warfare Electrical Engineering Department, U.S. Army Research and Development Laboratories.
15. R. E. Kalman. A new approach to linear filtering and prediction problems. *Transactions of the ASME, Journal of Basic Engineering*, pp. 35–45, March 1960.
16. Alan J. Lipton. Tutorial: Visual intelligence – what's next for video surveillance. In *Seventh International Conference on Control, Automation, Robotics, and Vision (ICARCV'02)*, Singapore, December 2002.
17. Alan J. Lipton. Activity-based forensic analysis of unstructured video data. In *Intelligence Support Systems for Lawful Interception (ISS)*, Washington, DC, December 2007. Telestrategies.
18. Alan J. Lipton, John Clark, Paul Brewer, Peter L. Venetianer, and Andrew J. Chosak. Objectvideo forensics: Activity-based video indexing and retrieval for physical security applications. In *Proceedings of IEE Conference on Intelligent Distributed Surveillance Systems*, pp. 56–60, London, 2004.
19. Seymour Papert. The summer vision project. Vision Memo 100, MIT — AI Group, July 1966.
20. Lawrence R. Rabiner. A tutorial on hidden markov models and selected applications in speech recognition. In *Proceedings of the IEEE*, 77: 257–286, February 1989.
21. Ashley Roe and Stephanie Silk. Where on the network? Security Solutions Online: http://securitysolutions.com/video/network_video_analytics_cameras, 1 April 2008.
22. Chris Stauffer and Eric Grimson. Learning patterns of activity using real-time tracking. *IEEE Transactions on Pattern Analysis and Machine Intelligence*, 22(8): 747–575, August 2000.
23. T. E. Boult, R. J. Micheals, X. Gao, P. Lewis, C. Power, W. Yin, and A. Erkan. Frame-rate omnidirectional surveillance and tracking of camouflaged and occluded targets. In *Proc. of the IEEE Workshop on Visual Surveillance*, June 1999.

24. Alan Turing. Computing Machinery and Intelligence (1950). In B. J. Copeland, ed., *The Essential Turing*. Oxford University Press, 2004.
25. S. A. Velastin, B. A. Boghossian, B. P. L. Lo, J. Sun, and M. A. Vicencio-Silva. Prismatica: toward ambient intelligence in public transport environments. *IEEE Transactions on Systems, Man and Cybernetics, Part A,* 35(1): 164–182, 2005.
26. P. Venetianer, M. Allmen, P. Brewer, A. Chosak, J. Clark, M. Frazier, N. Haering, T. Hirata, C. Horne, A. Lipton, W. Severson, J. Sfekas, T. Slowe, T. Strat, J. Tilki, and Z. Zhang. Video tripwire. US Patent No. 6,696,945, 2004.
27. P. Venetianer, A. Lipton, A. Chosak, N. Haering, and Z. Zhang. Video tripwire. US Patent No. 6,999,600, 2006.
28. P. Viola and M. Jones. Rapid object detection using a boosted cascade of simple features. In *Proc. IEEE CVPR Conference*, 2001.

Part II
Advances in Embedded Computer Vision

Chapter 4
Using Robust Local Features on DSP-Based Embedded Systems

Clemens Arth, Christian Leistner, and Horst Bischof

Abstract In recent years many powerful computer vision algorithms have been proposed, making feasible automatic or semi-automatic solutions to many popular vision tasks, such as camera calibration and visual object recognition. In particular, the driving force was the development of new powerful algorithms, especially in the area of local features. On the other hand, embedded vision platforms and solutions, such as smart cameras, have successfully emerged. Smart cameras offer enough power for decentralized image processing for various kinds of tasks, especially in the field of surveillance, but are still strictly limited in their computational and memory resources.

In this chapter, we investigate a set of robust local feature detectors and descriptors for application on embedded systems. We briefly describe the methods involved, that is, the DoG (difference of Gaussians) and MSER (maximally stable extremal regions) detector as well as the PCA-SIFT descriptor, and discuss their suitability for smart systems for camera calibration and object recognition tasks. The second contribution of this work is the experimental evaluation of these methods on two challenging tasks, namely, the task of robust camera calibration and fully embedded object recognition on a medium-sized database. Our approach is fortified by encouraging results which we present at length.

4.1 Introduction

In the last few years, computer vision has become one of the most powerful tools in engineering. Industrial and commercial demands are further pushing the development of high-performance vision algorithms, bringing up efficient solutions to existing problems and also many new applications into everyones life. This has led to the deployment of large networks of cameras and, in turn, a demand for local

Clemens Arth, Christian Leistner, Horst Bischof
Graz University of Technology, Graz, Austria, e-mail: {arth,leistner,bischof}@icg.tugraz.at

processing [4]. Therefore and due to their flexibility, scalability as well as passive operation, special interest has been placed on smart camera systems, for example, for industrial and surveillance applications. Embedded vision systems are already present in our everyday life. Almost everyone's mobile phone is equipped with a camera and, thus, can be treated as a small embedded vision system. Clearly this gives rise to new applications, like navigation tools for visually impaired persons or collaborative public monitoring using millions of artificial eyes.

Robust local features and descriptors have already been successfully applied to related tasks such as camera calibration or object recognition. They are designed to be invariant to illumination changes, image scale and rotation. Therefore, these features may be robustly matched over a substantial range of affine distortion and change in 3D viewpoint. Clearly, these properties require high demand in terms of computational power and memory. Hence, local feature- and descriptor-based systems for calibration or recognition have been mostly avoided in resource-constrained embedded systems. Nevertheless, it is necessary to deploy certain algorithms on these systems, especially to perform dedicated tasks from the area of surveillance. For example, recognition is a very important tool as the robust recognition of suspicious vehicles, persons or objects is a matter of public safety. That this makes the deployment of recognition capabilities on embedded platforms necessary, even if this includes some computationally complex and demanding algorithms.

In general, most computer vision algorithms are designed for use on standard desktop computers, having to meet almost no constraints in terms of memory and computational power consumption. Additionally, they mostly do not fit the fixed-point and SIMD architectures used by many embedded systems (e.g., fixed-point DSPs). Altogether, this has often made the full deployment of state-of-the-art algorithms a tedious task on resource-constrained embedded devices. As embedded systems are limited in enrolling their full potential without taking advantage of the state-of-the-art algorithms, we concentrate our work on connecting these two worlds in order to benefit from both approaches. In this work we investigate a set of highly-efficient robust local features and descriptors used in a wide range of popular computer vision applications. We discuss the suitability of these methods for implementation and usage on embedded systems and experimentally show their efficiency on two applications, namely, a camera calibration framework and a fully embedded object recognition system. Our encouraging results justify the usage of these algorithms for specific problems in the world of smart sensors.

Section 4.2 gives an overview about related work in the area of embedded systems. In Section 4.3 we briefly discuss the criteria for choosing algorithms for given tasks. Furthermore, we shortly describe our region detection and description algorithms, together with the algorithms for descriptor matching and for epipolar geometry calculation. An experimental evaluation of our implementations and examples of two applications, namely, camera calibration and object recognition, is given in Section 4.4. The remainder of this chapter in Section 4.5 contains some concluding remarks and an outlook on future work.

4.2 Related Work

In recent years smart cameras have attracted the interest of many research groups with applications in traffic monitoring [1], home care [17], gesture recognition [34], to mention a few. Prototypical platforms include, for example, the CMUCam3 [33], the WiCa [19] the SmartCam platform [7] and the MeshEye[TM]system [14]. Many applications require well calibrated systems, while fast and easy deployment is still a difficoult goal. Thus, solving the challenges of self-localization and self-calibration is very important for smart camera networks.

Both tasks (see also Section 4.3.6) require correspondences and, thus, local features and descriptors. Clearly, the performance of algorithms based on point correspondences is highly dependent on the quality of the detection process and on the type of descriptors used. Although Mikolajczyk et al. [27, 28] have shown that Difference of Gaussian (DoG) keypoints in combination with scale invariant feature transform (SIFT) descriptors [22] have proven to be very effective in terms of detectability and repeatability, most embedded systems use simpler corner detectors [15] or use additional active LEDs [2, 20] to perform calibration. Yet, Cheng et al. [8] as well as Mallett [23] were among the first to apply SIFT in embedded systems in order to perform multi-camera self-localization and calibration. In the work of Cheng et al. DoG keypoints are detected on high-resolution images, and a principle component analysis (PCA)-based compression method is performed on the corresponding descriptors to reduce the amount of data to be transmitted between camera nodes. The feasibility of their approach was shown in a multi-camera simulation to determine vision graphs and camera localization. Note that this way of using PCA is remarkably different from the one used to generate PCA-SIFT descriptors as introduced in Section 4.3.4. Furthermore, we point out that the huge amount of computations in this approach is a big issue and that the implementation of parts of the algorithms on a smart camera network presents a big challenge.

While the usage of local features and descriptors is not limited to the task of camera calibration, they have not been widely applied in the area of embedded systems, for example, for object recognition. Yet, to the best of our knowledge there exists no completely embedded object recognition system that is based on local interest regions and descriptors. Recently, Munich et al. built a library around Lowe's SIFT which has already been applied in several commercial products [29]. However, although they have implemented a full-scale object recognition system on DSPs and other platforms, details about implementation issues and performance evaluations are omitted. Using a modified kd-tree for efficient feature vector organization was proposed by Bishnu et al. [5]. An object database is built from so-called Euler vectors which are calculated from binary forms of object images. While an implementation and evaluation on hardware is not performed explicitly, the design of a hardware system and a pipelining structure is motivated in the work of Bishnu et al. [6] and Dey et al. [9].

A related approach was proposed by Yeh et al. [35]. In this work two images are taken with a mobile phone camera, one image with and one without the object sought. An interactive segmentation tool is used to isolate the object and to submit its image as a query to a web-database. After recognizing the object, the database engine provides the user with useful information about the object, be it a famous building or a shopping item. At least the step of object segmentation—and thereby describing the object—is performed on the smart phone. The main strength of this algorithm is that it is in general not limited to any type of object since the recognition is done remotely using a more powerful device. We still believe that the usage of local features and descriptors could make the framework more efficient, at least in terms of communication costs via compression of the amount of data to be transmitted.

To sum up, there is only little literature about the usage of interest point detectors and descriptors in the context of smart cameras.

4.3 Algorithm Selection

In this section we first describe the criteria for choosing dedicated algorithms for the given tasks based on our hardware platform. Furthermore, we describe the algorithms we have selected due to their suitability to solve the two examples given. We justify the usage of these algorithms and outline their special relevance and qualification for usage on smart systems. Several modifications to the algorithms are proposed to better fit the algorithms for usage on our prototypical hardware platform. We also shortly describe an efficient method for descriptor matching and the robust algorithm for calculating the epipolar geometry from a given image pair.

4.3.1 Hardware Constraints and Selection Criteria

Our hardware platform is similar to the one used in [1] and represents a typical and popular set-up used in many applications. Hence, all algorithms run on a single Texas Instruments™ TMS320C6414 DSP running at 600 MHz with 1 MB internal cache, the amount of external memory is 16 MB.

Given a special task, the challenge is choosing the best algorithms currently available to solve the problem most efficiently under consideration of additional hardware constraints. Clearly the selection of algorithms has to be done according to special application dependent criteria too. The best choice of algorithms must result in a system that is optimized in more than one aspect. For both applications we present in the next section there is more than one aspect to be considered during system design. For object recognition, it is important that the recognition performance is good (choosing the right type of object) even under adverse conditions, while the time spent for recognition should be minimized. In the second case, for camera calibration, communication costs between individual camera entities should be minimized, but the overall number of correct point correspondences (the matching performance) should still be kept at a high level to guarantee a good calibration result.

In the following we describe the set of algorithms we have chosen for our two tasks to be solved most efficiently and note their properties that make them suitable for our purposes.

4.3.2 DoG Keypoints

The first algorithm we have investigated is Lowe's difference of Gaussians (DoG) detector, which can be used to obtain accurate keypoints with high repeatability [22].

The DoG detector is mainly based on Gaussian filtering and differencing the resulting filtered images. The differences can be interpreted as an approximation of the scale normalized Laplacian [21, 22]. By doing so a scale space is built in multiple octaves, and maxima and minima in the scale space are determined. These extremas are keypoints, which indicate the presence of blob-like structures in images. The image size is downsampled by a factor of 2 with each doubling of the sigma of the Gaussian filter kernel (after each octave) to form the initial image for the next octave. For each keypoint a circular region around the keypoint is cropped whose size is dependent on the scale factor delivered during detection. By summing up the gradients in the image patch, the main gradient direction is determined and assigned as orientation to the keypoint.

A nice feature of the DoG detector is that it is almost purely based on image filtering and addition/subtraction operations. While a clever arrangement of filtering and search operations makes the algorithm also efficient in terms of memory usage, the algorithm is very well suited for DSP platforms, as they are mainly designed for fast filter operations. We implemented the Gaussian filtering in fixed-point as the hardware platform has no floating point unit and floating point operations have to be emulated in software. Due to the small amount of internal memory the filtered images and the difference images are consecutively swapped between the external memory and the internal cache of the DSP. To reduce the number of difference images to be stored in the stack for extrema search, the search is performed on each difference image stack immediately after creation. By doing so the difference image can be discarded immediately and only the valuable information about maxima and minima has to be kept. For determining the main orientation of a keypoint, a scale-normalized patch is cropped from the original image around the keypoint and resized to a fixed size to fix the runtime of this orientation assignment step. After calculating the gradients on this patch, the main gradient orientation is determined by finding the maxima in the accumulated orientation histogram. For all local peaks that are within 80% of the highest peak another new keypoint with the same scale and location but with different orientation is created. This significantly increases stability in matching for keypoints in highly textured areas with multiple dominant orientations.

4.3.3 MSER

MSER stands for *maximally stable extremal regions* and was first proposed by Matas et al. [26]. This region detector is complementary to the DoG-detector and is based on searching for regions which possess an extremal property of the intensity function inside and on their outer boundary.

In short, the MSER detector searches for regions that are brighter or darker than their surroundings, that is, are surrounded by darker, vice-versa brighter pixels. Note that in the following we will also refer to both types of regions as *positive* and *negative* regions, respectively. First, pixels are sorted in ascending or descending order of their intensity value, depending on the region type to be detected. The pixel array is sequentially fed into a union-find algorithm and a tree-like shaped data structure is maintained, whereas the nodes contain information about pixel neighborhoods, as well as information about intensity value relationships. Finally, nodes which satisfy a set of predefined criteria are sought by a tree traversis algorithm, which in our case has to be iterative due to our architectural hardware constraints.

An appealing feature of this algorithm is that it does not need any floating point arithmetics to be performed. Another big advantage of the MSER algorithm is that it is efficiently computable—at least on conventional desktop computers—and that the regions to be found are not restricted in terms of area or shape. Moreover, it is possible to identify regions across very large viewpoint changes because the extremal property of the regions in general does not change. For ease of implementation we have not implemented full-featured local affine frames [25], but used the ellipse fitting approach of Mikolajczyk [28]. After fitting an ellipse to the region, the image patch below the ellipse is deskewed and rotated to $0°$ for the calculation of the descriptors.[1]

A union-find based algorithm creates a tree-like data structure, and though recursive algorithms are not suitable for DSP platforms, an iterative tree-traversis algorithm has to be used. The shape of the tree is heavily dependent on the image processed, thus the runtime of the algorithm can not be estimated easily. Moreover, for building the data structure a large amount of memory is needed. Note, that other approaches for MSER calculation are also known which are based on multiple trees, so-called forests [30]. These algorithms require a lot of branching instructions, which are also not very suitable for execution on DSPs. The reason for choosing the MSER algorithm for implementation on the DSP is that its superior performance for identifying distinctive regions simply votes out all disadvantages. Moreover, when runtime is not a critical factor, the MSER algorithm might still be a valuable option.

---

[1] The drawback of this method is that two descriptors have to be calculated for each region, one for $0°$ and one for $180°$ due to the ambiguous orientation of the ellipse.

4.3.4 PCA-SIFT

Ke and Sukthankar [16] proposed to use a compact descriptor based on eigenspace analysis, the so-called PCA-SIFT descriptor. This descriptor has less in common with the original SIFT descriptor, proposed in [22], as one might suppose. The original SIFT descriptor is a histogram of oriented gradients, which are summed up within 16 rectangular areas to form a 128-dimensional descriptor. In contrast, Ke and Sukthankar calculated a PCA eigenspace on the plain gradient images of a representative number of over 20,000 image patches to find a more compact description, coevally preserving a maximum in information content. The descriptor of a new image tile is generated by projecting the gradients of the tile onto the precalculated eigenspace keeping only the d most significant eigenvectors.

This descriptor has several advantages, especially for our application. First, the algorithm mainly consists of multiply-accumulate (MAC) operations, which fits the properties of embedded platforms very well. Secondly, the descriptor is much more compact, because Ke and Sukthankar have shown the $d = 36$ dimensional descriptor to exhibit the same discriminatory power as the 128-dimensional SIFT descriptor. A third big advantage is that a further decrement of d results in only a slight loss in discriminatory power, thereby making the descriptor calculation itself scalable. The amount of storage for the large set of descriptors is also reduced by a factor of ≥ 4, because of the smaller amount of memory needed to store the individual descriptors. Finally, for application in a smart camera network, choosing the PCA-SIFT descriptor over the SIFT descriptor results in one more favorable effect, namely, the reduction of transmission costs of raw descriptors by a factor of ≥ 4.

In our application, a scale-normalized patch which exhibits the same dimensions as proposed in their original work is extracted from the original image and rotated to compensate the specific orientation. The dimensions are chosen such that we can use the same coefficients as Ke and Sukthankar [16]. Furthermore we converted their eigenspace projection matrices to a fixed-point version. By doing so we can take advantage of the benefits of fixed-point calculations on our platform [18]. The dimensionality of the resulting descriptor d can be adjusted, which allows for a tradeoff between discriminability and final recognition performance, but also between more and less computationally expensive calculation. The final descriptor is a d-dimensional vector of 1-byte elements.

4.3.5 Descriptor Matching

An important part of most systems using local features is a descriptor-matching engine. Efficient descriptor matching is a challenge on its own and a lot of distance metrics exist. One very popular metric is the Euclidean distance, which is defined as

$$\text{dist}(X,Y) = \left(\sum_{i=1}^{N} (x_i - y_i)^2 \right)^{1/2} \qquad (4.1)$$

with X and Y being vectors of length N, and x_i, y_i being the ith element of vector X, respectively Y. Matching of descriptors is relatively expensive. The naive exhaustive search has a complexity of $\mathcal{O}(nmd)$ with n being the number of descriptors in a database, m the number of descriptors to be matched and d the dimension of the descriptor vectors. Making d smaller is one possible solution to reduce the computational load, using kd-trees and approximate-nearest-neighbor search algorithms is another one.

Although a linear exhaustive search can be implemented very efficiently given embedded hardware properties, it is computationally very expensive. The exhaustive matching of descriptors in databases is impracticable for databases with more than several hundred descriptors. As has been shown recently, vocabulary tree based approaches are very suitable in this respect, as they allow for a approximated nearest neighbor search in medium dimensional spaces with a huge numbers of candidates. In the approach of Nistér and Stewénius [31], hundreds of thousands of descriptor vectors are quantized using k-means clustering in a hierarchical vocabulary tree for image retrieval, being capable of organizing a database of 1 million images. The results of an initial scoring scheme are verified by using the geometry of keypoints matched to further improve image retrieval quality. Combining the ideas of vector quantization and hierarchical clustering results in real-time behavior of matching.

Despite the considerable benefits of tree-like structures for solving this task, there is one main problem of tree-like data structures on embedded systems. Data-dependent control flow and control code containing random conditional statements is predominant in the implementation of these approaches. Needless to say these are mechanisms that cannot be executed very efficiently on DSPs.

4.3.6 Epipolar Geometry

The intrinsic projective geometry between two views is called *epipolar geometry*. It only depends on the cameras' internal parameters and relative pose. The epipolar geometry is independent of scene structure and is captured in the so-called fundamental matrix F, which is a 3×3 matrix of rank 2. For calculating the epipolar geometry between an image pair, point correspondences between the images have to be established. After having enough robust potential point correspondences, it is possible to compute the cameras extrinsic parameters and estimate the fundamental matrix F, where $(x')^T F x = 0$ and x' and x are the corresponding features in the first, respectively the second image. Depending on the quality of the matches, this works for both stereo and wide-baseline setups [3]. Note, however, that in order to achieve high accuracy, point correspondences in general position should be distributed uniformly. Hence, for slightly overlapping views, different methods have to be applied [32].

For most scenarios, though, one of the simplest yet efficient ways to estimate F is the normalized 8-point algorithm more precisely described in [12]. In order to handle the many possible outliers an iterative matching method RANSAC (RANdom SAmple Concensus) [10] is applied. For n iterations RANSAC takes randomly eight points and calculates the fundamental matrix using the 8-point algorithm. After that a distance d for each putative correspondence is calculated. We used the Sampson distance measure which yields quite good results . Then the number of inliers consistent with F is determined. Finally, F with the largest number of inliers is taken. For a more precise algorithm overview again see [12].

Because the calculation of the fundamental matrix is very sensitive to outliers, a robust outlier detection algorithm is necessary. The special qualification of the RANSAC based outlier detection algorithm for our purposes is that it is computationally inexpensive and it does not require large data storage.

4.4 Experiments

Now we will evaluate our algorithms on the two challenging tasks given, namely, camera calibration and object recognition. First we will describe the datasets and experimental setup used, then we list the timings for each separate module on our embedded platform, and afterwards we elucidate and discuss the results of our algorithms.

4.4.1 Camera Calibration

Our first test scenario is camera calibration. In the following we will describe our experimental setup and give notes about our configuration choices and why we have done so. Since camera calibration usually has to be done only once during deployment, setup time is not necessarily a critical factor. It is much more important that the number of point correspondences is high enough, and that the major amount of correspondences is correct. Moreover, in a camera network it is important to minimize the amount of data to be transmitted.

4.4.1.1 System Setup

As the MSER detector has been proven to be a good choice for the task of wide-baseline camera calibration, we choose the camera calibration task to test its performance together with the PCA-SIFT descriptor on our platform. A limiting factor in this task is image size and resolution. On the one hand, it is hard to calibrate from low resolution images, on the other hand, the usage of high resolution images results in a higher memory consumption, which is especially critical on embedded systems. Thus, we decided to split the 680×510 test images, which are depicted in Fig. 4.1, into 4 tiles, each of size 352×288 with a small overlap area. The images are separated by an approximately $30°$ viewpoint change. We are aware that this configuration is neither wide-baseline, nor does it provide a good testbed for proofing the strengths of the MSER detection algorithm together with a robust calibration algorithm. Anyhow, we simply want to demonstrate the approach so we did not choose a more difficult scenario. Furthermore, it is common to tile images into smaller parts if memory and computational resources are limited, thus this setup makes it possible to process and run our framework without much additional programming overhead.

Fig. 4.1 Cropped image tiles in the first row. Overlayed ellipses for the detected MSER regions in the second and third row for positive and negative regions, respectively. The images are separated by an approximately $30°$ viewpoint change.

We process both sets of image tiles sequentially on a single instance of our platform, only storing and exchanging the region coordinates and the corresponding descriptors as if they were passed between separate smart cameras. After calculating positive and negative MSERs, we calculate the PCA-SIFT descriptors on the deskewed patches for both types of regions separately. Also the subsequent matching of the descriptors of each type is done separately to avoid additional wrong matches. The descriptors are matched using exhaustive search and putative point correspondences are established. The RANSAC-based fundamental matrix calculation algorithm is finally used to eliminate outliers and to calculate the epipolar geometry of the image pair, as in Fig. 4.2.

Fig. 4.2 Our calibration scenario, on which we have calculated the fundamental matrix, and three corresponding epipolar lines

4.4.1.2 Calibration Results

In Fig. 4.1 the results of our MSER detection on two sample tiles of our image pair for positive and negative regions are depicted. The detection algorithm enumerates the same parts in both images as interest regions. In our calibration experiment the algorithm detects 951 regions in the first image and 976 regions in the second image, respectively. In Fig. 4.2 three corresponding epipolar lines are overlayed on our calibration test images. The average reprojection error is in the range of a few pixels.

4.4.1.3 Timing Results

In Table 4.1 the timing results for our implementation of the detector are listed. We ran the detection algorithm on the images used for our object recognition experiment. All results are based on an average detection of 358 regions per image and

597 descriptors.[2] We have not listed the amount of time necessary for calibrating an image pair with our complete calibration framework. The reason for doing so is that the time span needed is heavily dependent on the image data, that is, on the number of descriptors to be matched, and especially on the number of RANSAC iterations needed for robustly identifying and discarding outliers. For our calibration scenario, it takes our system less than a minute to calculate the epipolar geometry.

The runtime of all parts of the MSER detection algorithm is heavily dependent on the image data. Furthermore, it is somewhat slower than the DoG detector, due to its algorithmic workflow. Random memory accesses, the necessity of linked lists, and the tree-like shape of the data structure disunites the architectural strengths of the platform and the algorithm. Nevertheless, MSER is one of the most popular approaches and has been shown to perform very well for this task. Due to the fact that camera calibration has to be done only once during setup, the time needed for detection is not critical and thus the algorithm can be used for this purpose.

Table 4.1 Timing results for the MSER detection algorithm. The results are obtained detecting positive or negative regions separately for about 358 (positive or negative) regions and an average number of 597 descriptors to be calculated.

	Avg.Time [ms]	Std.Dev.
Tree data structure building	412.96	67.324
Tree traversis algorithm	2572.86	712.395
Ellipse fitting	51.38	28.293
PCA-SIFT calculation	343.17	144.945
Total:	**3380.37**	**768.890**
Ellipse fitting / MSER	0.13	0.021
PCA-SIFT calculation / descriptor	0.57	0.010

4.4.2 Object Recognition

In this application a medium-sized database is deployed on our embedded system. Our image database is a subset of the publicly available ALOI (Amsterdam Library of Object Images) database from Geusebroek et al. [11] (Fig. 4.3 shows some sample images). We preselected those 250 objects out of 1000 which deliver the highest number of DoG points. The main reason for doing so is that deploying this medium-sized object database on our system is already challenging, but to a greater extent because the database contains a lot of objects that cannot be sufficiently represented using DoG points alone, as the number of them is too small. To overcome this

---

[2] Descriptors are only calculated on regions for which the extracted image patch completely lies in the original image. Thus, the average number of descriptors is not twice the number of regions found.

problem multiple different detectors can be used, but for now we left this as an open issue.

All object images are resized to CIF resolution (352×288), for training as well as for the performance evaluations of our system. For building our database we use all descriptors at steps of 15°, while we calculate the recognition results at intermediate steps of 5° and omit testing the system at the angles learned. The training of the object recognition system is done on a standard desktop computer using MATLAB™. After building the vocabulary tree we upload it onto our smart camera platform, where all further evaluations are performed. The vocabulary and the tree structure is represented as raw blocks of data in memory which are accessible interpreting pointers from a binary executable on the platform. The binary program for recognizing objects is built using the Code Composer Studio 3.2 from Texas Instruments and uploaded together with all necessary data buffers using a JTAG emulator device. During evaluation, images are presented to the algorithm, which extracts local features, calculates descriptors, searches correspondences in the vocabulary tree, and finally returns the ID of the best object match.

Fig. 4.3 A subset of the 250 selected objects in our database from the ALOI (Amsterdam Library Object Images), viewed from 0°.

For the vocabulary tree, for all experiments k was chosen to be 2, which means that each vocabulary tree is a binary decision tree. Without loss of generality k can be chosen arbitrary to trade vocabulary tree depth against calculation costs and accuracy in practice. Although Nistér and Stewénius [31] have shown a large k to result in better recognition performance, our choice of $k = 2$ is inspired by implementation considerations of our vocabulary tree and the approximate-nearest-neighbor query. If $k = 2$, the query of a descriptor along the path in a vocabulary tree can be implemented by simple $if - then - else$ statements. Choosing k to be larger would result in a more complex control structure.

In our approach we calculate distances in feature space using the sum of squared distances (SSD) metric rather than the Euclidean metric. In doing so the partial ordering of elements is not changed (which essentially means that the voting result is not affected). However, we can omit calculating the square root which is a computationally expensive task on our embedded platform.

Due to the memory restrictions we further assume that the critical limit for our database residing in the external memory of the platform is 12.5 MB, as we also need a piece of memory to store other data buffers.

4.4.2.1 Vocabulary Tree Creation and Manipulation

The vocabulary tree obtained by the procedure described above contains the full amount of information, but is too large to meet our memory constraints. Due to the robustness of the local feature based approach a lot of redundancy can be removed. The most efficient way to achieve this is to prune the tree and replace the single votes by a set of votes from the pruned leafs. In other words, if leafs of the tree meet a given criterion they are collapsed into a single one which now votes for several objects. Note that there is a strong relation to decision trees in machine learning, where pruning is used to obtain a better generalization [13, 24]. We employ the strategy that all subtrees with a predetermined number i of inner nodes are pruned. Thus the partitioning is made coarser equally well in all regions of the feature space by simply merging leafs (and partitions respectively). We also refer to this method as *level-based* pruning. An example of this idea is depicted in Fig. 4.4.

In Fig. 4.5 the influence of the level-based pruning strategy and the resulting performance levels are visualized. In Fig. 4.6 the size of the resulting databases is shown. As can be seen, level-based pruning only slightly influences the recognition performance, but has a major impact on the database size. For the following experiments we choose the dimensionality of the descriptors to be 28 and the level-based pruning method with a level of 2. By doing so we generate a database with about 12.1 MB, still keeping an average recognition performance of about 90.6%. This setting is used to generate all following results.

4.4.2.2 Recognition Performance

To show the robustness of our pruning method and our vocabulary tree based approach, the recognition performance of our system for various dimensional PCA-SIFT descriptors without background noise was evaluated. The results are depicted in Fig. 4.7. The performance slightly decreases with a reduction in the number of dimensions. To simulate background noise, we projected the object images onto different background images, which are shown in Fig. 4.9. Some sample results of these projections are shown in Fig. 4.10. As can easily be seen, some of the objects are very small, thus they occupy less than 20% of the total image area. In Fig. 4.8, the recognition performance of our chosen setting (28-dim. PCA-SIFT, pruning level 2) for the four different background images is shown. It is easy to see that the approach performs best on the sea-view image as most parts of the image are low textured. On all other images, our approach performs almost equally well, with an average recognition rate of about 68% over the entire viewpoint range.

4.4.2.3 Timing Results and Memory Profile

To test the final performance of our algorithm on our platform we have measured the average time consumption of each individual step and evaluated the amount of memory spent on each task. We have divided the approach into several subsections which are listed in Table 4.2. The *scale space generation* step, consisting of *image filtering* and *image subtraction*, takes a constant amount of computation time as there is no dependency on the data being processed. All other steps of the approach are dependent on the number of DoG points found in the *minima/maxima search* and updated in the *orientation assignment* step. The timing results for the *descriptor calculation* and the *vocabulary tree query* step are based on the calculations necessary for 100 DoG points. Note that a detection rate of 50-200 points is reasonable. The high standard deviation in the *orientation assignment* is due to the possibility that multiple keypoints might be created or discarded and thus the time

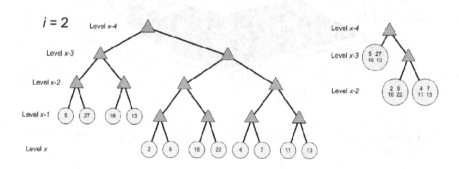

Fig. 4.4 Level-based leaf pruning given a predefined number *i* of levels.

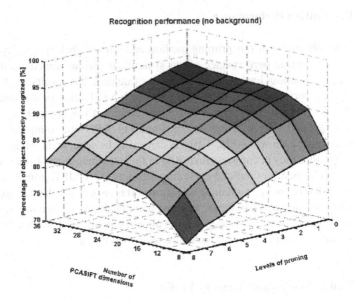

Fig. 4.5 Average recognition performance for the distance-based pruning method and different parameter settings.

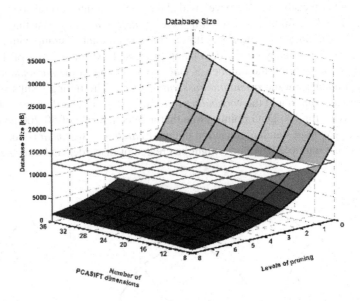

Fig. 4.6 Database size for the level-based pruning strategy. The size limit of 12.5 MB is depicted as a plane here.

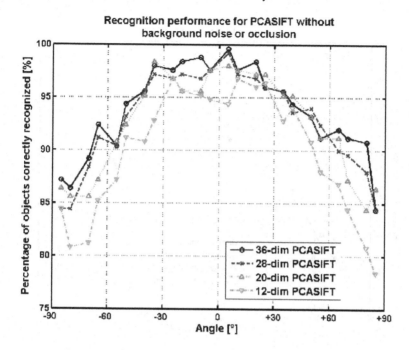

Fig. 4.7 Recognition performance for different dimensional PCA-SIFT descriptors. The performance only slightly decreases with the number of dimensions.

for assigning the orientation varies drastically. Based on the detection of about 100 DoG points, the algorithm can process 4 frames per second. As most of the parts of the algorithm have no fixed execution time, it is hard to estimate the system timing performance under real conditions. One way of predicting the worst case execution time is to limit the number of keypoints allowed to be detected. By placing an upper limit, say 250 keypoints, we can guarantee a worst case execution time be be calculated to 500 ms, which is 2 frames per second. Limiting the number of keypoints can be performed by putting a threshold on the DoG response and selecting the 250 keypoints having the highest DoG response.

Table 4.2 Timing results for the individual algorithmic parts of our approach. The *scale space generation* step can also described as a combination of *image filtering* and *image subtraction*.

Algorithm	Avg.Time [ms]	Std.Dev.
Scale space generation	35.78	0.014
Minima/maxima search	35.07	17.18
Orientation assignment	107.75	98.56
Descriptor calculation	75.59	11.40
Vocabulary tree query	3.62	1.14
Total:	257.82	127.73

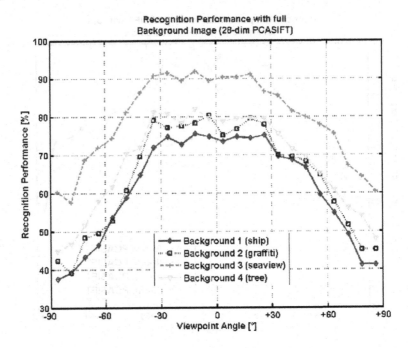

Fig. 4.8 Average recognition performance for projections onto the four background images for the settings chosen (28-dim. PCA-SIFT, pruning level 2).

Table 4.3 Memory consumption of the individual algorithmic steps. The size of the data buffer holding the final descriptors is based on the 28-dimensional descriptor used in our setup and a detection rate of 100 descriptors.

Algorithm	Memory Consumption [kB]
Scale space	1,386
PCA transformation matrices	219
Final descriptors	2.7
Vocabulary tree	12,471

In Table 4.3 the size of the individual memory buffers is listed. Due to the fixed spacing in the scale space and the fixed number of octaves, the *scale space* takes a fixed amount of 1386 kB. The size of the data buffers holding the transformation matrices for the PCA-SIFT descriptor takes about 219 kB. The amount of memory needed to store the descriptors increases linearly with their number. The size of the memory buffer holding the vocabulary tree is determined by the parameters chosen during the tree construction. The size of the data buffers for our tree is about 12.1 MB.

We have implemented almost all parts of the approach in fixed-point as this is basically necessary for algorithms to perform in acceptable time on our platform.

Fig. 4.9 The four different background images onto which we have projected the objects to further challenge our recognition system.

Elaborate investigations using the framework of Mikolajczyk et al. [28] have shown, that the loss in accuracy has no significant influence on the performance of the detector and descriptor. The only parts not implemented in fixed-point are the paraboloid fitting function used for accurate, interpolated keypoint detection, and the normalization of the descriptors after generation. The impact of these pieces of code is negligible, compared to the overall algorithm runtime. Note that we did not write any parts of the algorithms in assembly code or made any extensive use of other optimization techniques like intrinsics.

4.5 Conclusion

In this chapter we presented our investigation of a set of local features and their suitability for embedded systems. We used the state-of-the-art detectors, MSER and DoG, for selection of interest regions, and combined them with one of the most promising descriptors, the PCA-SIFT descriptor. All algorithms were fully implemented and tested on a single-chip based embedded platform and their suitability

Fig. 4.10 Some sample projection results. The amount of background noise is severe, some of the objects itself occupy less than 20% of the image area (352×288 pixels).

was shown on the popular tasks of camera calibration and object recognition. Doing so we further narrowed the gap between high-level state-of-the-art vision and resource-constrained embedded systems.

Future work will both concentrate on additional algorithm improvements and a system expansion to additional applications such as multi-camera tracking. Moreover, we aim to employ better region descriptors such as local affine frames in order to allow wide-baseline calibration and localization. In the context of object recognition, we want to investigate our algorithms in the context of mobile devices, that is, PDAs and mobile phone cameras. For object recognition algorithms to become a tool in everyday use, it is essential that these algorithms are at least partially usable on already existing devices. Thus we look forward to investigate our algorithms in the context of mobile, portable systems.

Acknowledgements This work was done in the scope of the EViS Project No. D-171 000 0037 and has been supported by the Austrian Joint Research Project *Cognitive Vision under projects S9103-N04 and S9104-N04.*

References

1. Arth, C., Bischof, H., Leistner, C.: TRICam: An Embedded Platform for Remote Traffic Surveillance. *IEEE Comput Soc Conf Comput Vis Pattern Recogn (Embedded Computer Vision Workshop)* (2006)
2. Barton-Sweeney, A., Lymberopoulos, D., Savvides, A.: Sensor Localization and Camera Calibration in Distributed Camera Sensor Networks. *Proc. of the International Conference on Broadband Communications, Networks and Systems (BROADNETS)*, pp. 1–10 (2006)
3. Bay, H., Ferrari, V., Van Gool, L.: Wide-Baseline Stereo Matching with Line Segments. *IEEE Comput Soc Conf Comput Vis Pattern Recogn* 1, pp. 329–336 (2005)
4. Bhardwaj, M., Chandrakasan, A., Garnett, T.: Upper Bounds on the Lifetime of Sensor Networks. *IEEE Int Conf Comm*, pp. 785–790 (2001)
5. Bishnu, A., Bhunre, P.K., Bhattacharya, B.B., Kundu, M.K.,Murthy, C.A., Acharya, T.: Content Based Image Retrieval: Related Issues Using Euler Vector. *Proc. of the IEEE International Conference on Image Processing* 2, pp. 585–588 (2002)
6. Bishnu, A., Bhattacharya, B.B., Kundu, M.K., Murthy, C.A., Acharya, T.: A Pipeline Architecture for Computing the Euler Number of a Binary Image. *J Syst Architect* 51 (8), pp. 470–487 (2005)
7. Bramberger, M., Doblander, A., Maier, A., Rinner, B., Schwabach, H.: Distributed Embedded Smart Cameras for Surveillance Applications. *Computer* 39 (2), pp. 68–75 (2006)
8. Cheng, Z., Devarajan, D., Radke, R.J.: Determining Vision Graphs for Distributed Camera Networks Using Feature Digests. *EURASIP Journal on Advances in Signal Processing* (2007)
9. Dey, S., Bhattacharya, B.B., Kundu, M.K., Acharya, T.: A Fast Algorithm for Computing the Euler Number of an Image and its VLSI Implementation. *Int Conf VLSI Des*, pp. 330–335 (2000)
10. Fischler, M.A., Bowles, R.C.: Random Sample Consensus: A Paradigm for Model Fitting with Applications to Image Analysis and Automated Cartography. *Comm ACM* 24 (6), pp. 381–395 (1981)
11. Geusebroek, J-M., Burghouts, G.J.,Smeulders A.W.M.: The Amsterdam Library of Object Images. *Int J Comput Vis* 61 (1), pp. 103–112 (2005)
12. Hartley, R., Zisserman, A.: Multiple View Geometry in Computer Vision. Cambridge University Press (2000)
13. Helmbold, D.P., Schapire, R.E.: Predicting Nearly as Well as the Best Pruning of a Decision Tree. *Computational Learing Theory*, pp. 61–68 (1995)
14. Hengstler, S., Prashanth, D., Fong, S., Aghajan, H.: MeshEye: a Hybrid-Resolution Smart Camera Mote for Applications in Distributed Intelligent Surveillance. *Proc. of the International Conference on Information Processing in Sensor Networks (IPSN)*, pp. 360–369 (2007)
15. Jannotti, J., Mao, J.: Distributed Calibration of Smart Cameras. *Proc. of the Workshop on Distributed Smart Cameras (DSC06)* (2006)
16. Ke, Y., Sukthankar, R.: PCA-SIFT: A More Distinctive Representation for Local Image Descriptors. *IEEE Comput Soc Conf Comput Vis Pattern Recogn*, pp. 506–513 (2004)
17. Keshavarz, A., Tabar, A.M., Aghajan, H.: Distributed Vision-Based Reasoning for Smart Home Care. *Proc. of the Workshop on Distributed Smart Cameras (DSC06)* (2006)
18. Kisačanin, B.: Examples of low-level computer vision on media processors. *Proc. IEEE CVPR, ECV Workshop,* (2005)
19. Kleihorst, R., Schueler, B., Danilin, A., Heijligers, M.: Smart Camera Mote with High-Performance Vision System. *Proc. of the Workshop on Distributed Smart Cameras (DSC06)* (2006)
20. Lee, J., Aghajan, H.: Collaborative Node Localization in Surveillance Networks using Opportunistic Target Observations. *Proc. of the ACM International Workshop on Video Surveillance and Sensor Networks (VSNN)*, pp. 9–18 (2006)
21. Lindeberg, T.: Feature Detection with Automatic Scale Selection. *Int J Comput Vis* 30 (2), pp. 77–116 (1998)

22. Lowe, D.G.: Distinctive Image Features from Scale-Invariant Keypoints. *Int J Comput Vis* **60** (2), pp. 91–110 (2004)
23. Mallett, J.: The Role of Groups in Smart Camera Networks. PhD Thesis, Massachusetts Institute of Technology (MIT) (2006)
24. Mansour, Y.: Pessimistic Decision Tree Pruning Based on Tree Size. *Proc. of the International Conference on Machine Learning (ICML)*, pp. 195–201 (1997)
25. Matas, J., Obdrzalek, S., Chum, O.: Local Affine Frames for Wide-Baseline Stereo. *Int Conf Pattern Recogn* **4**, pp. 363–366 (2002)
26. Matas, J., Chum, O., Urban, M., Pajdla, T.: Robust Wide Baseline Stereo from Maximally Stable Extremal Regions. *Proc. of the British Machine Vision Conference (BMVC)* **1**, pp. 384–393 (2002)
27. Mikolajczyk, K., Schmid, C.: A Performance Evaluation of Local Descriptors, *IEEE Trans Pattern Anal Mach Intell* **27** (10), pp. 1615–1630 (2005)
28. Mikolajczyk, K., Tuytelaars, T., Schmid, C., Zisserman, A., Matas, J., Schaffalitzky, F., Kadir, T., Van Gool, L.: A Comparison of Affine Region Detectors. *Int J Comput Vis* **65** (1-2), pp. 43–72 (2005)
29. Munich, M.E., Pirjanian, P., DiBernardo, E., Goncalves, L., Karlsson, N., Lowe, D.G.: Breakthrough Visual Pattern Recognition for Robotics and Automation. *IEEE Int Conf Robot Autom* (2005)
30. Murphy-Chutorian, E., Trivedi, M.M.: *N*-tree Disjoint-Set Forests for Maximally Stable Extremal Regions, *Proc. of the British Machine Vision Conference (BMVC)* **2**, p. 739 (2006)
31. Nistér, D., Stewénius, H.: Scalable Recognition with a Vocabulary Tree. *IEEE Comput Soc Conf Comput Vis Pattern Recogn* **2**, pp. 2161-2168 (2006)
32. Pflugfelder, R., Bischof, H.: Fundamental Matrix and Slightly Overlapping Views. *Int Conf Pattern Recogn* **1**, pp. 527–530 (2006)
33. Rowe, A., Rosenberg, C., Nourbakhsh, I.: A Second-Generation Low-Cost Embedded Color Vision System. *IEEE Comput Soc Conf Comput Vis Pattern Recogn (Embedded Computer Vision Workshop)* (2005)
34. Wolf, W., Ozer, B., Lv, T.: Smart Cameras as Embedded Systems. *Computer* **35** (9), pp. 48–53 (2002)
35. Yeh, T., Grauman, K., Tollmar, K., Darrell, T.: A Picture Is Worth a Thousand Keywords: Image-Based Object Search on a Mobile Platform. *CHI Extended Abstracts*, pp. 2025–2028 (2005)

Chapter 5
Benchmarks of Low-Level Vision Algorithms for DSP, FPGA, and Mobile PC Processors

Daniel Baumgartner, Peter Roessler, Wilfried Kubinger, Christian Zinner, and Karina Ambrosch

Abstract We present recent results of a performance benchmark of selected low-level vision algorithms implemented on different high-speed embedded platforms. The algorithms were implemented on a digital signal processor (DSP) (Texas Instruments TMS320C6414), a field-programmable gate array (FPGA) (Altera Stratix-I and II families) as well as on a mobile PC processor (Intel Mobile Core 2 Duo T7200). These implementations are evaluated, compared, and discussed in detail. The DSP and the mobile PC implementations, both making heavy use of processor-specific acceleration techniques (intrinsics and resource optimized slicing direct memory access on DSPs or Intel integrated performance primitives Library on mobile PC processors), outperform the FPGA implementations, but at the cost of spending all its resources to these tasks. FPGAs, however, are very well suited to algorithms that benefit from parallel execution.

5.1 Introduction

Nowadays, more and more computer vision methods find their way into new applications. Typical areas are automated inspection [8], advanced driver assistance systems [11], and robotics and autonomous systems [16, 23]. The main challenges for vision sensors to be used in intelligent vehicles are on the one hand coping with stringent real-time requirements and on the other hand having a reliable and power-aware system—normally solved using embedded systems.

Daniel Baumgartner, Wilfried Kubinger, Christian Zinner, Karina Ambrosch
Austrian Research Centers GmbH, Vienna, Austria
e-mail: {daniel.baumgartner, wilfried.kubinger, christian.zinner}@arcs.ac.at

Peter Roessler
University of Applied Sciences Technikum Wien, Vienna, Austria
e-mail: peter.roessler@technikum-wien.at

These two requirements lead a system designer in different directions. Vision systems usually have to cope with a huge amount of data and sometimes also with very sophisticated mathematics, leading to the need for a high-performance computer system or even a cluster of computers. On the other hand, reliability, cost and energy-awareness lead the designer to an embedded system solution, where small size, low energy consumption, long-time stability, and a wide temperature range for outdoor operation can be assumed. The drawback is a (perhaps significant) degradation in performance compared to the aforementioned solutions.

If one decides to utilize an embedded system for a computer vision application, there is currently the choice between either using digital signal processors (DSPs), field-programmable gate arrays (FPGAs), or mobile PC processors from different vendors. Compared to high-end DSPs, FPGAs are more expensive, the design and development of FPGA algorithms require more time and the processing power for sequential computations is slower than on DSPs—because of the higher clock frequency of DSPs. Recent DSPs are designed to fit a variety of market applications, with no consideration for any special algorithm [14]. Mobile PC processors are commonly used in mobile computers, notebooks, and some industrial or "embedded" PCs. Software developed and tested on a PC workstation can be easily migrated to an embedded platform based on a mobile PC processor.

The specific implementation of a computer vision system is, of course, highly application dependent. However, for many vision systems, functionality can be classified as follows: In the first step, called *image acquisition*, a digital 2D or 3D image (or sequence of images) is generated by one or multiple image sensors or cameras from different views and/or spectral bands. In the *image pre-processing* step basic enhancement and restoration techniques like noise reduction, contrast enhancement or correction of lens/sensor distortion are applied to the image. During *feature extraction* properties such as lines, edges, corners and blobs as well as features related to color, texture, shape or motion are extracted. The *segmentation* step refers to the selection of a specific set of points or regions of interest which are the subject for further processing. Finally, the *high-level processing* stage generates the final results of the system, e.g., the exact size and position of an object, the decision whether an object has passed or not passed an optical quality inspection system, the name of a person identified by a facial recognition system, and so on.

Keeping in mind that the design and verification effort to implement a certain kind of functionality in hardware (FPGA or an application-specific integrated circuit (ASIC)) is typically much higher than the effort for an equivalent software implementation (running on a general purpose CPU or DSP) leads to the following premises:

- "Simple" vision and image processing algorithms, where highly repetitive processes are applied to an image stream using only a few number of parameters are more suitable to be implemented in hardware than complex algorithms requiring many "if-then-else" decisions and branches and/or many parameters.
- Algorithms which are independent from applications are a potential subject of design reuse and thus are more cost efficient to be implemented in hardware than

algorithms that are tailored to a limited number of applications or even to a single application only.

Both simplicity and reusability are inherent to most low-level vision and image processing ("pre-processing") algorithms which turns them into much more suitable candidates to be implemented in hardware than higher-level algorithms [7, 8, 24]. For that reason, and in order to present algorithms which are useful to be implemented both in hardware as well as in software, the authors of this work focus on low-level algorithms only.

The remainder of this chapter is outlined as follows. In Section 5.2, we present prior work on performance comparisons of different implementations of low-level computer vision algorithms. Section 5.3 presents metrics we use for the benchmark. In Section 5.4, we describe four low-level vision algorithms, which have been used for the performance benchmark. Section 5.5 discusses the achieved results of the benchmark and Section 5.6 summarizes and concludes the chapter.

5.2 Related Work

Image processing algorithms are commonly developed and tested on a PC platform. To port the algorithm to an embedded system, questions about which hardware fits the needs of the algorithm and performance properties must be answered. Selecting an embedded hardware platform for image processing significantly influences performance [13].

The design considerations for FPGAs [8] are wide multiplication units, numerous logic elements, parallel hardware structures, handling of high data rates and the reconfiguration of FPGAs. Compared to high-end DSPs, an FPGA is more expensive, the design flow for FPGA algorithms requires more time and the processing power for sequential computations is slower than on DSPs. General purpose DSPs [6, 14] are designed to fit a variety of market applications, with no consideration for any special algorithm. DSPs have large word widths, common memory schemes, peripherals with standardized connections to other devices and very high clock frequency. A punctiform comparison is shown in [15], where a Monte Carlo simulation on both, a DSP and an FPGA was done. Both had nearly the same speed performance with the DSP having a slight advantage.

5.3 Benchmark Metrics

Typical image processing performance indicators are accuracy, robustness, sensitivity, adaptability, reliability, and efficiency [25].

This chapter discusses image processing performance with the main emphasis on efficiency (execution time and memory resources). The focus of our study is to compare and evaluate performance of the implementation of low-level vision algorithms on a DSP, an FPGA, and on a mobile PC processor. Based on these examples, the advantages and disadvantages of these technologies for realization of real-time computer vision applications are highlighted. Since most of our target applications have stringent real-time requirements, the performance of the resulting implementations is of great importance for a system designer. For the performance evaluation, we used the execution time per pixel of the algorithms (for a single full-scale input image) as a measure of the performance. Furthermore, the needed resources for the implementation are listed and discussed to give an insight into the hidden costs of the achieved performance results. Since image processing is a high performance application, power consumption is out of the scope of this chapter.

The execution time per pixel is still dependent to some degree on the size of the input image, at least on the platforms with a CPU such as DSP and PC. In [28] this effect is visualized in several diagrams. As a consequence, all test runs were done on input images with equal size for all platforms. In order to get precise performance data, high-resolution hardware timers were used to measure the execution times for the DSP and PC implementations.

5.4 Implementation

This section describes the four low-level vision algorithms that have been used for the performance benchmark. The implementation variants on an FPGA, a DSP and a mobile-PC platform are shown.

5.4.1 Low-Level Vision Algorithms

Gaussian pyramid [9]: Two dimensional low-pass filters, such as the Gaussian low-pass filter, work with a filter kernel, to calculate an average value for a destination pixel using a number of neighboring source pixels. The two dimensional Gaussian filter is defined by Eq. (5.1).

$$g(x,y) = \frac{1}{2\pi\sigma^2} e^{\frac{-(x^2+y^2)}{2\sigma^2}} \tag{5.1}$$

When dealing with digital images integer weighting factors are used. A typical 5×5 Gaussian filter matrix and the decimation of the pixels is shown in Fig. 5.1. The anchor point of the Gaussian filter kernel is marked by an "X." Obviously, for every calculated pixel two neighboring pixels in both dimensions are required. To avoid the need for special treatment of the border pixels, the function operates on a region of interest (ROI) that is two pixels smaller than the whole image in all four directions. This is a common approach in high performance implementations.

The Gaussian pyramid is a hierarchy of Gaussian low-pass filters, such that successive levels correspond to lower frequencies. With every Gaussian pyramid level the number of pixels in x- and y-coordinates is reduced by a factor of 2.

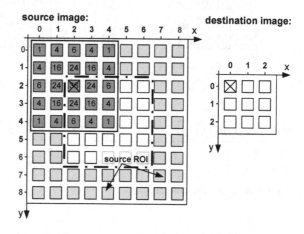

Fig. 5.1 Gaussian pyramid filter kernel with 5×5 pixels. The numbers in the dark square are the weighting factors for the pixels. All products are summed up and finally averaged to receive the value for the anchor point.

Bayer filter demosaicing [12]: A Bayer filter mosaic is a color filter array for arranging RGB color filters on a grid of photosensors. Its arrangement is used in most single-chip color image sensors and digital cameras. A Bayer filter demosaicing algorithm converts the raw image pixels from a Bayer color filter array into RGB values, as shown in Fig. 5.2. The Bayer color filter array refers to a particular arrangement of color filters. The demosaicing algorithm we implemented is shown in Eqs. (5.2). The color filter ID (*colID*) is used to determine the alignment of the camera's color filter to the current area of interest [5].

$$colID = 0 \begin{cases} R_{x,y} = r_{x,y} \\ G_{x,y} = \frac{g_{x,y+1}+g_{x+1,y}}{2} \\ B_{x,y} = b_{x+1,y+1} \end{cases} \quad colID = 1 \begin{cases} R_{x,y} = r_{x,y+1} \\ G_{x,y} = \frac{g_{x,y}+g_{x+1,y+1}}{2} \\ B_{x,y} = b_{x+1,y} \end{cases}$$

$$colID = 2 \begin{cases} R_{x,y} = r_{x+1,y} \\ G_{x,y} = \frac{g_{x,y}+g_{x+1,y+1}}{2} \\ B_{x,y} = b_{x,y+1} \end{cases} \quad colID = 3 \begin{cases} R_{x,y} = r_{x+1,y+1} \\ G_{x,y} = \frac{g_{x,y+1}+g_{x+1,y}}{2} \\ B_{x,y} = b_{x,y} \end{cases} \quad (5.2)$$

Sobel edge detector [9]: The Sobel operator is widely used in image processing, particularly within edge detection algorithms. The Sobel edge detector performs a gradient measurement over the x- and y- coordinates with separate filter kernels for each dimension.

$$C_V = \begin{pmatrix} -1 & 0 & 1 \\ -2 & 0 & 2 \\ -1 & 0 & 1 \end{pmatrix} \quad C_H = \begin{pmatrix} 1 & 2 & 1 \\ 0 & 0 & 0 \\ -1 & -2 & -1 \end{pmatrix} \quad C = |C_V| + |C_H| \quad (5.3)$$

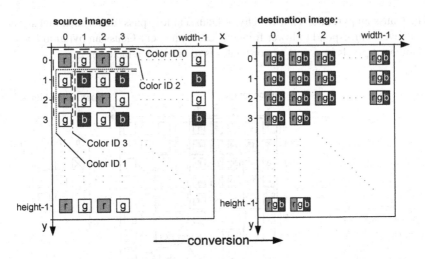

Fig. 5.2 Bayer filter demosaicing.

Regions with high spatial frequency correspond to edges. Typically, the Sobel filter kernel consists of a pair of 3×3 coefficients and is designed in such a way as to have a maximum response for edges running vertically and horizontally through the image. The result C is saturated to a value margin from 0 to 255.

Sum of absolute differences (SAD) [4]: The SAD algorithm is used to solve the correspondence problem between two image areas by calculating matching costs for blocks of pixels. This is performed by calculating the absolute difference between the pixels of two compared blocks and aggregating the results. In the application of stereo vision this is performed to compute the depth information of a scene. Here, two images taken from different viewpoints are compared and the object correspondence has to be solved by comparing pixel blocks along a specific range, called the disparity range. The quality of the result depends on the SAD block size (e.g., 8×8 or 9×9). For a more detailed description of the SAD algorithm see Chapter 6.

5.4.2 FPGA Implementation

FPGA implementations of the low-level algorithms described in Section 5.4.1 were used in three applications; see [1, 7, 8]. For these applications the processing sequence of image data follows the approach shown in Fig. 5.3.

For the low-level algorithms, image data of only a few adjacent rows must be processed in parallel. Thus, less memory is required to process these algorithms. This is in contrast to most high-level algorithms, which typically need access to much larger regions of an image. Moreover, processing parameters of higher-level algorithms often depend on results from further processing steps. Thus, high-level image processing typically requires large amounts of memory.

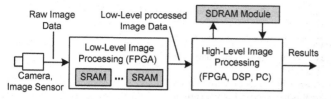

Fig. 5.3 Processing sequence of image data as implemented in [7, 8].

Today's high-end FPGAs offer a large number of small SRAM-based memories on-chip. For example, the Xilinx Virtex-5 FPGA family provides devices which contain more than 600 SRAM blocks, each 18 kbits in size [26]. By using such SRAM resources, partitioning of low-level and high-level image processing algorithms for the applications described in [7, 8] was done as follows:

- Due to the low amount of memory needed, low-level algorithms were implemented in an FPGA by using on-chip SRAM resources. Since the several algorithms use different SRAM blocks, all algorithms can be processed in parallel.
- High-level algorithms are implemented partly in an FPGA, in a DSP-based system or a standard PC, all using a large external SDRAM-based memory module. Since a single memory device is used, parallelization of the several high-level algorithms is limited when compared to the implementation of the FPGA-based low-level algorithms.

In the context of this chapter we focus on the implementation of the low-level algorithms. Fig. 5.4 shows the interfaces of a low-level image processing module as implemented in the FPGA designs described in [7, 8].

Fig. 5.4 Interfaces of the low-level image processing modules as implemented in [7, 8].

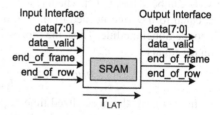

The meaning of the several interface signals shown in Fig. 5.4 is described in Table 5.1.

5.4.2.1 Sobel Edge Detector

Fig. 5.5 shows the internal data flow of a Sobel filter which is implemented according to Fig. 5.4 (the control logic which handles the data_valid, end_of_row and end_of_frame signals is not shown in Fig. 5.5).

Table 5.1 Interface definitions of the FPGA-based low-level image processing modules

Signal Name	Description
data[7:0]	Pixel data
data_valid	Indicates, when high, that data on data[7:0] is valid
end_of_row	Indicates, when high, that the current pixel on data[7:0] is the last pixel of the current row
end_of_frame	Indicates, when high, that the current pixel on data[7:0] is the last pixel of the current frame

The filter is composed of several 8-bit registers (R) and some SRAM-based buffers forming a large pipeline. Each buffer holds a number of $(n-2)$ 8-bit pixels where n is the number of pixels by row (e.g., 256). With each clock cycle the whole pipeline is shifted by one pixel and a new pixel is read in from the input data_in[7:0] of the pipeline. That way, the outputs of the six 8-bit registers (R), the outputs of the two buffers and data_in[7:0] hold the pixel values of the 3×3 filter kernel area. For example, to apply the vertical Sobel operator to the center pixel of the 3×3 area the coefficient matrix given by Eq. (5.3) (left side) is used. Afterwards, the absolute value of the result is saturated to 255 in order to limit the final result to 8 bits. Applying the coefficient matrix, calculation of the absolute value and the final saturation is performed in one clock cycle. Hence, every time a new pixel is received from data_in[7:0], a Sobel-filtered pixel is generated on the output interface signal data_out[7:0], which results in a processing time for a single pixel (without considering any latency) of $t = \frac{1}{f_{CLK}}$ where f_{CLK} is the clock frequency of the Sobel module. By using an Altera Stratix EP1S60 FPGA [2] a clock frequency of 133 MHz can be achieved [8]. The latency T_{LAT} between data_in[7:0] and data_out[7:0] is equal to the time needed to shift in a complete row plus two additional pixels into the Sobel module. Thus, the processing time needed to process all pixels of an image equals

$$t_{IMG} = T_{LAT} + \frac{1}{f_{CLK}} \cdot \text{rows} \cdot \text{columns} \qquad (5.4)$$

In summary, the normalized time required to apply the (either vertical or horizontal) Sobel operator to a single pixel is given by

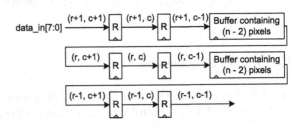

Fig. 5.5 Internal data flow of a Sobel filter kernel with 3×3 pixels.

$$t_{PIX} = \frac{T_{LAT}}{\text{rows} \cdot \text{columns}} + \frac{1}{f_{CLK}} \tag{5.5}$$

The implementation requires about 210 LEs (Logic Elements) which is less than 0.4% of the total number of LEs available in that device. Assuming $n = 256$ pixels per row, a number of two M4K SRAM blocks, each 512 bytes in size, is required to implement the two row buffers of the Sobel filter, which is about 0.4% of the M4K blocks available. Timing data and resource count of the Sobel filter are summarized in Table 5.2.

Table 5.2 Timing and resource count of an FPGA-based Sobel filter implementation

	3×3 Sobel Vertical	3×3 Sobel Horizontal
FPGA device	Altera EP1S60	Altera EP1S60
# of LEs	210	220
% of LEs	0.4	0.4
# of M4K SRAM blocks	2	2
% of M4K SRAM blocks	0.4	0.4
f_{CLK}	133 MHz	133 MHz
T_{LAT}	1.94 μs	1.94 μs
t_{PIX}	7.55 ns	7.55 ns

5.4.2.2 Gaussian Pyramid

Implementation of a single level of a 5×5 Gaussian pyramid (see Section 5.4.1) follows the approach shown in Fig. 5.5. Due to the 5×5 pixel area, 20 registers (R) as well as four row buffers are required to perform the calculation. However, since each level of a Gaussian pyramid reduces the height and width of the resulting image by a factor of 2, only half of the pixels contained in each row must be stored in the row buffers, which reduces the amount of SRAM memory by two. For a single 5×5 Gaussian pyramid, T_{LAT} equals the time needed to shift in two complete rows plus three additional pixels. Implementing the 5×5 Gaussian pyramid in an Altera Stratix EP1S60 FPGA results in a maximum clock frequency of 133 MHz; see [8]. Timing and resource data of a single Gaussian pyramid (assuming $n = 256$ pixels) is shown on the left side of Table 5.3. Note, that the processing time t_{PIX} of a single Gaussian pyramid is about four times the processing time of the Sobel filter. This results from the fact that due to the reduction of the image size, a pixel is generated by the image processing block on every fourth clock cycle only.

5.4.2.3 Bayer Filter Demosaicing

The Bayer filter described in Section 5.4.1 was implemented using an Altera Stratix-II EP2S30 device; see [3, 7]. Two registers (R) and one SRAM buffer holding

Table 5.3 Timing and resource count of the FPGA-based single 5×5 Gaussian pyramid and Bayer filter

	Single 5×5 Gaussian Pyramid	Bayer Filter
FPGA device	Altera EP1S60	Altera EP2S30
# of LEs	460	150
% of LEs	0.8	0.4
# of M4K SRAM blocks	4	1
% of M4K SRAM blocks	0.7	0.7
f_{CLK}	133 MHz	140 MHz
T_{LAT}	3.86 μs	14.29 ns
t_{PIX}	30.13 ns	7.14 ns

$(n-1)$ 8-bit pixels are required to perform the calculation according to Eqs. (5.2). The output interface of the Bayer filter is slightly different from Fig. 5.4. In detail, data_out[7:0] is replaced by the three signals data_red_out[7:0], data_green_out[7:0] and data_blue_out[7:0]. For the Bayer filter, T_{LAT} is equal to 2 clock cycles caused by two register stages. Timing and resource count of the Bayer filter (with $n = 256$ pixels) are summarized on the right side of Table 5.3.

5.4.2.4 SAD Algorithm

The 9×9 SAD algorithm, as described in Section 5.4.1, was implemented and synthesized for an Altera Stratix II EP2S130 using a block size of 9×9. Detailed information on the implementation can be found in Chapter 6. The latency time $T_{LAT,IMG}$ is necessary once per image and $T_{LAT,LINE}$ every line. Both latencies are required to fill the pipeline structure and enable the calculation of one hundred SADs in parallel for the whole disparity range. In summary, the normalized time required to apply the SAD algorithm to blocks of 9×9 pixels is given by Eq. (5.6). Furthermore, the total time required to calculate the SAD block match on a complete image (e.g., 800×400 pixels) is given by Eq. (5.7). The SAD's timing and resource data is shown in Table 5.4.

$$t_{SAD-Block} = \frac{T_{LAT,IMG}}{\text{disparity} \cdot \text{rows} \cdot \text{columns}} + \frac{T_{LAT,LINE}}{\text{disparity} \cdot \text{rows}} + \frac{1}{f_{CLK} \cdot \text{disparity}} \quad (5.6)$$

$$t_{SAD-IMG} = T_{LAT,IMG} + T_{LAT,LINE} \cdot \text{columns} + \frac{1}{f_{CLK}} \cdot \text{rows} \cdot \text{columns} \quad (5.7)$$

Table 5.4 Timing and resource count of an FPGA-based 9×9 SAD blockmatching implementation

	9×9 SAD Blockmatch	
FPGA device	Altera EP2S130	
# of LEs	75453	
% of LEs	56.9	
# of M4K SRAM blocks	104	
% of M4K SRAM blocks	17.0	
f_{CLK}	110 MHz	@100 blocks parallel
$T_{LAT,IMG}$	66.00 μs	@800$\times$400 pixels
$T_{LAT,LINE}$	1.27 μs	@ 800 pixel per line
$t_{SAD-Block}$	0.111 ns	@ (800-(100 disparity)) $\times$ (400-(9 blocksize)) calculation steps for a 800$\times$400 pixel image

5.4.3 DSP Implementation

The selected digital signal processor TMS320C6414T-1000 [21] is from Texas Instruments. It is a device from the C6000 family and one of the cutting-edge fixed point DSPs in this series. It runs with a clock of 1 GHz and provides up to 8,000 million MAC (multiply-accumulate) operations per second.

5.4.3.1 Gaussian Pyramid

An example will show the performance improvement of partly hand-optimized code. Some tests are carried out with the function that calculates one level of a Gaussian pyramid '*PfePyrDown_Gauss5x5_8u_C1R()*'. The digital filtering of an image requires MAC operations on every pixel with a sliding scope over the image. The first unoptimized implementation of the Gaussian pyramid is the reference code in portable ANSI C, which we call the "functional behavior." The filter coefficients are derived from an array. All coefficients are multiplied with the corresponding pixels. The products are summed up and divided by the sum of the coefficients derived from the array, as shown in Listing 5.1. The Gaussian Filter is a neighborhood operation, which means that an ROI is used. During the test, the image size of 256×256 pixels is used, where the ROI window has a size of 252×252 pixels, because a border of 2 pixels is required for the algorithm. This results in a destination image with the size of 126×126 pixels and obtains a performance of 86.11 ns/pixel. The functions '*PfeGetPix8u()*' and '*PfeSetPix8u()*' are a part of the PfeLib, which is an embedded performance primitives library [28].

Code Optimization

A common method to gain execution time performance is to inline subfunctions. It means that the C/C++ source code for the called function is inserted at the place of the function call. This technique is useful for platforms with multistaged-pipelines and especially for C6000 DSPs that are featuring instruction-level-parallelism using very long instruction words (VLIW). Execution time on VLIW processors is improved, because function calls inside of loops hinder the optimizing compiler in parallelizing loops [17].

As shown in Listing 5.1, the algorithm to perform the Gaussian pyramid consists of four nested loops, two loops for x- and y-coordinates and the other two loops for the filter coefficients array. To reduce the number of loops, the filter array is replaced by separate 'const' coefficients which are multiplied by every corresponding pixel of the source image. By removing the inner two loops execution time decreases from 86.11 to 41.67 ns/pixel.

Software functions on DSPs typically can have their performance improved by using specific intrinsics [18]. Intrinsics are special built-in functions which the compiler can directly translate into machine code. Intrinsics can be used in loops without disturbing the compiler to perform software pipelining. However, once intrinsics are used in the code it is not ANSI C-compliant anymore.

In the next optimization step of the Gaussian pyramid algorithm, compiler intrinsics are introduced. It is important that the inner loop can be processed quickly, because it is often executed. As mentioned before, every pixel is loaded separately from memory. For speedup, the intrinsic '_mem4_const' can be used, which allows loading four freely aligned bytes from memory and is equivalent to four separate loads of pixels. The bytes are stored in a 32-bit local variable that contains four pixels. However, splitting up this 4×8-bit variable for a separate multiplication would result in a slow-down in overall performance. The intrinsic '_dotpu4' allows access to SIMD (single instruction multiple data) machine code, which does 4 8-bit multiplications in parallel and sums the results. This is all performed within one CPU cycle. After the specific intrinsics have been applied and a successful compile run has been accomplished, the result can be observed in the compiler-generated assembly feedback file (see Listing 5.2).

Listing 5.1 Functional behavior of the Gaussian pyramid

```
// loop over image lines
for (y=0; y<pImgSrc->u32Height; y+=2)
{
  // loop over pixels of current line
  for (x=0; x<pImgSrc->u32Width; x+=2)
  {
    nPixel=0;
    for (j=0; j<szMask.u32Height; j++)
    {
      for (i=0; i<szMask.u32Width; i++)
```

```
    {
        nPixel_tmp=PfeGetPix8u(pImgSrc,
                               x−ptAnchor.x+i,
                               y−ptAnchor.y+j);
        nPixel+=nPixel_tmp*Flt[i][j];
    }
  }
  nPixel/=Flt_const;
  // write pixel to memory
  PfeSetPix8u(pImgDst,(x/2),(y/2),nPixel);
  }
}
```

Listing 5.2 Compiler-generated assembly feedback

	A−side	B−side
Loop source line	: 201	
Loop opening brace source line	: 202	
Loop closing brace source line	: 235	
Known Minimum Trip Count	: 1	
Known Max Trip Count Factor	: 1	
Loop Carried Dependency Bound(^)	: 22	
Unpartitioned Resource Bound	: 5	
Partitioned Resource Bound(*)	: 7	
Resource Partition:	A−side	B−side
.L units	0	1
.S units	1	2
.D units	4	3
.M units	5	5
.X cross paths	7*	3
.T address paths	6	6
Long read paths	0	0
Long write paths	0	0
Logical ops (.LS)	0	0
Addition ops (.LSD)	11	1
Bound(.L .S .LS)	1	2
Bound(.L .S .D .LS .LSD)	6	3

The next improvement gaining performance is to use software pipelining. Software pipelining is a technique creating machine code and scheduling it in such a way that instructions from several consecutive executions of a loop are executed in parallel. As a basic step in creating pipelined code, the code should be analyzed by hand or by the compiler, which the C64x compiler performs automatically. Restrictions [18] for software pipelining are that loops should not have any branches or function calls.

To force software pipelining of the innermost loop, the information in Listing 5.2 is important. *'Loop Carried Dependency Bound():22'* is based on ordering constraints among the assembly instructions. The keyword *'restrict'* helps to decrease the loop carried dependency. Decreasing it means that every loop iteration becomes more independent from the others. *'restrict'* is a type qualifier for a pointer, which tells the compiler that the referenced data can only by accessed via this pointer.

After introducing the keyword *'restrict'* and declaring some variables *'const'*, the *'Loop Carried Dependency Bound()'* decreases to 2 and the software pipeline information *'ii = 6 Schedule found with 5 iterations in parallel'* is given as feedback. *'ii = 6 Schedule found with 5 iterations in parallel'* means that the piped loop kernel needs six cycles, but within these six cycles the DSP processes five different loop iterations in parallel. The *'ii-value'* of the innermost loop has the greatest influence on performance.

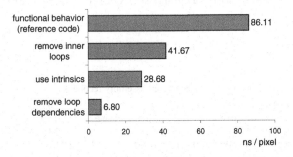

Fig. 5.6 Optimization summary for calculating one level of a Gaussian pyramid on a C64x DSP.

Fig. 5.6 shows an optimization summary of the Gaussian pyramid with a performance gain by a factor of 12.66. The performance values are measured with the device cycle-accurate simulator [19] embedded in Code Composer Studio 3.1.0 from Texas Instruments.

Finally, additional compiler options help to speed up the algorithm. These options for the C64x compiler are to deactivate code size reducing, to perform software pipelining, perform loop unrolling and elimination of all local and global assignments. The last option that impacts speed is to disable the debug information [17]. At this point, achieving further optimizations would mean rewriting the whole function in assembly by hand. But the additional effort is quite high and TI's C compiler can do an excellent job after the developer is able to derive the benefits from the compiler feedback—so there may be very little room for further enhancements.

Memory Access Optimization

Modern DSP systems have various types of hierarchical memories and caches that differ significantly in their sizes, latency times, and data bandwidths. Fast on-chip memory is always a very limited resource, thus, the memory configuration and data access pattern also have significant influence on the achieved performance. In the following, three different test setups are used and evaluated.

Firstly, the complete source image data is stored in the IRAM (internal RAM). Secondly, if the image data exceeds the available space in the IRAM (the TMS-320C6414T-1000 is equipped with 1 MB IRAM), the complete image data is stored in the ERAM (external RAM) and only slices of the image are transferred to the IRAM by the DMA controller. This technique is called ROS-DMA (resource optimized slicing with direct memory access) [27] and is provided by the Pfe-Lib [28]. ROS-DMA is a generalized approach of DMA double buffering that can be easily activated for almost all image processing routines inside of the PfeLib. And in the third setup, the complete image data are stored in the ERAM without using special techniques to transfer data into the IRAM, but with activated L2 Cache (256kB).

Fig. 5.7 compares the performance of these three cases. The source image has a size of 256×256 pixels, where each pixel value is represented by 8 bits. The tests are carried out with the Gaussian pyramid function and leads us to a destination image size of 126×126 pixels. The performance data is shown in nanoseconds per output pixel.

The case "complete image data in IRAM" is, as expected, the fastest variant and is realistic for an image size of up to 640×480 pixels on the TMS320C6414T-1000. Further, the implementation using the ROS-DMA technique is only a bit slower, which shows that the ROS-DMA [27] technique is able to reduce the performance gap between IRAM and ERAM better than using ordinary L2 cache.

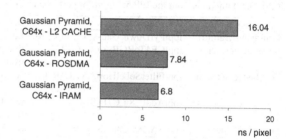

Fig. 5.7 Execution times of the Gaussian pyramid function under different memory configurations on a C64x DSP: IRAM, ERAM + ROS-DMA, ERAM + L2 Cache.

5.4.3.2 Other Functions

A similar strategy for improving performance is also applied to the functions for Bayer filter demosaicing and Sobel edge detecting. This is possible because these low-level algorithms have a similar structure, except the use of intrinsics and their convenient arrangement, which depends on the algorithm itself. The SAD 8×8 algorithm is derived from the Texas Instruments Image/Video Processing Library v2.0 [20], which contains various assembly-optimized functions that are C-callable. The achieved execution times of these functions are discussed in Section 5.5.

5.4.4 Mobile PC Implementation

The PC processor chosen for this comparison is an Intel Mobile Core 2 Duo with 2 GHz clock frequency (model T7200). Compared to desktop CPUs, this model has better energy efficiency. Thus, it is commonly used in notebook PCs, but also in industrial and so-called "embedded" PCs, which also makes it an interesting candidate for computer vision applications.

The degree of software optimization has a significant influence on the achievable performance of recent PC CPUs. Here, the situation is similar to that of DSPs. In the case of low-level image processing, this means that dedicated software libraries providing target-specific hand-optimized code are essential. For the test runs we used a library that is provided by the processor manufacturer itself, namely the Intel performance primitives (IPP) [10]. We consider the IPP library the state-of-the-art on the PC platform. It uses various SIMD extensions, such as the SSE, SSE2, SSE3 of modern PC CPUs. Most of the library's functions are inherently capable of threading, i.e., they can use all cores of multicore CPUs. Table 5.5 lists the functions used for the performance test on the PC platform. The chosen IPP functions provide a level of functionality that is either identical or very similar to their respective counterparts for the DSP and FPGA platforms.

Table 5.5 Functions from the IPP 5.3 used for performance measurements on the PC platform

Operation	IPP function(s)	Comment
Gaussian pyramid	ippiPyrDown_Gauss5x5_8u_C1R()	Equivalent functionality
Bayer demosaicing	ippiCFAToRGB_8u_C1C3R()	Interpolation method differs slightly from Eqs. (5.2)
Sobel edge detector	ippiFilterSobelHoriz_8u_C1R(), ippiFilterSobelVert_8u_C1R(), ippiAddC_8u_C1IRSfs()	A combination of these 3 IPP functions was used to get an equivalent functionality as described in Section 5.4.1
Sum of abs. diff.	ippiSAD8x8_8u32s_C1R	SAD of 8×8 blocks

Most of the test runs on the PC platform were executed using the test framework of the PfeLib [28]. This was possible because PfeLib is inherently portable. When it is executed on the PC, it wraps to the IPP whenever possible. This method was used for all algorithms except for the SAD 8×8 function, where a dedicated test routine was written. An important issue in the field of computer vision is the generally poor real-time capability of PC platforms. On the one hand, this problem arises from using high-level operating systems such as MS Windows or Linux. Our test runs were performed under Windows XP. On the other hand, the various transparent data and program caches on the PC make it hard to get predictable execution times. This leads to the situation that on a PC the worst case execution time (WCET) of a particular image processing operation can be orders of magnitude higher than in the average or best case. We took care that the performance values published in Section 5.5 are always results of best case scenarios.

5.5 Results

Figs. 5.8 and 5.9 show the performance for PC, FPGA, and DSP implementations of the low-level image processing algorithms. For the DSP implementations, two implementation variants (using IRAM, ERAM + ROSDMA) are shown. The ERAM is clocked with 133 MHz. For speed measurements on the DSP, the Code Composer Studio of Texas Instruments and the integrated C6414 Device Cycle Accurate Simulator were used. For the FPGA, performance was evaluated using Synplify for logic synthesis and Altera Quartus for place and route as well as for static timing analysis. The mobile PC performance values are derived from the IPP [10] running on an Intel Core 2 Duo Processor T7200, with 2×2.0 GHz and 2 GB RAM.

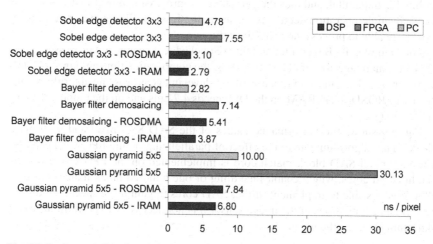

Fig. 5.8 Performance benchmark for PC, FPGA and DSP implementations

Upon first glance, the DSP outperforms the FPGA for all three algorithms in Fig. 5.8. The mobile PC implementations behave similarly, either better or slightly worse than the DSP. However, some facts must be considered. FPGA low-level

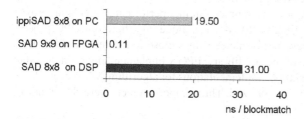

Fig. 5.9 Performance Benchmark for PC (8×8), FPGA (9×9) and DSP (8×8) implementations of SAD block match. The FPGA outperforms the DSP although the DSP uses the data from the fast L1 Cache.

image processing is done by directly receiving data from an image sensor or a camera (see left side of Fig. 5.3). As long as the algorithm is able to cope with the speed of the image sensor/camera there is no need for higher processing speeds. Hence, it does not make sense to speed up processing for these algorithms in this scenario, since the image sensor/camera is not able to deliver the image data faster anyway. Obviously, this contrasts with the implementation of the higher-level algorithms (right side of Fig. 5.3), which operate by using a large memory device. For this class of algorithms it surely would make sense to increase either the performance of the algorithms or the speed of the data transfers from the memory device.

Further, for our benchmarks 100% of the available DSP and mobile PC performance is spent on the processing of a single low-level image algorithm. However, for a complex vision system, many operations must be processed by the DSP or mobile PC in parallel, and thus the percentage of processing power that is available for each single operation decreases substantially. Instead, FPGA image processing blocks are able to process data concurrently.

For example, if a Bayer filter and three Sobel edge detectors are processed on an FPGA for an image size of 800×400 pixels, the computation time amounts to 2.418 ms per image. The same combination of low-level image processing algorithms with the use of ROSDMA+ERAM on the DSP needs 4.71 ms and on the mobile PC 5.49 ms per image.

Fig. 5.9 shows the performance values of the SAD 8×8 pixel and 9×9 pixel block match algorithm, where the effect of parallelizing on the FPGA is apparent. The 9×9 pixel SAD block match core is implemented on the FPGA as a row of one hundred cores, which enables handling of one hundred block matches in parallel. It is possible to implement further SAD cores to gain more speed, but due to performance limitations of the image sensor it is not necessary to perform the SAD algorithm faster on the image.

5.6 Conclusions

In this chapter the implementations of several low-level vision algorithms were evaluated, compared, and discussed. Cutting-edge hardware was used for the DSP, FPGA, and mobile PC processor platforms.

For the DSP implementations we pointed out that performance can be improved by the use of intrinsics and the ROSDMA technique. On the mobile PC processor it was possible to achieve performance values close to the results of the DSP implementations by the use of the IPP library. FPGA implementations, on the other hand, outperform the DSP and PC implementations for algorithms when ever a large number of operations can be parallelized. Three important facts were shown in this work:

- Low-level algorithms such as filter kernels (image denoising, enhancement, reconstruction or pixel matching) which can be run in parallel (where the pixels are processed on-the-fly) fit best to FPGAs.

- High-level algorithms which consist of complex branches (if, else) or control loops and operate on data widths which are a multiple of 8 bits are preferred for implementing on DSPs.
- Powerful image libraries which are available for PC platforms enable short design times. However, compared to DSP and FPGA implementations, the performance is not always the best.

In this chapter we focused our investigations on a performance benchmark of some low-level vision algorithms on selected platforms. However, cost and power consumption issues were not analyzed at all. More information on that issue can be found, for example, in [13].

Acknowledgements The research leading to these results has received funding from the European Community's Sixth Framework Programme (FP6/2003-2006) under grant agreement No. FP6-2006-IST-6-045350 (robots@home).

References

1. Ambrosch, K., Humenberger, M., Kubinger, W., Steininger, A.: Hardware implementation of an SAD based stereo vision algorithm. *Proc. Comput. Vis. and Pattern Recognition Work.*, (2007), doi: 10.1109/CVPR.2007.383417.
2. Altera Corporation, 101 Innovation Drive, San Jose, CA 95134: *Stratix Device Handbook*, Vol. 1, Apr 2003.
3. Altera Corporation, 101 Innovation Drive, San Jose, CA 95134: *Stratix II Device Handbook*, Vol. 1, Jan 2005.
4. Azad, P., Gockel, T., Dillmann, R.: *Computer Vision*, Elektor-Verl. GmbH (2007).
5. Basler Cooperation, *Basler A600f User's Manual*, Document Number DA00056107 (2005).
6. Bosi, B., Savaria, Y., Bois, G.: Reconfigurable pipelined 2-D convolvers for fast digital signal processing, *IEEE Trans. Very Large Scale Integr. Syst.*, **7(3)**, pp. 299-308 (1999).
7. Eckel, C., Bodenstorfer, E., Nachtnebel, H., Roessler, P., Fuertler, J., Mayer, K.: Hochschwindigkeitsmera mit intelligenter Datenvorverarbeitung. *Proc. of the Austrochip 2006*, pp. 103-108 (2006), ISBN 3-200-00770-2.
8. Fuertler, J., Roessler, P., Brodersen, J., Nachtnebel, H., Mayer, K., Cadek, G., Eckel, C.: Design considerations for scalable high-performance vision systems embedded in industrial print inspection machines, *EURASIP Journal on Embed. Syst.* (2007) doi:10.1155/2007/71794.
9. Gonzalez, R.C., Woods, R.E.: *Digital Image Processing*, Second Ed., Pearson Educa. Int. (2002).
10. Intel Corporation, 2200 Mission College Blvd, Santa Clara, CA 95054: *Intel Integrated Performance Primitives for Intel Architecture*, Doc. Number:A70805-014, Version-014, (2004).
11. Jones, W.D.: Keeping cars from crashing. *IEEE Spectr.* **38(9)**, (2001).
12. Kimmel, R.: Demosaicing: Image reconstruction from color CCD samples. *IEEE Trans. on Image Process.*, pp. 1221-1228 (1999).
13. Kisačanin, B.: Examples of low-level computer vision on media processors. *Proc. IEEE CVPR, ECV Workshop*, 2005.
14. Koc, I.S.: Design considerations for real-time systems with DSP and RISC architectures. *Proc. of the EUSIPCO2005 13th Eur. Signal Process. Conf.*, (2005).
15. Monaghan, S., Cowen, C.P., Reconfigurable Multi-Bit Processor for DSP Applications in Statistical Physics, Master Thesis, Department of Electric Systems Engineering, University of Essex (1993).

16. Murphy, R.R.: Rescue robotics for Homeland Security. *Commun. of the ACM,* pp. 66-68 (2004).
17. Texas Instruments Incorporated. *TMS320C6000 Optimizing Compiler User's Guide,* Jul 2005, Lit. Number: SPRU187N, http://www.ti.com/litv/pdf/spru187n.
18. Texas Instruments Incorporated. *TMS320C6000 Programmer's Guide,* Mar 2006, Lit. Number: SPRU198I, http://www.ti.com/litv/pdf/spru198i.
19. Texas Instruments Incorporated. *TMS320C6000 Instruction Set Simulator,* Apr 2007, Lit. Number: SPRU600I, http://www.ti.com/litv/pdf/spru600i.
20. Texas Instruments Incorporated. *TMS320C64x+ DSP Image/Video Processing Library* (v2.0), Oct 2007, Lit. Number: SPRUF30, http://www.ti.com/litv/pdf/spruf30.
21. Texas Instruments Incorporated. *TMS320C6414T, TMS320C6415T, TMS320C6416T Fixed-Point Digital Signal Processors,* Jan 2008, Lit. Number: SPRS226K, http://focus.ti.com/lit/ds/sprs226l/sprs226l.pdf.
22. Tilera Corporation, 2333 Zanker Road, San Jose, California 95131: *TILE64 Processor,* http://www.tilera.com/products/processors.php. Cited 21 Feb 2008.
23. Travis, W., Daily, R., Bevly, D.M., Knoedler, K., Behringer, R., Hemetsberger, H., Kogler, J., Kubinger, W., Alefs, B.: SciAutonics-Auburn Engineering's low-cost, high-speed ATV for the 2005 DARPA Grand Challenge. *Journal of Field Robotics* **23**, pp. 579-597 (2006).
24. Williams, R.: Using FPGAs for DSP image processing, *FPGA and Struct. ASIC Journal* (2004), available from http://www.fpgajournal.com/. Cited 5 Feb 2008.
25. Wirth, M., Fraschini, M., Masek, M., Bruynooghe, M.: Performance evaluation in image processing, *EURASIP Journal on Appl. Signal Process.* (2006) doi: 10.1155/ASP/2006/45742.
26. Xilinx Incorporation, 2100 Logic Drive, San Jose, CA 95124-3400: *Virtex-5 Family Overview,* Datasheet DS100 (v3.0), Feb 2007.
27. Zinner, C., Kubinger, W.: ROS-DMA: A DMA double buffering method for embedded image processing with resource optimized slicing. *Proc. of RTAS 2006,* pp. 361-372 (2006).
28. Zinner, C., Kubinger, W., Isaacs, R.: PfeLib – A performance primitives library for embedded vision, *EURASIP Journal on Embed. Syst.* (2007) doi:10.1155/2007/49051.

Chapter 6
SAD-Based Stereo Matching Using FPGAs

Karina Ambrosch, Martin Humenberger, Wilfried Kubinger,
and Andreas Steininger

Abstract In this chapter we present a field-programmable gate array (FPGA) based stereo matching architecture. This architecture uses the sum of absolute differences (SAD) algorithm and is targeted at automotive and robotics applications. The disparity maps are calculated using 450×375 input images and a disparity range of up to 150 pixels. We discuss two different implementation approaches for the SAD and analyze their resource usage. Furthermore, block sizes ranging from 3×3 up to 11×11 and their impact on the consumed logic elements as well as on the disparity map quality are discussed. The stereo matching architecture enables a frame rate of up to 600 fps by calculating the data in a highly parallel and pipelined fashion. This way, a software solution optimized by using Intel's Open Source Computer Vision Library running on an Intel Pentium 4 with 3 GHz clock frequency is outperformed by a factor of 400.

6.1 Introduction

In the field of automotive applications there is a growing need for sensors that can detect obstacles at a wide range of distances. For adaptive cruise control (ACC) and collision warning systems there are already embedded radar sensors in use [8]. Clearly, embedded stereo vision sensors can also be used for this kind of obstacle detection, producing much more detailed information than radar sensors. Due to their high mechanical reliability, stereo vision sensors were already deployed for the navigation of autonomous vehicles as in the DARPA Grand Challenge [21] or for the NASA/JPL Mars Exploration Rover mission [11]. However, the calculation of three-

Karina Ambrosch, Martin Humenberger, Wilfried Kubinger
Austrian Research Centers GmbH, Vienna, Austria
e-mail: {martin.humenberger, wilfried.kubinger}@arcs.ac.at

Andreas Steininger
Vienna University of Technology, Vienna, Austria, e-mail: steininger@ecs.tuwien.ac.at

dimensional depth maps has been considered computationally too complex for low-cost solutions. Thus, stereo vision is still limited to special-purpose applications.

Besides the cost factor, automotive hardware platforms have to meet additional requirements, such as size and power consumption constraints. Another very challenging requirement is the temperature range of automotive equipment, which is from -40°C to +85°C even at the most protected places within the car. This temperature range has to be maintained without the need for active cooling, because moving parts intensely reduce the reliability of the system and Peltier Elements violate the requirement for low power consumption.

The use of a stereo vision system that meets all these requirements would not be limited to the automotive domain. Other applications, e. g., in the robotics domain, have similar requirements.

The calculation of three-dimensional depth maps on signal processors that meet these requirements is very time consuming. Fortunately, many stereo vision algorithms do not enforce a purely sequential implementation and are therefore amenable to parallelized solutions, leading to FPGAs (field-programmable gate arrays) as a highly attractive realization platform.

We simulated and synthesized a stereo vision core algorithm implemented in VHDL for the Altera EP2S130, an FPGA that is suitable for this kind of application. The algorithm is based on the sum of absolute differences (SAD) algorithm [1]. Due to the flexible implementation, its resource usage can be adjusted to keep it small enough to enable the pre- and post-processing of the images on the same FPGA, without locking onto a specific FPGA size. With a disparity range of up to 150 pixels it performs well enough for the detection of close fast-moving objects.

Section 6.2 presents the related work in the field of hardware-based stereo vision. Section 6.3 gives an overview of stereo vision algorithms and their composition. Furthermore, the detailed functionality of the SAD algorithm is described. In Section 6.4 the hardware implementation of the SAD algorithm is presented and possible optimizations are pointed out. The test configuration of the experimental evaluations as well as the discussion and comparison of our results is given in Section 6.5. Finally, we close this chapter with our concluding remarks in Section 6.6.

6.2 Related Work

Various examples of stereo vision algorithms implemented on FPGAs have been reported in the literature.

Implementations that use more than one FPGA [7, 10, 20] can be excluded for our purpose, because the hardware costs are too high and the board size does not fit as well. The same applies for works that are using PCI cards in personal computers [3, 12, 15].

Woodfill et al. have proposed a stereo vision sensor, called DeepSea G2 vision system [22], that is based on an application-specific integrated circuit (ASIC). The sensor contains the DeepSea ASIC, as well as a PowerPC chip, an Analog Devices

Blackfin digital signal processor (DSP), and an FPGA that handles the communication between the devices. Thus, the advantages of the fast ASIC are outweighed by the high costs of the additional components. Therefore, this system is not suitable for our purpose.

Yi et al. [24] proposed a stereo vision system based on a Xilinx Virtex II, which uses the SAD algorithm. The system can process images with a size of 270×270 at a frame rate of 30 fps. But the maximum disparity of 34 pixels is not considered as sufficient for tracking close objects at high speed, which is crucial for collision warning systems. The same applies for the system described by Murphy et al. [13], which can process 320×240 images at 150 fps, but only with a disparity range of 20 pixels.

The systems proposed in [9] and [14] use a single FPGA, but also with too limited disparity range for our purpose.

Han and Hwang have proposed a system [4] that can process images with a resolution of 640×480 at a frame rate of 60 fps and a maximum disparity of 128 pixels for the use in a household mobile robot. At 128 pixels the maximum disparity is large enough to detect close objects and still have enough resolution for the detection of more distant ones. Because the full chip surface of the Xilinx XC2V3000 is consumed, there is no space left for the pre- and post-processing of the image data or the detection of occluded regions using a left/right consistency check.

Other works use a graphics processing unit (GPU) for the stereo matching. Yang and Pollefeys [23] proposed a system using the GPU of a GeForce4 graphics card achieving 50-70 M disparity evaluations per second, using a multiresolutions approach. When using a resolution of 512×512 for the input images and the resulting disparity map, the system reaches a frame rate of 4.8 fps at a disparity range of 100 pixels. Another GPU-based stereo vision system was proposed by Prehn [17]. He used a GeForce 8800 GTS graphics card reaching 18 fps at an image size of 450×375 when using a block size of 7×7 for the SAD algorithm and a disparity range of 59 pixels. In addition to the fact that using a high-end graphics card does not usually correlate with the aforementioned power consumption constraints, it requires the use of a personal computer.

6.3 Stereo Vision Algorithm

The task of a stereo vision algorithm is to analyze the images taken by a pair of cameras and to extract the displacement of the objects in both images. This displacement is counted in pixels and called disparity. All these disparities form the disparity map, which is the output of a stereo vision algorithm and enables the calculation of distances to objects using triangulation.

Stereo vision algorithms can be roughly divided into feature-based and area-based algorithms. Feature-based algorithms use characteristics in the images such as edges or corners, comparing their similarities to solve the correspondence problem. The displacement between those features is used to build the disparity map and its density is directly related to the number of features found. Area-based algorithms match blocks of pixels to find correspondences in the images. In the ideal case, each pixel can be found in the corresponding image as long as the search for the correct match keeps it within the image borders. The quality of the disparity map depends highly on the textures in the images. Common methods for the matching in area-based algorithms are the sum of squared differences (SSD) [1] and sum of absolute differences (SAD). There exist various other algorithms for area-based matching, but most of them are computationally too expensive for our purpose.

In our work we use area-based matching, because the matching steps are independent of the calculation history and thus can be calculated in parallel for all analyzed disparities. The first part of the matching procedure is the calculation of the disparity space image [2], which contains the matching costs (absolute differences) for each disparity. For the detection of close objects, a high disparity range is desirable, but its maximum value is limited by the processing resources. Therefore, we evaluated the resource usage for disparity ranges reaching from 5 to 150 pixels when using 8-bit grayscale images.

Close objects can also be detected using a smaller disparity range, where the minimum value is not zero, but at a dynamically chosen minimum value. This minimum disparity is detected for each object in the image. If there is a new object in the image, the algorithm needs to recover from the mismatch. Miyajima et al. [10] proposed a relatively large system using four Altera Stratix S80 FPGAs, which still has a worst-case time to recovery of 233 ms. Even with the high resource usage the recovery time is unacceptable for automotive applications, because in this time span a car driving 130 km/h will have already moved a distance of 8.4 m. In dense traffic—especially at large crossings—the number of new objects in one second can be pretty high. If in such a situation the frame rate of the stereo vision system drops to 4.3 fps, this is insufficient for our purpose even if we had these enormous hardware resources available. This is the reason why we prefer to use a large disparity range than a small but dynamic one.

As shown in [5], the SSD algorithm performs only a little better than the SAD algorithm, not justifying the high hardware resources required for the implementation of the square operation. Thus, we use the SAD algorithm for the calculation of the matching costs in our implementation. SAD is defined as

$$SAD = \sum_{n=-L}^{L} \sum_{m=-L}^{L} |I_{x+n,y+m} - I'_{x'+n,y'+m}| \tag{6.1}$$

where $L = (s-1)/2$, while I is the primary and I' is the secondary image being matched against each other, having x,y or x',y' respectively as the center coordinates of the current SAD block. The algorithm block size s affects the quality of the disparity map, but its maximum is limited by the FPGA's resources. Thus, we analyzed block sizes from 3×3 up to 11×11 and evaluated the quality of the generated disparity maps.

After calculating the SAD, we select the best match using the winner takes all (WTA) algorithm. Here, the block with the lowest matching costs is searched for and its position is chosen as the pixel value for the disparity map.

We perform the matching using the right image as the primary one. To perform a left/right consistency check for the detection of occluded areas, it is necessary to calculate the disparity using the left image as the primary as well. This can be performed by exchanging and horizontally flipping the input images, using the same hardware for the calculation.

The chosen algorithm is only a core stereo vision algorithm. To enable its efficient implementation, it is necessary that the input images are rectified, fulfilling epipolar geometry, which is the main task for the pre-processing stage. In epipolar geometry each object point in one of the stereo images can be found on a specific line, called the epipolar line, in the other image, as depicted in Fig. 6.1. Here, the epipolar lines are given as the lines between the pixel points p_R, p_L and the epipoles E_R, E_L. The epipoles are the intersection points, where the line between the cameras' focus points O_R, O_L crosses the image planes. When the images are rectified, the epipolar lines are equal to the image rows, i.e., the epipoles are ad infinitum. Thus, the search for correspondences in the images can be limited to one dimension, ensuring a less complex implementation of the stereo matching algorithm.

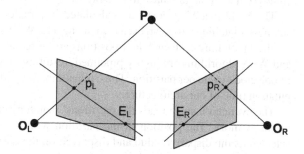

Fig. 6.1 Unrectified epipolar geometry.

6.4 Hardware Implementation

6.4.1 Architecture

The architecture is split into three major pipeline stages, the input, calculation, and the evaluation stage.

The first stage is the input stage, which supplies the image data for the computation. Therefore, it reads the data of the rectified images from the 8-bit input port and stores it in internal memory. This image memory consists of one memory block per image line and holds as many image lines as required by the SAD's block size plus one additional image line. The memory blocks are accessed cyclically, and while the input stage writes the new image line into one memory block, the calculation stage can read from the others. This way, the calculation stage can access all stored image lines in one clock cycle, resulting in a memory data width of *block height* $\times 8bit$. At the beginning of each disparity map calculation the input stage has to fill all memory blocks before the calculation stage can be started.

The calculation stage computes the SAD and the WTA algorithms iteratively. This means that the disparity range is split into n partitions, each with a disparity range of $d_{\text{partition}}$ pixels, and the matching is performed for each partition separately. Thus the maximum disparity d_{max} is defined as

$$d_{\text{max}} = n \times d_{\text{partition}} - 1. \tag{6.2}$$

Using an iterative implementation gives the advantage of being able to scale the architecture for a better tradeoff between consumed logic and frame rate. The key to the architecture's high performance is the pipelining of the whole computation. Pipelines enable a highly parallel execution, but also require initialization times at the computation's start. The reason why we compute one line per round rather than one pixel per round, is to keep these pipeline initializations at a minimum. The price for this performance increase is a higher demand for memory, because the interim values of the whole line have to be stored.

The SAD matching costs are calculated in parallel for each partition and the smallest matching costs are selected using the WTA algorithm. The partitions' smallest matching costs and their positions are stored in internal memory. The SAD and WTA algorithms are highly pipelined, resulting in an average calculation time of one clock cycle per partition. Thus, the number of partitions determines the computation time of our architecture.

The evaluation stage reads the partitions' matching costs and positions from internal memory. The position of the partition with the smallest matching costs is selected as the disparity value and displayed on the output port. This is performed using the same computation time as the calculation stage, saving hardware resources and avoiding idle times. Furthermore, the memory data width is kept constant at 16 bit for both the positions and the matching costs memory.

We assume that the data transfer to or from external memory for the pre-/post-processing stages is performed by another hardware block to keep the algorithm more flexible.

Fig. 6.2 depicts the block diagram of the hardware architecture.

6.4.2 Optimizing the SAD

A straightforward implementation of the SAD algorithm leads to a blockwise calculation. Here, the absolute differences for each single block are calculated and aggregated. Fig. 6.3 shows the block diagram of this implementation technique.

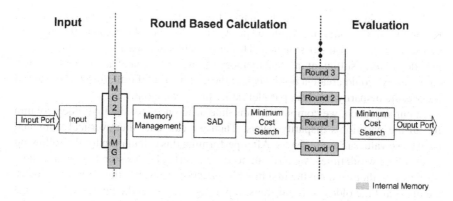

Fig. 6.2 Architecture of the stereo vision hardware algorithm.

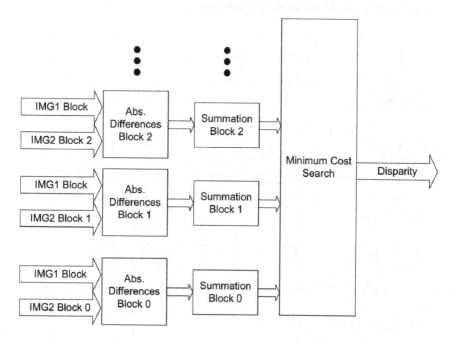

Fig. 6.3 Unoptimized SAD.

Kanade et al. [6] have proposed a calculation method for the SAD that splits the computation of a single block into the calculation of the SAD's vertical sums and their aggregation. This way the next block's value for same disparity level can be computed by calculating only the next row's sum and aggregating the shifted vertical sums.

This calculation method can be mapped onto FPGAs with slight modifications. Kanade et al. compute the whole disparity space image, storing it in the memory before searching for the best match. This approach is not possible on FPGAs, since they do not have sufficient internal memory for the storage, and accessing the external memory would create a bottleneck in the architecture. Furthermore, we want to process the disparity levels in parallel rather than sequentially.

In our approach, we compute the absolute differences for the first block column for all the partition's disparity levels. Then we calculate their vertical sums and keep these values in the registers. After performing this calculation for the following pixels block width times, we have all necessary vertical sums stored in the registers to aggregate them and get the first block's matching costs. For the following blocks, we disregard the oldest vertical sums, replacing them with the next pixel's vertical sums. Thus, after the calculation of the first block's matching costs is performed, the complexity is now linear in the block dimension rather than exponential.

Fig. 6.4 shows the block diagram of this approach.

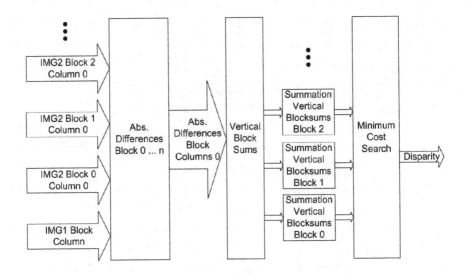

Fig. 6.4 Optimized SAD.

6.4.3 Tree-Based WTA

The WTA algorithm searches for the smallest matching cost's position. For this search we decided to use a tree-based search, as depicted in Fig. 6.5. Here, the matching costs for the whole disparity range are arranged into groups. For each group the smallest value as well as its relative position in the group are selected and stored. This is performed several times, readjusting the values' positions according to the group's position within the disparity range. Finally, the global minimum value forms the tree's root. Its position is selected as the pixel's disparity.

The advantage of using a tree-based search is not only to reduce the complexity of the search operation. It also fits the dataflow within the FPGA very well. Thus, it can be highly pipelined and the throughput increased up to one disparity range per clock cycle.

To find the best tradeoff between resource usage and throughput, we evaluated several different group sizes. A small group size leads to higher resource usage, but the reduction caused by large group sizes is negligible compared to the resources consumed by the SAD. Thus, we kept the focus on the throughput and used a binary search tree in our WTA implementation.

There exist two WTA algorithms in our architecture. The first one examines the partitions' disparity ranges in the calculation stage and the second one the values for the partitions' results in the evaluation stage. Both implementations are similar, with the only exception being that the WTA in the evaluation stage handles the position values already in its first stage, while the calculation stage's has no need for this until the second stage.

6.5 Experimental Evaluation

6.5.1 Test Configuration

We evaluated our stereo matching architecture using the Teddy images from the Middlebury dataset [18]. The image size is 450×375 and they were converted to 8-bit grayscale. Fig. 6.6 shows the image set and its corresponding ground truth.

To show the impact of good optimization for hardware based algorithms, we synthesized the optimized as well as the unoptimized SAD implementation using five calculation rounds and contrasted the resource usage for a disparity range from 5 up to 150 pixels.

To illustrate the relationship between frame rate and hardware resources, we synthesized the architecture using different numbers of calculation rounds, reaching from 1 to 5 for a disparity range of 100 pixels or 99 for three rounds, respectively.

Furthermore, we analyzed the use of different block sizes and their impact on the hardware resources consumed by the optimized SAD as well as the quality of the generated disparity maps. To evaluate the disparity map quality, we performed a left/right consistency check allowing a maximum deviation of three pixels for both disparity maps, removing the inconsistent results caused by occluded areas or incorrect matches. For the remaining pixels we calculated the root mean square (RMS) over the deviations to the ground truth. Additionally, we analyzed the number of found and consistent pixels, as well as the number of correct matches that are within a maximum deviation of 1 pixel.

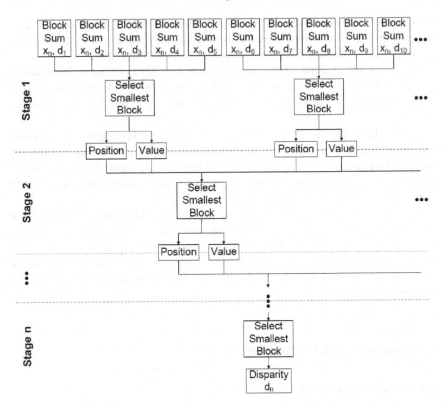

Fig. 6.5 Tree-based WTA.

The Teddy image ground truth from the Middlebury data set is scaled by a factor of 4. Hence, we scaled our disparity maps in the same way for a better comparison of the presented images.

6.5.2 Results

The results for the optimized as well as the unoptimized SAD are illustrated in Fig. 6.7. Depending on the calculated disparity range, the optimization factor reaches from 1.5 for five disparity levels up to 3.65 for 150. This illustrates that good hardware-specific algorithm optimization can have a major impact on resource usage. Even if the pipeline length is increased and the algorithm gets more complicated, this is more than outweighed by the reduced number of aggregations.

The optimization factor is not a constant since the more sophisticated algorithm leads to higher static resource usage, being independent of the selected disparity

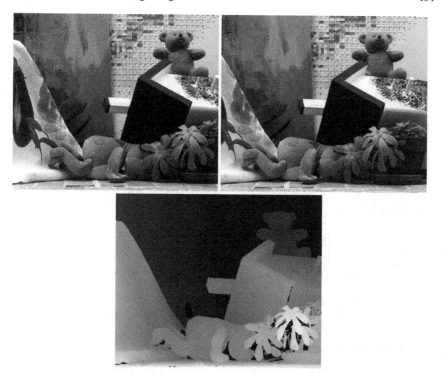

Fig. 6.6 Teddy images from the Middlebury dataset. Top: camera images. Bottom: ground truth image.

range and therefore enforcing smaller optimization factors for small disparity ranges. In any case, the optimization is good enough to show a positive optimization factor even at five disparity levels.

The dependence of the resource usage of the optimized SAD in terms of logic elements as well as internal memory, the corresponding frame rate, and the design's frequency versus the number of calculation rounds is depicted in Fig. 6.8. The results show that the frame rate is not directly proportional to the number of calculation rounds. While the initialization times can be neglected for this analysis and the number of clock cycles per generated disparity map is reduced proportional to the calculation rounds, the system clock frequency is decreased due to the design's higher complexity and the resulting longer interconnects between the logic cells. The memory consumption is bound to the number of calculation rounds, since a higher number results in a higher count of intermediate results that have to be stored for the evaluation stage. The size of the memory blocks is bound to the power of 2 and therefore only increases if the block size exceeds such a boundary, which is not the case for round numbers 4 and 5.

Even if the achieved frame rates are significantly higher than most camera frame rates, a further reduction may not be desirable. Most cameras provide the data for

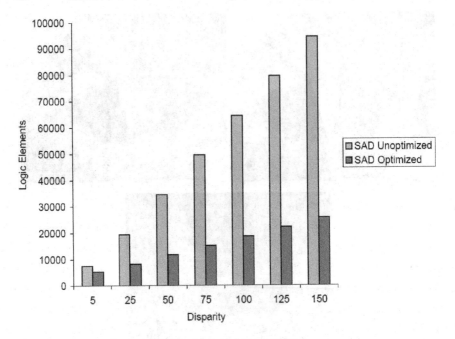

Fig. 6.7 Resource usage of the optimized and unoptimized SAD.

each image in a burst, having a considerably higher data rate than required by their frame rate. Due to the fact that the performance of an FPGA-based system depends on its pipelining and step-wise computations lead to idle times of resources, buffering the camera data in external memory would work against the FPGA's data flow and therefore cannot be advisable.

By using internal memory only, the memory operates at system frequency.

The results for the optimized SAD versus the block size are shown in Fig. 6.9. Since the optimized SAD computes only one vertical and one horizontal block sum, the consumed logic elements are not proportional to the number of pixels in the blocks, but to the block's dimensions. The system frequency and the frame rate show small deviations, which are not directly correlated to the block size. They are effects caused by the design's layout during the synthesis and the routing within the FPGA, which is not a deterministic process. The memory consumption is linear to the block height and the memory is again operated at system frequency.

Fig. 6.10 shows the disparity maps generated for the different block sizes in a simulation of the hardware. Depending on the block size, the disparity maps are pretty noisy at 3×3 and smooth at 11×11. The disparity maps show that the SAD algorithm is not able to match the house's roof due to its low textured surface at all analyzed block sizes. For this application, an even larger block size would be desirable, but at 11×11 the disparity map already shows a synthetic smoothness, which would be further enforced by larger block sizes leading to deformed images.

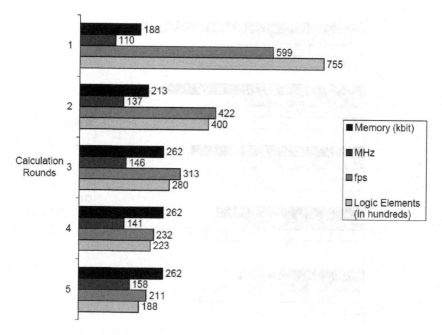

Fig. 6.8 Resource usage, memory consumption, frame rate, and system frequency of the optimized SAD depending on the calculation rounds.

Another technique for the computation of low textured surfaces is to use a post-processing stage that uses the disparity of the objects' edges to interpolate the unmatched surfaces in between. When using an SAD algorithm, this seems to be the more promising solution.

For avoiding border effects, the disparity was not calculated for the first 100 pixels, since sufficient image information would not be available in the secondary image to perform the matching for the whole disparity range. Hence, these image areas are black and disregarded in the further evaluation.

For these five disparity maps we also evaluated their quality as depicted by Fig. 6.11. The numbers of found pixels and correct matches reveal an asymptotic behavior, while the deviations' RMS is constantly decreased according to the block size except for block size 11×11. This shows, again, the smoothing characteristic of the SAD depending on its block size. The slight increase in RMS between block size 9×9 and 11×11 marks the turnaround, when image smoothness starts leading to a deformed disparity map.

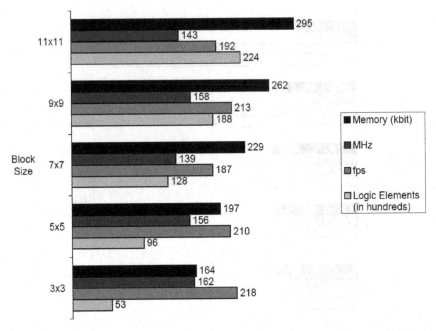

Fig. 6.9 Resource usage, memory consumption, frame rate and system frequency of the optimized SAD depending on the block size.

6.5.3 Comparison

The total computation of a stereo image pair takes 183,747 clock cycles, when using only one calculation round. When synthesized in this configuration with Altera Quartus II, the FPGA can operate with a maximum frequency of 110 MHz. Thus, the total computation takes 1.67 ms and the achieved frame rate is about 600 fps.

The algorithm consumes 60,362 arithmetic look-up tables, which is just about 57% of the available FPGA resources and equivalent to 75,453 logic elements. There is a high amount of hardware resources left for the pre- and post-processing of the images, although we are not using a latest-generation FPGA.

The maximum memory usage is 294,912 bits or 4.4% of the chip's internal memory or 11.8% of the 4 kbit block RAM. Thus, there is sufficient internal memory available such as required for the implementation of the pre- and post-processing stages.

For a better evaluation of the performance benefits of our FPGA-based hardware implementation compared to processor based systems, we implemented the same algorithm in software as well. This software implementation is an optimized implementation using Intel's Open Source Computer Vision Library [16]. Furthermore, in this implementation the computation of the SAD's aggregations was optimized using integral images [19]. Integral images are an optimization method that improves

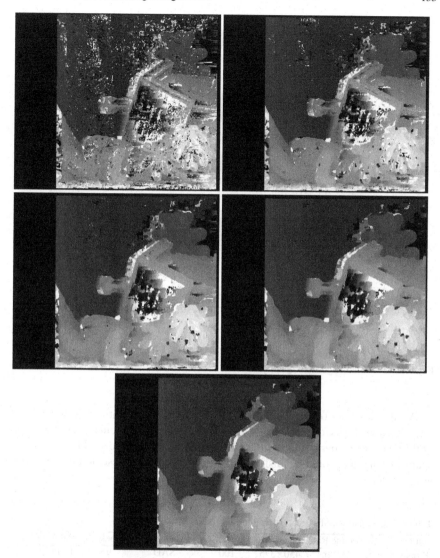

Fig. 6.10 Disparity maps generated from the Middlebury dataset's teddy images using different block sizes. Top left: 3×3. Top right: 5×5. Middle left: 7×7. Middle right: 9×9. Bottom: 11×11.

software-based SAD implementations very well, being less suitable for FPGA implementations due to the integral images' high memory consumption. The test platform was an Intel Pentium 4 with 3 GHz clock frequency and 1 GB memory. The processing time for one image pair was 673 ms resulting in a frame rate of 1.48 fps. This is about 400 times slower than our hardware implementation and it seems obvious that even with the algorithmic and software optimizations, the processor-based system cannot outperform the FPGA-based solution.

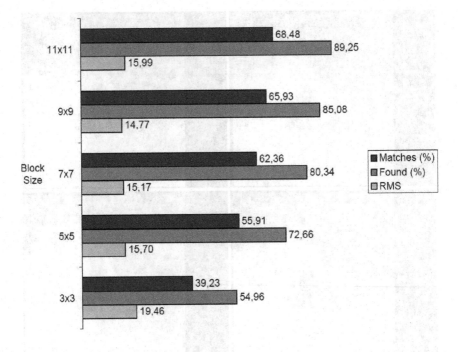

Fig. 6.11 Evaluated Algorithm Quality.

We also compared our system with other FPGA implementations as shown in Table 6.1. Since the used stereo vision algorithms are very different and so the quality of the resulting disparity maps differs as well, direct comparisons of logic elements against frame rate would be misleading, even if all authors presented their resource usage in detail.

Table 6.1 Comparison of stereo vision implementations.

Author	Frame Rate	Image Size	Max. Disp.	Algorithm	Block Size	Platform
Proposed impl.	599 fps	450×375	100	SAD	9×9	1 FPGA
Software impl.	1.48 fps	450×375	100	SAD	9×9	PC
Murphy et al.	150 fps	320×240	150	Census Transf.	13×13	1 FPGA
Niitsuma et al.	30 fps	640×480	27	SAD	7×7	1 FPGA
Lee et al.	122 fps	320×240	64	SAD	16×16	1 FPGA
Kim et al.	30 fps	1300×640	NA	Trellis based	NA	2 FPGAs
PARTS	42 fps	320×240	24	LW Phase Corr.	NA	16 FPGAs
Masrani et al.	30 fps	640×480	dyn	LW Phase Corr.	NA	4 FPGAs
Niitsuma et al.	840 fps	320×240	121	SAD	7×7	1 FPGA + PC
Miyajima et al.	18.9 fps	640×480	200	SAD	7×7	2 FPGAs + PC
Yang et al.	4.8 fps	512×512	100	SSD	16×16	GPU
Prehn	18 fps	450×375	59	SAD	7×7	GPU
DeepSea	200 fps	512×480	52	Census Transf.	NA	ASIC

6.6 Conclusions

We proposed a cost-efficient hardware implementation of a real-time stereo vision algorithm using an FPGA for the calculation of disparity maps. Our algorithm leaves enough resources such as are required for the implementation of pre- and post-processing stages. It performs well enough for the detection of fast-moving objects when using a large disparity range.

The results of our experimental evaluation show that the algorithm's resource usage increases exponentially when increasing the frame rate. On the other hand, increasing the block size leads to a more linear increase of consumed logic elements due to the SAD's optimized implementation. The evaluation of the disparity maps' quality depicted the advantages of high block sizes, but also revealed their limiting factors.

By using an FPGA-specific optimization for the SAD and a tree-based search for the WTA algorithm, we enable a highly pipelined implementation. The pipelining allowed us to completely outperform an already optimized software implementation. This shows that FPGAs or ASICs are an excellent choice for the realization of low-cost real-time stereo vision systems for automotive or robotics applications.

Acknowledgements The research leading to these results has received funding from the European Community's Sixth Framework Programme (FP6/2003-2006) under grant agreement No. FP6-2006-IST-6-045350 (robots@home).

References

1. Banks, J., Bennamoun, M. and Corke, P.: Non-parametric techniques for fast and robust stereo matching, *Proc. IEEE Conf. Speech Image Technol. Comput. Telecommun.* (1997).
2. Bobick, A. and Intille, S.: Large occlusion stereo, *Intern. J. Comput. Vis.* **33**(3), 181–200 (1999).
3. Corke, P. and Dunn, P.: Real-time stereopsis using FPGAs, *Proc. IEEE Conf. Speech Image Technol. Comput. Telecommun.* (1997).
4. Han, D. and Hwang, D.: A novel stereo matching method for wide disparity range detection, *Lect. Notes Comput. Sci.* **3656**, 643–650 (2005).
5. Kanade, T.: Development of a video-rate stereo machine, *Proc. 1994 ARPA Image Underst. Work.* (1994).
6. Kanade, T., Yoshida, A., Kazuo, O., Kano, H. and Tanaka, M.: A stereo machine for video-rate dense depth mapping and its new applications, *Proc. 1996 Conf. Comput. Vis. Pattern Recognit. Work.* (1996).
7. Kim, S., Choi, S., Won, S. and Jeong, H.: The coil recognition system for an unmanned crane using stereo vision, *Proc. 30th Conf. IEEE Ind. Electron. Soc.* (2004).
8. Le Beux, S., Marquet, P., Labbani, O. and Dekeyser, J.: FPGA implementation of embedded cruise control and anti-collision radar, *Proc. 9th EUROMICRO Conf. Digit. Syst. Des.* (2006).
9. Lee, Su., Yi, J. and Kim, J.: Real-time stereo vision on a reconfigurable system, *Lect. Notes Comput. Sci.* **3553**, 299–307 (2005).
10. Masrani, D.K. and MacLean, W.J.: A real-time large disparity range stereo-system using FPGAs, *Proc. IEEE Intern. Conf. Comput. Vis. Syst.* (2006).

11. Matthies, L., Maimone, M., Johnson, A., Cheng, Y., Willson, R., Villalpando, C., Goldberg, S., Huertas, A., Stein, A. and Angelova, A.: Computer vision on Mars, *Intern. J. Comput. Vis.* **75(1)**, 67–92 (2007).

12. Miyajima, Y. and Maruyama, T.: A real-time stereo vision system with FPGA, *Lect. Notes Comput. Sci.* **2778**, 448–457 (2003).

13. Murphy, C., Lindquist, D., Rynning, A.M., Cecil, T., Leavitt, S. and Chang, M.: Low-cost stereo vision on an FPGA, *Proc. 15th IEEE Symp. FPGAs Cust. Comput. Mach.* (2007).

14. Niitsuma, H. and Maruyama, T.: Real-time detection of moving objects, *Lect. Notes Comput. Sci.* **3203**, 1155–1157 (2004).

15. Niitsuma, H. and Maruyama, T.: High-speed computation of the optical flow, *Lect. Notes Comput. Sci.* **3617**, 287–295 (2005).

16. Intel Open Source Computer Vision Library, Intel Corporation, Santa Clara, CA., www.intel.com/technology/computing/opencv/. Cited 13 Feb 2008.

17. Prehn, S.: GPU Stereo Vision, Project Thesis, Robotics Research Lab, University of Kaiserslautern (2007).

18. Scharstein, D. and Szeliski, R.: High-accuracy stereo depth maps using structured light, *Proc. 2003 Conf. Comput. Vis. Pattern Recognit.* (2003).

19. Veksler, O.: Fast variable window for stereo correspondence using integral iImages, *Proc. 2003 Conf. Comput. Vis. Pattern Recognit.* (2003).

20. Woodfill, J. and Von Herzen, B.: Real-time stereo vision on the PARTS reconfigurable computer, *Proc. 5th IEEE Symp. FPGAs Cust. Comput. Mach.* (1997).

21. Woodfill, J.I., Gordon, G. and Buck, R.: The Tyzx DeepSea high-speed stereo vision system, *Proc. 2004 Conf. Comput. Vis. Pattern Recognit. Work.* (2004).

22. Woodfill, J.I., Gordon, G., Jurasek, D., Brown, T. and Buck, R.: The Tyzx DeepSea G2 vision system: A taskable, embedded stereo camera, *Proc. 2006 Conf. Comput. Vis. Pattern Recognit. Work.* (2006).

23. Yang, R. and Pollefeys, M.: Multi-resolution real-time stereo on commodity graphics hardware, *Proc. 2003 Conf. Comput. Vis. Pattern Recognit.* (2003).

24. Yi, J., Kim, J., Li, L., Morris, J., Lee, G. and Leclercq, P.: Real-time three-dimensional vision, *Lect. Notes Comput. Sci.* **3189**, 309–320 (2004).

25. Zhang, Z.: Determining the epipolar geometry and its uncertainty: A review, *Intern. J. Comput. Vis.* **27(2)**, 161–195 (1998).

Chapter 7
Motion History Histograms for Human Action Recognition

Hongying Meng, Nick Pears, Michael Freeman, and Chris Bailey

Abstract In this chapter, a compact human action recognition system is presented with a view to applications in security systems, human-computer interaction, and intelligent environments. There are three main contributions: Firstly, the framework of an embedded human action recognition system based on a support vector machine (SVM) classifier and some compact motion features has been presented. Secondly, the limitations of the well-known motion history image (MHI) are addressed and a new motion history histograms (MHH) feature is introduced to represent the motion information in the video. MHH not only provides rich motion information, but also remains computationally inexpensive. We combine MHI and MHH into a low-dimensional feature vector for the system and achieve improved performance in human action recognition over comparable methods that use tracking-free temporal template motion representations. Finally, a simple system based on SVM and MHI has been implemented on a reconfigurable embedded computer vision architecture for real-time gesture recognition.

7.1 Introduction

Visual recognition of different classes of motion within the context of embedded computer vision systems has wide-ranging applications. Examples include intelligent surveillance of human and road traffic activity, biometric security, such as gait recognition, and visually driven interaction and context awareness in "smart" environments, both of which are related to the application areas of "ambient intelligence" and "ubiquitous computing."

Hongying Meng
University of Lincoln, Lincoln, UK, e-mail: hmeng@lincoln.ac.uk

Nick Pears, Michael Freeman, Chris Bailey
University of York, York, UK, e-mail: {nep, mjf, chrisb}@cs.york.ac.uk

139

The work presented here focuses on the use of video for classifying general human motions, with a view to deploying our system in a smart home environment and using it to recognize gestural commands. In particular, our methods are designed to be appropriate for deployment in a real-time, embedded context. In this sense, we have developed compact, descriptive motion representations and low complexity classification algorithms, all of which may be implemented on our flexible stand-alone video processing architecture, which is based upon field-programmable gate arrays (FPGAs).

Aggarwal and Cai [1] present an excellent overview of human motion analysis. Of the appearance based methods, template matching has gained increasing interest recently [2, 6, 8, 12, 14, 15, 20, 21, 22, 24, 26, 27, 28, 30]. These methods are based on the extraction of a 2D or 3D shape model directly from the images, to be classified (or matched) against training data. Motion-based models do not rely on static models of the person, but on human motion characteristics. Motion feature extraction is the key component in these kinds of human action recognition systems.

In this chapter, we build a compact human action recognition system based on a linear support vector machine (SVM) [5, 25] classifier. We address the limitations of the motion history image (MHI) [3] and introduce a new feature, which we call the motion history histograms (MHH) [16]. This representation retains more motion information than MHI, but also remains inexpensive to compute. We extract a compact feature vector from the MHH and then combine it with the histogram of the MHI feature in our human action recognition system and get very good performance.

We have started to implement our systems within an FPGA-based embedded computer vision architecture, which we call "Videoware," although in our current implementation, we use MHI features only and embedded implementation of our new MHH feature is ongoing.

The rest of this chapter is organized as follows: In Section 7.2, we give an overview of related work. In Section 7.3, we give a brief introduction of the framework of the SVM based human action recognition system. In Section 7.4, we firstly introduce some fundamental motion features, of which the MHI is the classical example. Furthermore, we give a detailed description of the new MHH feature, which is designed to be more descriptive than MHI features in order to give improved classification performance. In Section 7.5, we discuss the possible feature combination and dimension reduction methods in our framework. In Section 7.6, experimental results derived from a MATLAB implementation of our SVM based human action recognition system are evaluated. In Section 7.7, we give a simple example implementation and evaluation of an MHI/SVM based gesture recognition system on our reconfigurable embedded computer vision architecture, which we call "Videoware." Finally, we present conclusions.

7.2 Related Work

The idea of temporal templates was introduced by Bobick and Davis [3, 19]. They used motion energy images (MEI) and MHI to recognize many types of aerobics exercise. In [4], they also proposed the motion gradient orientation (MGO) to explicitly encode changes in an image introduced by motion events. Davis [7] also presented a useful hierarchical extension for computing a local motion field from the original MHI representation. The MHI was transformed into an image pyramid, permitting efficient fixed-size gradient masks to be convolved at all levels of the pyramid, thus extracting motion information at a wide range of speeds. The hierarchical MHI approach remains a computationally inexpensive algorithm to represent, characterize, and recognize human motion in video.

Schuldt et al. [24] proposed a method for recognizing complex motion patterns based on local space-time features in video and they integrated such representations with SVM classification schemes for recognition. The work of Efros et al. [9] focuses on the case of low resolution video of human behaviors, targeting what they refer to as the 30 pixel man. In this setting, they propose a spatio-temporal descriptor based on optical flow measurements, and apply it to recognize actions in ballet, tennis and football datasets.

Weinland et al. [26] introduced motion history volumes (MHV) as a free-viewpoint representation for human actions in the case of multiple calibrated and background-subtracted video. They presented algorithms for computing, aligning, and comparing MHVs of different actions performed by different people from a variety of viewpoints. Ke et al. [12] studied the use of volumetric features as an alternative to the local descriptor approaches for event detection in video sequences. They generalized the notion of 2D box features to 3D spatio-temporal volumetric features. They constructed a real-time event detector for each action of interest by learning a cascade of filters based on volumetric features that efficiently scanned video sequences in space and time. Ogata et al. [21] proposed modified motion history images (MMHI) and used an eigenspace technique to realize high-speed recognition of six human motions. Wong and Cipolla [27] proposed a new method to recognize primitive movements based on MGO extraction and, later, used it for continuous gesture recognition [28].

Recently, Dalal et al. [6] proposed histogram of oriented gradient (HOG) appearance descriptors for image sequences and developed a detector for standing and moving people in video. Dollár et al. [8] proposed a similar method where they use a new spatio-temporal interest point detector to obtain a global measurement instead of the local features in [9]. Niebles et al. [20] also use spatial-time interest points to extract spatial-temporal words as their features. Yeo et al. [30] estimate motion vectors from optical flow and calculate frame-to-frame motion similarity to analyze human action in video. Blank et al. [2] regarded human actions as three dimensional shapes induced by silhouettes in space-time volume. They adopted an approach for analyzing 2D shapes and generalized it to deal the idea with volumetric space-time action shapes. Oikonomopoulos et al. [22] introduced a sparse representation of image sequences as a collection of spatio-temporal events that were localized at points that were salient both in space and time for human action recognition.

We note that, in some of these methods, the motion features employed are relatively complex [2, 6, 8, 9, 12, 20, 22, 24, 26, 30], which implies significant computational cost when building the features. Some of them require segmentation, tracking or other prohibitive computational cost processes [2, 3, 4, 7, 21, 27, 28], which currently makes them not suitable for real-time embedded vision applications. In our work, we aim for a solution which uses compact representations, is fast to compute, and yet gives an improved classification performance over existing compact and fast methods.

7.3 SVM-Based Human Action Recognition System

In our system, we have employed a linear SVM classifier [5], for two main reasons: (i) low complexity classification and hence suitable for real-time embedded applications, (ii) very good performance in many real-world classification problems.

The schematic of our SVM based human action recognition system is shown in Fig. 7.1, where the training path is given by the solid arrows and the testing path is given by the dotted arrows. It is composed of four parts: source (data), motion features, dimension reduction, and learning. The motion features can be MHI, MMHI, MGO, and our new feature which we call motion history histograms (MHH).

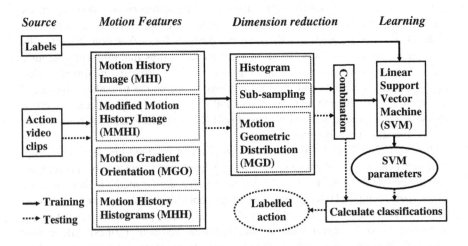

Fig. 7.1 SVM based human action recognition system. Compact motion features are extracted from human action video clips without corner detection, tracking or segmentation. These feature vectors are compressed by dimension reduction methods. Then they are efficiently combined into the linear SVM classifier. The parameters of the SVMs obtained from training are used in the classification process.

In the training part of this system, combined motion feature vectors, extracted from fundamental motion features, are used for training SVM classifiers. The parameters computed are then used in the recognition part. Note that this diagram represents an architecture (rather than a specific implementation) in which any subset of motion features may be used and possibly combined in a specific implementation. This flexibility exists to deal with limitations in the specific embedded hardware available, such as FPGA gate count, memory, processing speed, data communication capability and so on.

Although the SVM performs well with very high dimensional feature vectors, we reduce the dimension of the feature vector to aid embedded deployment of our algorithm. For this, we use simple algorithms, which are easily implemented on our FPGA architecture, such as down-sampling or block averaging operations.

The training of the SVM classifier is done off-line using video data, also collected off-line. After that, the parameters computed for the classifier are embedded in our FPGA-based architecture.

In the following sections, we will give detailed information on this system.

7.4 Motion Features

In order to generate compact, descriptive representations of motion which are simple to extract, several techniques have been proposed to compact the whole motion sequence into a single image. The most popular of such "temporal template" motion features are the motion history image (MHI), the modified motion history image (MMHI), and the motion gradient orientation (MGO). Here, we give a brief introduction to the these features.

7.4.1 Temporal Template Motion Features

A motion history image (MHI) [3] is the weighted sum of past images and the weights decay back through time. Therefore, an MHI image contains the past images within itself, where the most recent image is brighter than the earlier ones. Normally, an MHI $H_\tau(u,v,k)$ at time k and location (u,v) is defined by

$$H_\tau(u,v,k) = \begin{cases} \tau, & D(u,v,k) = 1 \\ \max\{0, H_\tau(u,v,k-1) - 1\}, & \text{otherwise} \end{cases} \quad (7.1)$$

where the motion mask $D(u,v,k)$ is a binary image obtained from subtraction of frames, and τ is the maximum duration a motion is stored. In general, τ is chosen as the constant 255, allowing the MHI to be easily represented as a grayscale image with one byte depth. Thus an MHI pixel can have a range of values, whereas a motion energy image (MEI) is its binary version, which can easily be computed by thresholding $H_\tau > 0$.

Ogata et al. [21] use a multivalued differential image to extract information about human posture because differential images encode human posture information more than a binary image, such as a silhouette image. They called the feature MMHI.

The MGO feature was proposed by Bradski and Davis [4] to explicitly encode changes in an image introduced by motion events. The MGO is computed from an MHI and a MEI. While an MHI encodes how the motion occurred, an MEI encodes where the motion occurred, the MGO, therefore, is a concatenated representation of motion (where and how it occurred).

We have tested the performance of these three features on our SVM based human action recognition system and found that the MHI had the best classification performance of 63.5% on a large challenging dataset [15]. This overall performance is far from good enough. In the following, we will look at the MHI feature further in order to find a way to improve it.

7.4.2 Limitations of the MHI

An example of an MHI is shown in Fig. 7.2, where (a) is one frame from the original hand waving action video clip and (b) is the MHI of this action.

In order to have a detailed look at the MHI, we have selected the pixels on the vertical line in the MHI of Fig. 7.2 (b). If some action happened at frame k on pixel (u,v), then $D(u,v,k) = 1$, otherwise $D(u,v,k) = 0$. The locations of these pixels are $(60,11),(60,12),\ldots,(60,80)$. For a pixel (u,v), the motion mask $D(u,v,:)$ of this pixel is the binary sequence:

$$D(u,v,:) = (b_1,b_2,\ldots,b_N), \quad b_i \in \{0,1\} \tag{7.2}$$

where $N+1$ is the total number of frames.

All of the motion masks on the vertical line in Fig. 7.2 (b) are shown in Fig. 7.3. Each row is $D(u,v,:)$ for one fixed pixel (u,v) and a white block represents '1' and

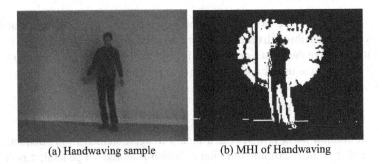

(a) Handwaving sample   (b) MHI of Handwaving

Fig. 7.2 Example of an MHI. Part (a) is one frame from the original hand waving action video clip and (b) is the MHI of this action. The vertical line in (b) has the pixels from $(60,11)$ to $(60,80)$.

Fig. 7.3 $D(:,:,:)$ on the vertical line of Fig. 7.2(b) is shown. Each row is $D(u,v,:)$ for one fixed pixel (u,v). A white block represents '1' and a black block '0'. For example, $D(60,50,:)$ is the "binarized frame difference history" or "motion mask" of pixel $(60,50)$ through time.

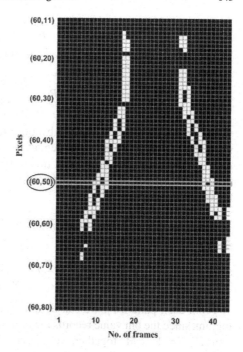

black block represents '0' in the sequences. The motion mark $D(60,50,:)$ has the following sequence:

$$00000000011010000000000000000000000001010000 \qquad (7.3)$$

From the definition of MHI in Eq. (7.1) it can be observed that, for each pixel (u,v), MHI actually retains the time since the last action occurred. That is, only the last '1' in the Sequence (7.3) is retained in the MHI at pixel $(60,50)$. It is clear that previous '1's in the sequence, when some action occurred, are not represented. It is also clear that almost all the pixels have more than one '1' in their sequence.

7.4.3 Definition of MHH

The above limitation of the MHI has motivated us to design a new representation (the MHH) in which all of the information in the sequence is used and, yet, it remains compact and simple to use.

We define the patterns P_i in the $D(u,v,:)$ sequences, based on the number of connected '1's:

$$P_1 = 010$$
$$P_2 = 0110$$
$$P_3 = 01110$$

$$\vdots$$

$$P_M = 0\underbrace{1\ldots1}_{M}0$$

(7.4)

We denote a subsequence $C_{I,k}$ by Eq. (7.5), where I and k are the indexes of starting and ending frames, and denote the set of all subsequences of $D(u,v,:)$ as $A\{D(u,v,:)\}$. Then, for each pixel (u,v), we can count the number of occurrences of each specific pattern P_i in the sequence $D(u,v,:)$, as shown in Eq. 7.6, where χ is the indicator function.

$$C_{I,k} = b_I, b_{I+1}, \ldots, b_k, \quad (1 \leq I < k \leq N) \tag{7.5}$$

$$\mathrm{MHH}(u,v,i) = \Sigma_{(I,k)}\, \chi_{\{C_{I,k}=P_i|C_{I,k}\in A\{D(u,v,:)\}\}} \tag{7.6}$$
$$(1 \leq I < k \leq N,\ 1 \leq i \leq M)$$

From each pattern P_i, we can build a grayscale image and we call this its histogram, since the bin value records the number of this pattern type. With all the patterns P_i, $(i = 1, \ldots, M)$ together, we collectively call them motion history histograms (MHH) representation.

For a pattern P_i, $\mathrm{MHH}(:,:,i)$ can be displayed as an image. In Fig. 7.4, four patterns P_1, P_2, P_3, and P_4 are shown, which were generated from the hand waving action in Fig. 7.2. By comparing the MHH in Fig. 7.4 with the MHI in Fig. 7.2, it is interesting to find that the MHH decomposes the MHI into different parts based on patterns. Unlike the hierarchical MHI described by Davis [7], where only small size MHIs were obtained, MHH records the rich spatial information of an action.

The choice of the number M depends on the video clips. In general, the bigger the M is, the better the motion information will be. However, the values within the MHH rapidly approach zero as M increases. In our experiment, no more than half of the training data had the sixth pattern P_6 and so we chose $M = 5$. Furthermore we note that a large M will increase the storage requirement for our hardware based system.

The computation of MHH is inexpensive and can be implemented by the procedure in Fig. 7.5. $D(u,v,k)$ is the binary sequence on pixel (u,v) that is computed by thresholding the differences between frame k and frame $k-1$. $I(u,v)$ is a frame index that stands for the number of the starting frame of a new pattern on pixel (u,v). At the beginning, $I(u,v) = 1$ for all (u,v). That means a new pattern starts from frame 1 for every pixel. $I(u,v)$ will be updated to $I(u,v) = k$ while $\{D(u,v,I(u,v)), \ldots, D(u,v,k)\}$ builds one of the patterns $P_i(1 \leq i \leq M)$ and, in this case, $\mathrm{MHH}(u,v,i)$ increases by 1.

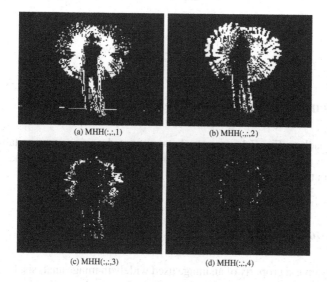

(a) MHH(:,:,1)   (b) MHH(:,:,2)

(c) MHH(:,:,3)   (d) MHH(:,:,4)

Fig. 7.4 MHH example. Four patterns P_1, P_2, P_3, and P_4 were selected. This results were generated from the handwaving action in Fig. 7.2. Each pattern P_i, MHH(:,:,i) has the same size as the original frame.

Algorithm (MHH)

Input: Video clip $f(u,v,k)$, $u=1,...,U$, $v=1,...,V$, frame $k=0,1,...,N$
Initialization: Pattern M, MHH$(1{:}U,1{:}V,1{:}M)=0$, $I(1{:}U,1{:}V)=1$
For $k=1$ to N (For 1)
 Compute: $D(:,:,k)$
 For $u=1$ to U (For 2)
  For $v=1$ to V (For 3)
   If Subsequence $C_j=\{D(u,v,I(u,v)),...,D(u,v,k)\}=P_i$
    Update: MHH$(u,v,P_i)=$MHH$(u,v,P_i)+1$
   End *If*
   Update: $I(u,v)$
  End (For 3)
 End (For 2)
End (For 1)
Output: MHH$(1{:}U,1{:}V,1{:}M)$

Fig. 7.5 Procedure of MHH algorithm.

7.4.4 Binary Version of MHH

Recall that the MEI is a binary version of the MHI. Similarly, we can define the binary version of an MHH. To do this, we first define the binary version of an MHH as MHH$_b$, as

$$\text{MHH}_b(u,v,i) = \begin{cases} 1, & \text{MHH}(u,v,i) > 0 \\ 0, & \text{otherwise} \end{cases} \tag{7.7}$$

7.5 Dimension Reduction and Feature Combination

Referring back to Fig. 7.1, once we have extracted one or more suitable motion features, we use several techniques to reduce the dimension of the data. These are described in the following subsections.

7.5.1 Histogram of MHI

The histogram is a property of an image used widely in image analysis. For example, for a grayscale image, it shows the frequency of particular grayscale values within the image. Note that MHIs can be rendered as grayscale images, where a value of a pixel in the MHI records time information, namely when some motion most recently occurred at this particular pixel location. Thus the histogram of MHI represents the intensity of motion history. Other features, such as MMHI and MGO, do not offer this property, while the MHH itself is already a histogram.

7.5.2 Subsampling

Subsampling (or downsampling) is the process of reducing the sampling rate of a signal. This is usually done to reduce the data rate or the size of the data. Images typically have a large data size and so subsampling is a general method often used to reduce data size. Subsampling can be done by selecting odd or even rows and columns. Wavelet transforms or other filters are often used to extract the low frequency components of the image to get a compact image on larger scales. In this work, we use subsampling to reduce computational complexity. This can be applied for all the motion features described here, such as MHI, MMHI, MGO, and MHH.

7.5.3 Motion Geometric Distribution (MGD)

The size of the MHH_b representation can be rather large for some embedded implementations and also we seek a more compact representation, which captures the geometric distribution of the motion across the image. Thus we sum each row of MHH_b (for a given pattern, P_i) to give a vector of size V rows. We obtain another vector by summing columns to give a vector of size U rows. Thus using all M levels in the binarized MHH hierarchy, we obtain a motion geometric distribution (MGD) vector of size $M \times (U + V)$, which is relatively compact, when compared to the size of the original MHH and MHI features. The MGD vector can thus be represented by Eq. (7.8):

$$MGD = \{\Sigma_u \text{MHH}_b(u,v,i), \Sigma_v \text{MHH}_b(u,v,i)\}$$
$$(i = 1, 2, \ldots, M)$$
(7.8)

In our work, we prefer to compute the MGD by using the MHH_b feature instead of the MHH feature directly. From our experiments, it has been found that the values within the MHH decrease significantly for the large patterns. The values for P_4 and P_5, for example, are much smaller than those of P_1, P_2 and P_3. Thus, if we use the MHH directly to compute the MGD, a normalization process is necessary in order to treat all the patterns equally. However, this normalization process is not an easy task for our hardware implementation because of limited memory and the requirement to implement a floating-point processing ability. In contrast, computation of the MGD from the MHH_b feature does not need a normalization process and yet we retain a satisfactory performance.

7.5.4 Combining Features

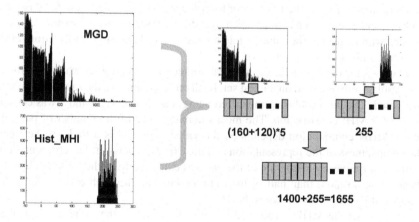

Fig. 7.6 Combination between MGD of the MHH and histogram of the MHI from a same video example. The frame has the size of 160×120. MGD of MHH and histogram of MHI have the size of $(160 + 120) \times 5 = 1400$ and 255, respectively.

We want to efficiently use the motion features extracted in order to achieve an improved classification performance, relative to other compact systems. Based on the simplicity requirement of the system, our two feature vectors are combined in the simplest way by concatenating these two feature vectors into a higher dimensional vector. Fig. 7.6 shows an example of a combination between the MGD of the MHH and the histogram of the MHI from the same video.

7.6 System Evaluation

In this section, we present the experimental results derived from a MATLAB implementation of our SVM based human action recognition system.

7.6.1 Experimental Setup

For the evaluation of our system, we use a challenging human action recognition database, recorded by Christian Schuldt [24], which is both large and publicly available. It contains six types of human actions (walking, jogging, running, boxing, hand waving, and hand clapping) performed several times by 25 subjects in four different scenarios: outdoors (s1), outdoors with scale variation (s2), outdoors with different clothes (s3), and indoors (s4).

This database contains 2391 sequences. All sequences were taken over homogeneous backgrounds with a static camera with 25 Hz frame rate. The sequences were downsampled to the spatial resolution of 160×120 pixels and have a time length of 4 seconds on average. To the best of our knowledge, this is the largest video database with sequences of human actions taken over different scenarios. All sequences were divided with respect to the subjects into a training set (8 persons), a validation set (8 persons), and a test set (9 persons).

In our experiment, the classifiers were trained on a training set while classification results were obtained on the test set. In all our experiments, the same parameters were used. The threshold in frame differencing was chosen as 25 and τ was chosen as 255 for MHI construction. The most suitable choice of the number of patterns M for MHH computation depends on the video clips and is a trade-off between the compactness of the representation and the expressiveness of the representation. Building a frequency histogram of the patterns extracted from the training clips indicates that no more than half of the training data had the sixth pattern. Thus the number of patterns was chosen to be $M = 5$.

The size of the MHI is $160 \times 120 = 19,200$, which is the same width as that of the frames in the videos. In our experiment, the SVM is implemented using the SVM^{light} software [11]. In SVM training, choosing a good parameter C value is not so straightforward and can significantly affect classification accuracy [10], but in order to keep our system simple, the default value of C in SVM^{light} is used in all of the experiments.

Fig. 7.7 shows examples in each type of human action in this dataset. In order to compare our results with those as [12] and [24], we use the exact same training

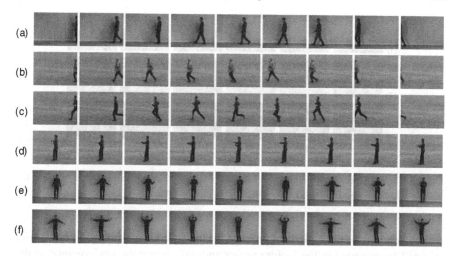

Fig. 7.7 Six types of human action in the database: (a) walking (b) jogging (c) running (d) boxing (e) hand-clapping (f) hand-waving.

set and testing set in our experiments. The only difference is that we did not use the validation dataset in training. Our experiments are carried out on all four different scenarios. In the same manner as [12], each sequence is treated individually during the training and classification process. In all of the following experiments, the parameters are kept same.

7.6.2 Performance of Single Features

We have tested the performance of the fundamental motion features MHI, MMHI and MGO in our system. Fig. 7.8 shows these three motion features extracted from the action examples shown in Fig. 7.7. In order to keep our system simple for hardware implementation, we use the simplest method to transform the motion features (MHI, MMHI and MGO) into a plain vector based on the pixel scan order (row by row) to feed SVM classifier.

Firstly, we tested the system performance on the four different subsets of the whole dataset. The results can be seen in Fig. 7.9. The correctly classified percentage on these data subsets indicates how many percent of the action clips in the testing set were correctly recognized by the system. It is clear that the MHI feature gave the best classification performance in all four subsets while the MGO feature gave poor results for all four data subsets. We also can see that subset s2 (outdoors with scale variation) is the most difficult subset in the whole dataset.

From the experiments, it can be seen that this type of system can get reasonable results. The MHI based system looks better than the MMHI system in the experiments. The disadvantage for MMHI is that it can only work well in the case

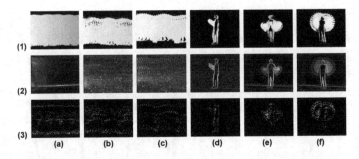

Fig. 7.8 The (1) MHI, (2) MMHI and (3) MGO for the six actions in the dataset: (a) walking (b) jogging (c) running (d) boxing (e) hand-clapping (f) hand-waving

of an uncluttered and static background. If there is background motion or noise, this will be recorded in the feature vector and will reduce the performance of the classification.

For the whole dataset, the classification confusion matrix is a good measure for the overall performance in this multiclass classification problem. Table 7.1 shows the classification confusion matrix based on the method proposed as [12]. Table 7.2 shows the confusion matrix obtained by our system based on MHI. The confusion matrices show the motion label (vertical) versus the classification results (horizontal). Each cell (i, j) in the table shows the percentage of class i action being recognized as class j. Thus the main diagonal of the matrices show the percentage of correctly recognized actions, while the remaining cells show the percentages of misclassification. The trace of the matrix shows the overall classification rate. In Table 7.1, the trace is 377.8 and since there are six classes, the overall mean classification rate is $377.8/6 = 63\%$.

In comparison with Ke's method, we use a simple MHI feature rather than large volumetric features in which the dimension of a feature vector might be a billion, yet the performance of our system is marginally better on this dataset.

In the second step, we test some low dimensional features based on the fundamental motion features. Subsampling is easy to implement in hardware by any factor of 2 and this can be done in both rows and columns of the motion feature.

Fig. 7.9 Correctly classified percentage for separate data subset: s1 (outdoors), s2 (outdoors with scale variation), s3 (outdoors with different clothes) and s4 (indoors).

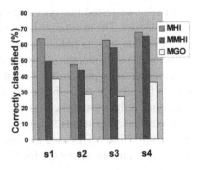

Table 7.1 Ke's confusion matrix [12], trace = 377.8, mean performance = 63%.

	Walk	Jog	Run	Box	Clap	Wave
Walk	**80.6**	11.1	8.3	0.0	0.0	0.0
Jog	30.6	**36.2**	33.3	0.0	0.0	0.0
Run	2.8	25.0	**44.4**	0.0	27.8	0.0
Box	0.0	2.8	11.1	**69.4**	11.1	5.6
Clap	0.0	0.0	5.6	36.1	**55.6**	2.8
Wave	0.0	5.6	0.0	2.8	0.0	**91.7**

Table 7.2 MHI's confusion matrix, trace = 381.2, mean performance = 63.5%.

	Walk	Jog	Run	Box	Clap	Wave
Walk	**53.5**	27.1	16.7	0.0	0.0	2.8
Jog	46.5	**34.7**	16.7	0.7	0.0	1.4
Run	34.7	28.5	**36.1**	0.0	0.0	0.7
Box	0.0	0.0	0.0	**88.8**	2.8	8.4
Clap	0.0	0.0	0.0	7.6	**87.5**	4.9
Wave	0.0	0.0	0.0	8.3	11.1	**80.6**

Tables 7.3 and 7.4 show the results based on downsampling by a factor of 64 (a factor of 8 for both row and column) and the histogram of MHI. From the experiments, we find that this dimensional reduction is detrimental for the MHI. Also, it can be seen that subsampling of MHI obtains a similar performance to Ke's method. This feature performed well in distinguishing the last three groups. On the other hand, the histogram of MHI did not perform well in terms of overall performance but has the power to distinguish the first three groups, which demonstrates that the two methods encode different information.

Table 7.3 MHI_S's confusion matrix, trace = 377.7, mean performance = 62.95%.

	Walk	Jog	Run	Box	Clap	Wave
Walk	**56.9**	18.1	22.2	0.0	0.0	2.8
Jog	45.1	**29.9**	22.9	1.4	0.0	0.7
Run	34.7	27.8	**36.1**	0.0	0.0	1.4
Box	0.0	0.0	0.0	**89.5**	2.1	8.4
Clap	0.0	0.0	0.0	5.6	**88.9**	5.6
Wave	0.0	0.0	0.0	12.5	11.1	**76.4**

Fig. 7.10 shows examples in each type of human action and their associated MHI and MHH motion features. For the MHH, it is hard to deal with the whole feature in our hardware system as, with the number of patterns set to 5, the MHH has a

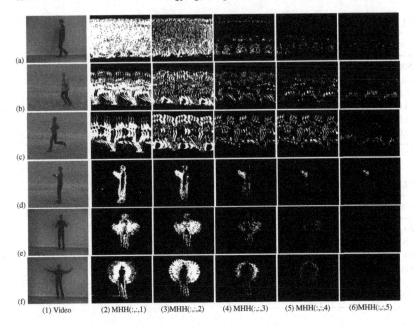

(1) Video   (2) MHH(:,:,1)   (3)MHH(:,:,2)   (4) MHH(:,:,3)   (5) MHH(:,:,4)   (6)MHH(:,:,5)

Fig. 7.10 The six database human actions and associated MHH features: (a) walking (b) jogging (c) running (d) boxing (e) handclapping (f) hand-waving.

Table 7.4 Hist. of MHI's confusion matrix, trace = 328.6, mean performance = 54.8%

	Walk	Jog	Run	Box	Clap	Wave
Walk	**62.5**	32.6	0.0	1.4	1.4	2.1
Jog	12.5	**58.3**	25.0	0.0	0.0	4.2
Run	0.7	18.8	**77.1**	0.0	0.0	3.5
Box	4.9	2.8	0.7	**17.5**	61.5	12.6
Clap	4.9	2.1	0.7	11.1	**75.0**	6.3
Wave	5.6	3.5	6.9	20.1	25.7	**38.2**

relatively high dimension of $5 \times 160 \times 120 = 96000$. Thus, we constructed a small sized MHH_s by averaging the pixels in an 8×8 block, so that the size of all MHH feature vectors is reduced to $20 \times 15 \times 5 = 1500$. Our MGD feature also has a small size of $(160 + 120) \times 5 = 1400$.

Table 7.5 and Table 7.6 show the results when using features MHH_s and MGD respectively. From these two tables, it is very clear that both MHH_s and MGD improve the overall performance. But they failed to classify the "jogging" class. The reason is that these video clips are quite similar to "walking" and "running." It is hard to distinguish between them correctly even by human observation.

Table 7.5 MHH$_s$'s confusion matrix, trace = 417.3, mean performance = 69.55%.

	Walk	Jog	Run	Box	Clap	Wave
Walk	**88.9**	1.4	6.3	0.7	1.4	1.4
Jog	56.9	**2.1**	38.2	0.7	2.1	0.0
Run	22.2	0.7	**75.7**	0.0	1.4	0.0
Box	0.0	0.0	0.0	**96.5**	0.7	2.8
Clap	0.0	0.0	0.0	4.2	**93.1**	2.8
Wave	0.0	0.0	0.0	22.2	16.7	**61.1**

Table 7.6 MGD's confusion matrix, trace = 432.6, mean performance = 72.1%.

	Walk	Jog	Run	Box	Clap	Wave
Walk	**85.4**	4.9	2.8	2.8	2.8	1.4
Jog	65.3	**9.2**	23.6	2.1	0.0	0.0
Run	18.8	8.3	**68.8**	1.4	0.0	2.8
Box	0.0	0.0	0.0	**91.6**	2.8	5.6
Clap	1.4	0.0	0.0	6.3	**92.4**	0.0
Wave	0.0	0.0	0.0	7.6	6.9	**85.4**

7.6.3 Performance of Combined Features

In the previous subsection, we found that different features had different power in distinguishing classes of action. In order to overcome their own disadvantages, we combine them in the feature space. Table 7.7 shows the confusion matrix obtained from our system when combined features were used. From this table, we can see that the overall performance has a significant improvement over Ke's method, which is based on volumetric features. Note that good performance is achieved in distinguishing all of the six actions in the dataset.

Table 7.7 MGD & Hist. of MHI's confusion matrix, trace = 481.9, mean performance = 80.3%.

	Walk	Jog	Run	Box	Clap	Wave
Walk	**66.0**	31.3	0.0	0.0	2.1	0.7
Jog	13.9	**62.5**	21.5	1.4	0.0	0.7
Run	2.1	16.7	**79.9**	0.0	0.0	1.4
Box	0.0	0.0	0.0	**88.8**	2.8	8.4
Clap	0.0	0.0	0.0	3.5	**93.1**	3.5
Wave	0.0	0.0	0.0	1.4	6.9	**91.7**

We compared our results with other methods on this challenging dataset and summarize the correctly classified rates in Table 7.8. From this table, we can see that MHH has made a significant improvement in comparison with MHI. Further-more, the MGD feature gives a better performance than the MHH itself. The best performance, which gives significantly better classification results, came from the combined feature, which is based on the histogram of the MHI and the MGD.

Table 7.8 Overall correctly classified rate (%) for all the methods on this open, challenging dataset. Some of them did not use the difficult part of dataset(Δ), while some of them did an easier task($*$).

Method	Rate(%)
SVM on local features [24]$*$	71.7
Cascade of filters on volumetric features [12]	63
SVM on MHI [15]	63.5
SVM_2K on MHI & MMHI [14]	65.3
SVM on MHH$_s$	69.6
SVM on MGD	72.1
SVM on HWT of MHI & Hist. of MHI [17]	70.9
SVM on MGD & Hist. of MHI	**80.3**
SVM on spatio-temporal feature [8]Δ	81.2
Unsupervised learning on spatial-temporal words [20] $*$	81.5
KNN on nonzero motion block similarity [30]$\Delta*$	86.0

It should be mentioned here that some results [8, 20, 30] are better than ours on this dataset. However, these results are not directly comparable with ours. For example, Dollar et al. [8] achieved a correct classification rate of 81.2%, but the authors omitted the most difficult part of the dataset (subset 2, outdoor with scale variation).

Niebles et al. [20] obtained similar results with 81.5% and Yeo et al. [30] obtained 86.0%, but they did an easier task of classifying each complete sequence (containing four repetitions of same action) into one of six classes, while our method was trained as the same way as [9, 12, 14, 15, 17]; that is, to detect a single instance of each action within arbitrary sequences in the dataset. Furthermore, Yeo et al. [30] did not use the difficult subset 2 of the dataset, as was the case with Dollar et al. [8].

7.7 FPGA Implementation on Videoware

We have developed a hardware architecture called "Videoware" [23], which can be reconfigured for a wide range of embedded computer vision tasks. At present, we have not tested our MHH representations within our embedded "Videoware" archi-tecture, but we did test the performance of an MHI/SVM based gesture recognition in an embedded context [18].

Our approach has been to implement a video component library (VCL) of generic image processing, computer vision and pattern recognition algorithms in an FPGA

Fig. 7.11 Videoware processing architecture.

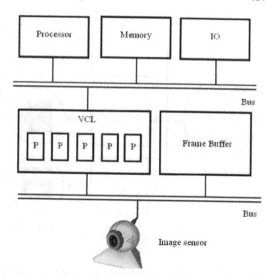

based architecture as shown in Fig. 7.11. The low level, high bandwidth processes, such as smoothing and feature extraction, are implemented as hardware IP-cores, whilst higher level, lower bandwidth processes, such as task-oriented combination of visual cues, are implemented in a software architecture as shown schematically in Fig. 7.12. The advantage of this modular approach is that a systems processing performance can be reconfigured for a particular application, with the addition of new or replicated processing cores.

"Videoware" has been implemented on a custom made FPGA board as shown in Fig. 7.13. This board is based on a Xilinx Spartan-III device [29], with 2 MB of external RAM and 8 MB of external ROM (this memory is also used to configure the FPGA via a configuration engine). The FPGA size can be selected to match a system's requirements, the board accepting three alternative devices: XC3S1500 (1.5M gates), XC3S2000 (2 M gates) and XC3S4000 (4 M gates). In addition to this a number of interface boards have also been developed to allow the easy connection of a camera [13], communications interfaces (e.g., LEDs, RS232), and additional external memory modules.

The action recognition processing pipeline that we have implemented is shown in Fig. 7.14. A difference operator is performed on the current and previous frames, updating a motion history image. The inner product of the MHI and the SVM classification data sets is then performed, the result of each accumulator then has a specific offset applied before a threshold is performed, selecting the stored action that most closely matches the observed motion. In the current implementation this process is operated in a one shot mode, however, this could be easily expanded to include motion detection to start and stop this process, i.e., when the difference between two frames exceeds a threshold the MHI is generated, when it falls below this threshold the inner product and threshold operations are then performed.

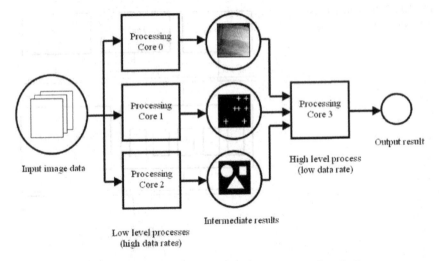

Fig. 7.12 Video component library configured to form a virtual processing pipeline.

Fig. 7.13 Amadeus ubiquitous system environment
(USE) board.

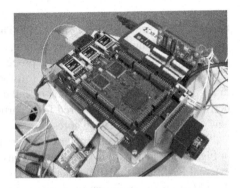

The current hardware implementation uses a 20 MHz system clock and can capture and process 100×80 image data at 12.5 frames per second, i.e., one frame every 80 ms. The system is capable of processing 200×160 images, with the addition of extra memory. In order to test the performance of the FPGA implementation of our human action recognition system, we recorded a hand motion dataset. In this dataset, there are only three types of hand motions: horizontal motion, vertical motion, and "other motion." We also recognize a "no-motion" case as an extra class.

For each class, we recorded 20 video samples, with the frame size set to 100×80 pixels. We recorded the video clips with a variety of backgrounds to test the system robustness to this variability. Fig. 7.15 shows some samples in this dataset.

In our experiment, 15 samples were randomly chosen from each class for training and the other 5 were used for testing. We repeated the experiments 10 times. We carried out the training on a PC using SVM^{light} (the default values were used for all the parameters in this software). Firstly, we extracted MHI features from each video clip. Then we trained three binary linear SVM classifiers based on these features

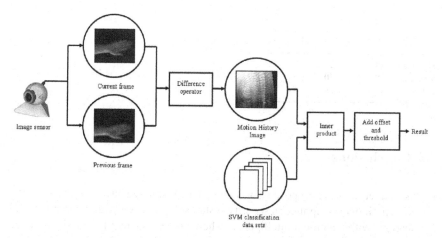

Fig. 7.14 Motion recognition processing pipeline.

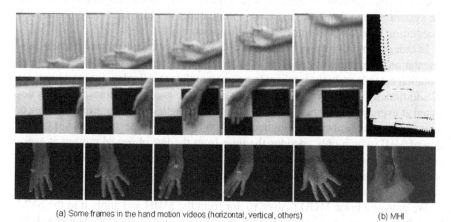

(a) Some frames in the hand motion videos (horizontal, vertical, others)   (b) MHI

Fig. 7.15 Some samples in the hand motion dataset and their MHI features.

to give a 3 parameter matrix containing the weight vector w and bias b. These parameters were stored in the internal memory of the FPGA chip and were used for gesture classification. During the classification, three values were obtained from each SVM classifier and the one with the largest (most positive) value is used to label the motion.

Table 7.9 shows the average classification rate. The average rate of correct classification for all gestures is 80%, which is almost identical to our PC based (MATLAB) result on the same data.

Table 7.9 Hand motion recognition average confusion matrix

	Horizontal	Vertical	Others
Horizontal	**94**	2	4
Vertical	18	**70**	12
Others	4	18	**76**

7.8 Conclusions

In this chapter, we have proposed a new compact SVM based human action recognition system. It may be applied in security systems, human-computer interaction, and applications within ambient intelligence, where embedded, real-time vision may be deployed. The proposed method does not rely on accurate tracking as many other works do, since most of the tracking algorithms incur an extra computational cost for the system. Our system is based on simple features in order to achieve high-speed recognition in real-world embedded applications.

In order to improve the performance of the system, we have proposed a new representation for motion information in video and this is called the MHH. The representation extends previous work on temporal template (MHI related) representations by additionally storing frequency information as the number of times motion is detected at every pixel, further categorized into the length of each motion. In essence, maintaining the number of contiguous motion frames removes a significant limitation of MHI, which only encodes the time from the last observed motion at every pixel. It can be used either independently or combined with the MHI to give human action recognition systems with improved performance over existing comparable compact systems, which do not employ complex articulated models for tracking.

We extract a basic MGD feature vector from the MHH and apply it in the SVM based human action recognition system. In comparison with local SVM methods by Schuldt [24] and a cascade of filters on volumetric features by Ke [12], our feature vectors are computationally inexpensive. Even though we do not use a validation dataset for parameter tuning in SVM training, we have demonstrated a significant improvement (around 10%) in the recognition performance, when our method is applied to a large, challenging public dataset.

A recognition system using the simple MHI features has been implemented on our FPGA-based embedded computer vision system called "Videoware," with encouraging performance. For the future work, we will implement an improved embedded system, based on combining features from both MHH and MHI, as described in this chapter.

References

1. Aggarwal JK, Cai Q (1999) Human motion analysis: a review. *Comput Vis Image Underst* 73(3):428–440, doi: 10.1006/cviu.1998.0744.
2. Blank M, Gorelick L, Shechtman E, Irani M, Basri R (2005) Actions as space-time shapes. In: *Int. Conf. on Comput. Vis.(ICCV)* pp, 1395–1402.
3. Bobick AF, Davis JW (2001) The recognition of human movement using temporal templates. *IEEE Trans Pattern Anal Mach Intell* 23(3):257–267.
4. Bradski GR, Davis JW (2002) Motion segmentation and pose recognition with motion history gradients. *Mach Vis Appl* 13(3):174–184.
5. Cristianini N, Shawe-Taylor J (2000) *An Introduction to Support Vector Machines (and Other Kernel-Based Learning Methods).* Cambridge University Press, Cambridge, UK.
6. Dalal N, Triggs B, Schmid C (2006) Human detection using oriented histograms of flow and appearance. In: *Euro. Conf. on Comput. Vis.(ECCV) (2),* pp, 428–441.
7. Davis JW (2001) Hierarchical motion history images for recognizing human motion. In: *IEEE Workshop on Detection and Recognition of Events in Video,* pp, 39–46.
8. Dollár P, Rabaud V, Cottrell G, Belongie S (2005) Behavior recognition via sparse spatio-temporal features. In: *VS-PETS,* pp, 65–72, doi: 10.1109/VSPETS.2005.1570899.
9. Efros AA, Berg AC, Mori G, Malik J (2003) Recognizing action at a distance. In: *Int. Conf. on Comput. Vis.(ICCV),* pp, 726–733.
10. Hastie T, Rosset S, Tibshirani R, Zhu J (2004) The entire regularization path for the support vector machine. http://citeseer.ist.psu.edu/hastie04entire.html.
11. Joachims T (1998) Making large-scale support vector machine learning practical. In: B Schölkopf AS C Burges (ed) *Advances in Kernel Methods: Support Vector Machines,* MIT Press, Cambridge, MA, citeseer.ist.psu.edu/joachims98making.html.
12. Ke Y, Sukthankar R, Hebert M (2005) Efficient visual event detection using volumetric features. In: *Int. Conf. on Comput. Vis.(ICCV),* pp, 166–173, beijing, China, Oct. 15-21, 2005.
13. Kodak (2006) Kodak kac-9628 image sensor 648(h) x 488(v) color CMOS image sensor. http://www.kodak.com/ezpres/business/ccd/global/plugins/acrobat/en/productsummary /CMOS/KAC-9628ProductSummaryv2.0.pdf.
14. Meng H, Pears N, Bailey C (2006) Human action classification using SVM_2K classifier on motion features. In: *Lect. Note. Comput. Sci.(LNCS),* Istanbul, Turkey, vol. 4105, pp, 458–465.
15. Meng H, Pears N, Bailey C (2006) Recognizing human actions based on motion information and SVM. In: *2nd IET International Conference on Intelligent Environments,* IET, Athens, Greece, pp, 239–245.
16. Meng H, Pears N, Bailey C (2007) A human action recognition system for embedded computer vision application. In: *Comput. Vis. and Pat. Rec (CVPR),* doi: 10.1109/CVPR.2007.383420.
17. Meng H, Pears N, Bailey C (2007) Motion information combination for fast human action recognition. In: *2nd International Conference on Computer Vision Theory and Applications (VISAPP07), Barcelona, Spain.,* pp, 21–28.
18. Meng H, Freeman M, Pears N, Bailey C (2008) Real-time human action recognition on an embedded, reconfigurable video processing architecture. *J. of Real-Time Image Processing,* doi: 10.1007/s11554-008-0073-1.
19. Moeslund T, Hilton A, Kruger V (2006) A survey of advances in vision-based human motion capture and analysis. *Comput Vis Image Underst* 103(2-3):90–126.
20. Niebles J, Wang H, Fei-Fei L (2006) Unsupervised learning of human action categories using spatial-temporal words. In: *British Machine Vision Conf. (BMVC),* pp, III:1249.
21. Ogata T, Tan JK, Ishikawa S (2006) High-speed human motion recognition based on a motion history image and an eigenspace. *IEICE Trans. on Inform. and Sys.* E89(1):281–289.
22. Oikonomopoulos A, Patras I, Pantic M (2006) Kernel-based recognition of human actions using spatiotemporal salient points. In: *Comput. Vis. and Pat. Rec. (CVPR) workshop 06,* Vol.3, pp, 151–156, http://pubs.doc.ic.ac.uk/Pantic-CVPR06-1/.
23. Pears N (2004) Projects: Videoware - video processing architecture. http://www.cs.york.ac.uk /amadeus/videoware/.

24. Schuldt C, Laptev I, Caputo B (2004) Recognizing human actions: a local SVM approach. In: *Int. Conf. on Pat. Rec (ICPR)*, Cambridge, UK.
25. Vapnik V (1995) *The Nature of Statistical Learning Theory*. Springer-Verlag, New York.
26. Weinland D, Ronfard R, Boyer E (2005) Motion history volumes for free viewpoint action recognition. In: *IEEE International Workshop on Modeling People and Human Interaction (PHI'05)*, http://perception.inrialpes.fr/Publications/2005/WRB05.
27. Wong SF, Cipolla R (2005) Real-time adaptive hand motion recognition using a sparse Bayesian classifier. In: *Int. Conf. on Comput. Vis.(ICPR) Workshop ICCV-HCI*, pp, 170–179.
28. Wong SF, Cipolla R (2006) Continuous gesture recognition using a sparse Bayesian classifier. In: *Int. Conf. on Pat. Rec (ICPR)*, Vol. 1, pp, 1084–1087.
29. Xilinx (2007) Spartan-3 FPGA family complete data sheet. http://direct.xilinx.com/bvdocs /publications/ds099.pdf.
30. Yeo C, Ahammad P, Ramchandran K, Sastry S (2006) Compressed domain real-time action recognition. In: *IEEE International Workshop on Multimedia Signal Processing (MMSP06)*, IEEE, Washington, DC.

Chapter 8
Embedded Real-Time Surveillance Using Multimodal Mean Background Modeling

Senyo Apewokin, Brian Valentine, Dana Forsthoefel, Linda Wills, Scott Wills, and Antonio Gentile

Abstract Automated video surveillance applications require accurate separation of foreground and background image content. Cost-sensitive embedded platforms place real-time performance and efficiency demands on techniques to accomplish this task. In this chapter, we evaluate pixel-level foreground extraction techniques for a low-cost integrated surveillance system. We introduce a new adaptive background modeling technique, multimodal mean (MM), which balances accuracy, performance, and efficiency to meet embedded system requirements. Our evaluation compares several pixel-level foreground extraction techniques in terms of their computation and storage requirements, and functional accuracy for three representative video sequences. The proposed MM algorithm delivers comparable accuracy of the best alternative (mixture of Gaussians) with a $6\times$ improvement in execution time and an 18% reduction in required storage on an eBox-2300 embedded platform.

8.1 Introduction

Techniques for automated video surveillance utilize robust background modeling algorithms to identify salient foreground objects. Typically, the current video frame is compared against a background model representing elements of the scene that are stationary or changing in uninteresting ways (such as rippling water or swaying branches). Foreground is determined by locating significant differences between the current frame and the background model.

Senyo Apewokin, Brian Valentine, Dana Forsthoefel, Linda Wills, Scott Wills
Georgia Institute of Technology, Atlanta, GA, USA

Antonio Gentile
University of Palermo, Palermo, Italy

Corresponding author e-mail: linda.wills@ece.gatech.edu

The availability of low-cost, portable imagers and new embedded computing platforms makes video surveillance possible in new environments. However, situations in which a portable, embedded video surveillance system is most useful (e.g., monitoring outdoor and/or busy scenes) also pose the greatest challenges. Real-world scenes are characterized by changing illumination and shadows, multimodal features (such as rippling waves and rustling leaves), and frequent, multilevel occlusions. To extract foreground in these dynamic visual environments, adaptive multimodal background models are frequently used that maintain historical scene information to improve accuracy. These methods are problematic in real-time embedded environments where limited computation and storage restrict the amount of historical data that can be processed and stored.

In this chapter, we examine several representative pixel-based, fixed-camera background modeling techniques in this real-time embedded environment. They are evaluated in terms of computational cost, storage, and extracted foreground accuracy. The techniques range from simple, computationally inexpensive methods, such as frame differencing and mean/median temporal filters [2], to more complex methods, including the multimodal mixture of Gaussians (MoG) [9] approach. In this comparative evaluation, we include a new proposed approach, multimodal mean (MM), for real-time background modeling. Our technique achieves accuracy comparable to multimodal MoG techniques but with a significantly lower execution time. For our testbed, we employ commercial off-the-shelf components to build a low-cost, low-power, and portable embedded platform. Our results demonstrate that our proposed MM algorithm achieves competitive real-time foreground accuracy under a variety of outdoor and indoor conditions with the limited computation and storage of a low-cost embedded platform.

This chapter is organized as follows. First, in Section 8.2, we summarize common backgrounding techniques. Then we present our new adaptive technique, multimodal mean, in Section 8.3. In Section 8.4, we describe an experiment in which several representative pixel-based techniques are evaluated in terms of performance, storage requirements, and accuracy. In Section 8.5, we discuss results of these experiments on two embedded platforms (the eBox-2300 and the HP Pavilion Slimline PC) and Section 8.6 summarizes conclusions.

8.2 Related Work

A variety of techniques exist for background subtraction; see [2, 6, 7] for recent comprehensive surveys. *Frame differencing* compares pixels in the current video frame with corresponding pixels in the previous frame. If the difference between the pixels is above a given threshold, then that pixel is identified as foreground. While computationally inexpensive, this method is prone to the foreground aperture problem [10] and cannot handle dynamic background elements, such as swaying tree branches.

Sliding window-based (or *nonrecursive* [2]) techniques keep a record of the *w* most recent image frames. The background is represented as the mean or median of the frames in the buffer. Foreground is determined either by determining if the current image pixel deviates by a fixed threshold away from the background model or, if it is within some standard deviation of the background. This type of technique is more memory intensive as it requires *w* image frames of storage per processed image.

Recursive techniques [2] utilize only the current frame and parametric information accumulated from previous frames to separate background and foreground objects. These techniques typically employ weighted means or approximated medians and require significantly less memory than the sliding window techniques. An *approximated median* is computed in [5]. The background is initialized by declaring the first image frame as the median. When a new video frame is acquired, the current image pixel values are compared with those of the approximated median pixel values. If a pixel value is above the corresponding median value, then that approximate median pixel value is incremented by one, otherwise it is decremented by one. It is assumed that the approximated median frame will eventually converge to the actual median after a given number of image frames are analyzed [5]. In [4] and [11], a *weighted mean* is used, which takes a percentage of the background pixel and a percentage of the current pixel to update the background model. This percentage is governed by a user-defined learning rate that affects how quickly objects are assimilated into the background model.

Issues can arise with the described techniques when there are moving background objects, rapidly changing lighting conditions, and gradual lighting changes. The mixture of Gaussians (MoG) and Wallflower approaches are designed to better handle these situations by storing *multimodal representations* of backgrounds that contain dynamic scene elements, such as trees swaying in the wind or rippling waves. The MoG approach maintains multiple data values for each pixel coordinate. Each data value is modeled as a Gaussian probability density function (pdf) with an associated weight indicating how much background information it contains. With each new image frame, the current image pixel is compared against the pixel values for that location. A match is determined based on whether or not the current pixel falls within 2.5 standard deviations of any of the pixel distributions in the background model [9].

Wallflower [10] uses a three-tiered approach to model foreground and background. Pixel, region, and frame-level information are obtained and analyzed. At the pixel-level, a linear predictor is used to establish a baseline background model. At the region-level, frame differencing, connected component analysis and histogram backprojection are used to create foreground regions. Multiple background models are stored at the frame-level to handle a sharp environmental change such as a light being switched on or off.

These techniques have limitations in either foreground extraction accuracy or real-time performance when applied to busy or outdoor scenes in resource-constrained embedded computing systems. Frame differencing and recursive backgrounding methods do not handle dynamic backgrounds well. Sliding window methods require significant memory resources for accurate backgrounding. The MoG approach requires significant computational resources for sorting and computations of standard deviations, weights, and pdfs.

In this chapter, we propose a new backgrounding technique that has the multimodal modeling capabilities of MoG but at significantly reduced storage and computational cost. A related approach [1] implements multimodal backgrounding on a single-chip FPGA using a collection of temporal lowpass filters instead of Gaussian pdfs. A similar background weight, match, and updating scheme as the MoG is maintained, with simplifications to limit the amount of floating-point calculations. In contrast to MoG and [1], we use a linear parameter updating scheme as opposed to nonlinear updates of weights and pixel values, and we make use of information about recency of background pixel matches. Updating the background model information in this manner allows for efficient storage of a pixel's long-term history.

8.3 Multimodal Mean Background Technique

We propose a new adaptive background modeling technique, called *multimodal mean*, which models each background pixel as a set of average possible pixel values. In background subtraction, each pixel I_t in the current frame is compared to each of the background pixel means to determine whether it is within a predefined threshold of one of them. Each pixel value is represented as a three-component color representation, such as an RGB or HSI vector. In the following, $I_{t.x}$ represents the x color component of a pixel in frame t (e.g., $I_{t.red}$ denotes the red component of I_t). The background model for a given pixel is a set of K mean pixel representations, called *cells*. Each cell contains three mean color component values. An image pixel I_t is a background pixel if each of its color components I_t is within a predefined threshold for that color component E_x of one the background means.

In our embedded implementation, we choose $K = 4$ cells and use an RGB color representation. Each background cell B_i is represented as three running sums for each color component $S_{i,t.x}$ and a count $C_{i,t}$ of how many times a matching pixel value has been observed in t frames. At any given frame t, the mean color component value is then computed as $\mu_{i,t.x} = S_{i,t.x}/C_{i,t}$.

More precisely, I_t is a background pixel if a cell B_i can be found whose mean for each color component x matches within E_x the corresponding color component of I_t:

$$\left(\bigwedge_x |I_{t.x} - \mu_{i,t-1.x}| \le E_x \right) \wedge (C_{i,t-1} > T_{FG}), \tag{8.1}$$

where T_{FG} is a small threshold number of times a pixel value can be seen and still considered to be foreground. (In our experiments, $T_{FG} = 3$ and $E_x = 30$, for $x \in \{R, G, B\}$.)

When a pixel I_t matches a cell B_i, the background model is updated by adding each color component to the corresponding running sum $S_{i,t.x}$ and incrementing the count $C_{i,t}$. As the background gradually changes, for example, due to lighting variations), the running averages will adapt as well. In addition, to enable long-term adaptation of the background model, all cells are periodically *decimated* by halving both the sum and the count every d (the decimation rate) frames. To be precise, when I_t matches a cell B_i, the cell is updated as follows:

$$S_{i,t.x} = (S_{i,t-1.x} + I_{t.x})/2^b \tag{8.2}$$
$$C_{i,t} = (C_{i,t-1} + 1)/2^b \tag{8.3}$$

where $b = 1$ if $t \bmod d = 0$, and $b = 0$, otherwise.

Decimation is used to decay long-lived background components so that they do not permanently dominate the model, allowing the background model to adapt to the appearance of newer stationary objects or newly revealed parts of the background. It also plays a secondary role in the embedded implementation in preventing counts from overflowing their limited storage. In the experiments reported in this chapter, the decimation rate d is 400, so decimation occurs in the longer test sequences at a rate of once every 20–25 seconds to enable long-term adaptation.

When a pixel I_t does not match cells at that pixel position, it is declared to be foreground. In addition, a new background cell is created to allow new scene elements to be incorporated into the background. If there are already K background cells, a cell is selected to be replaced based on the cells overall count $C_{i,t}$ and a recency count $R_{i,t}$ which measures how often the background cells mean matched a pixel in a recent window of frames. A sliding window is approximated by maintaining a pair of counts $(r_{i,t}, s_{i,t})$ in each cell B_i. The first $r_{i,t}$, starts at 0, is incremented whenever B_i is matched, and is reset every w frames. The second $s_{i,t}$, simply holds the maximum value of $r_{i,t}$ computed in the previous window:

$$r_{i,t} = \begin{cases} 0 & \text{if } t \bmod w = 0 \\ r_{i,t-1} + 1 & \text{if } B_i \text{ matches } I_t \text{ and } t \bmod w \neq 0 \end{cases} \tag{8.4}$$

$$s_{i,t} = \begin{cases} r_{i,t-1} & \text{if } t \bmod w = 0 \\ s_{i,t-1} & \text{otherwise.} \end{cases} \tag{8.5}$$

Recency $R_{i,t} = r_{i,t} + s_{i,t}$ provides a measure of how often a pixel matching cell B_i was observed within a recent window. The $s_{i,t}$ component allows information to be carried over across windows so that recency information is not completely lost at window transitions. When a new cell is created and added to a background model that already has K cells, the cell to be replaced is selected from the subset of cells seen least recently, i.e., cells whose recency $R_{i,t} < w/K$. From this set, the cell with the minimum overall count $C_{i,t}$ is selected for replacement. If all cells have a recency count $R_{i,t} > w/K$ (in the rare event that all cells are observed equally often over an entire window), then the cell with lowest $C_{i,t}$ is replaced. (In our experiments, we chose $w = 32$.)

8.4 Experiment

The backgrounding techniques are evaluated using representative test sequences. Two hardware platforms are used to evaluate the background modeling algorithm performance. Each technique is compared in terms of image quality and accuracy (false positives and false negatives) as well as execution cost (execution time and storage required). The evaluated techniques include:

- frame differencing
- approximated median
- sliding window median
- weighted mean
- sliding window mean
- mixture of Gaussians (MoG)
- multimodal mean (MM)

The test suite includes two standard test sequences and a longer outdoor sequence captured using an inexpensive webcam (see Table 8.1). All sequences have a frame size of 160×120.

Table 8.1 Test sequences.

Sequence	# Frames	Sampled Frame
Waving tree	281	247
Bootstrapping	1000	299
Outdoors	201	190

The standard sequences, "waving tree" and "bootstrapping," are from the Wallflower benchmarks [10], using the same sampled frame and associated ground truth found in the published benchmarks. They contain difficult challenges for backgrounding algorithms. "Waving tree" contains dynamic background in the form of a wind-blown tree with swaying branches and leaves. "Bootstrapping" lacks a "foreground-free" preamble for construction of the initial background model. This requires learning the background in the presence of continually changing foreground. These sequences are choreographed to present specific backgrounding problems. We also collected a longer sequence with dynamic background and the continuous presence of foreground objects. This sequence contains an outdoor scene with varying illumination, moving trees, and subjects moving in varying patterns and positions. It was captured at 640×480 resolution at one frame per second. Afterward, the sequence was resized to 160×120, a sample frame was selected, and its ground truth was manually derived.

Table 8.2 lists the algorithm parameters used in the experiments. Experiment parameters and thresholds were held constant for all sequences. The MoG method incorporated $K = 4$ Gaussians while the MM method utilized $K = 4$ cells. The sliding window implementations use a buffer size of four for comparable memory requirements.

Table 8.2 Algorithm parameters.

Algorithm	Parameters
Mean/median (SW)	$|window| = 4$
Weighted mean	$\alpha = 0.1$ for $u_t = (1 - \alpha) \times u_{t-1} + \alpha x_t$
Mixture of Gaussians (MoG)	$K = 4$ modes, initial weight $w = 0.02$, learning rate $\alpha = 0.01$, weight threshold $T = 0.85$
Multimodal mean	$K = 4, E_x = 30$ for $x \in \{R, G, B\}, T_{FG} = 3, d = 400, w = 32$

8.4.1 Embedded Platform: eBox-2300 Thin Client

Our first execution platform is an eBox-2300 Thin Client VESA PC [3] running Windows Embedded CE 6.0. The eBox incorporates a fanless Vortex86 SoC [8] (includes a 200 MHz $\times$86 processor that dissipates < 3 Watts) plus 128 MB SDRAM (PC133), three USB ports, a 10/100 Ethernet port, and a compact flash slot. The platform is $11.5 \times 11.5 \times 3.5$ cm in size, weighs 505g, and is designed for low power operation. Because of its limited 128 MB internal memory, we constructed a customized lightweight kernel occupying approximately 19 MB. Image sequences are also downloaded onto the internal memory prior to the evaluation of each series.

Each backgrounding technique is implemented in C and compiled for Windows CE using Microsoft Studio. Algorithm data storage is limited to 40 MB. This affects the variable window size for sliding window methods and the number of modes for multimodal techniques.

8.4.2 Comparative Evaluation Platform: HP Pavilion Slimline

Our second evaluation platform is an HP Pavilion Slimline S3220N PC. It has an AMD Athlon 64 X2 Dual-Core processor with 512 KB cache and a 512 KB L2 cache. It also has an NVIDIA GeForce 6150 LE graphics processor, 1024 MB of DDR memory and a 250 GB hard drive. It runs Microsoft Windows Vista and we used Microsoft Visual Studio 2005 for application development.

8.5 Results and Evaluation

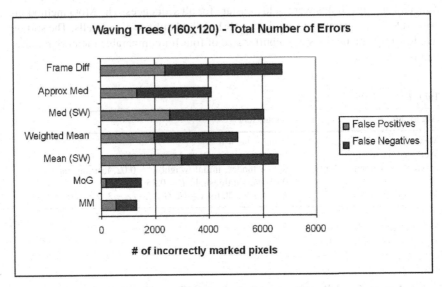

Fig. 8.1 Backgrounding algorithm accuracy on the "waving trees" sequence.

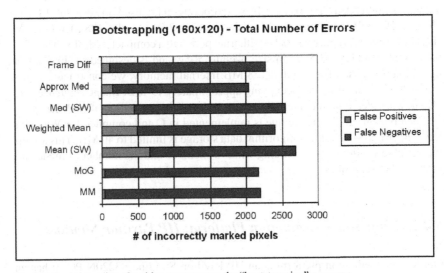

Fig. 8.2 Backgrounding algorithm accuracy on the "bootstrapping" sequence.

The accuracy of each backgrounding method is compared in Figs. 8.1 through 8.4. False positives indicate foreground identified outside the highlighted (white)

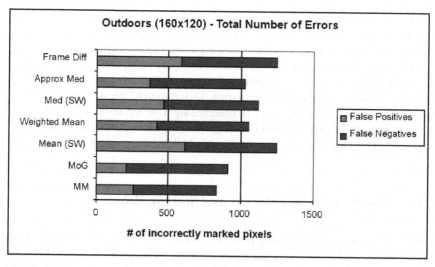

Fig. 8.3 Backgrounding algorithm accuracy on "Outdoors" sequence.

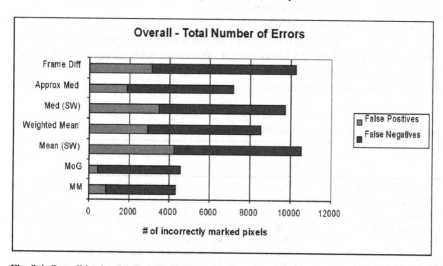

Fig. 8.4 Overall backgrounding algorithm accuracy.

regions of the ground truth. False negatives result from background detected in ground truth identified foreground. While these counts do not provide a complete measure of foreground usefulness (e.g., often incomplete foreground can be "filled in"), lower numbers of false positives and negatives are usually desirable. Generally, MoG and MM demonstrate comparable accuracy that is superior to the other methods.

Fig. 8.5 displays the image quality for each backgrounding technique. Multi-modal methods (MoG and MM) generally exhibit the lowest number of errors across the sequences. False positives are significantly lower for the multimodal methods.

In "waving trees," only the multimodal techniques incorporate the moving tree into the background. In "bootstrapping," all techniques are able to detect elements of the foreground identified in the ground truth. Unfortunately, the sliding window and weighted mean methods also identify reflected light on the floor (false positives). "Outdoors" features a large number of foreground elements as well as moving trees. Both multimodal techniques have significantly higher false positive accuracy.

8.5.1 eBox Performance Results and Storage Requirements

Table 8.3 lists average processing times per frame, average frame rates, and storage requirements for each method executing on the eBox test platform. Because the sequence frames originated from standard files rather than camera output, I/O requirements are not included in these figures.

The results showed that our MM method executes 6.2× faster than the MoG technique, while providing comparable image quality and accuracy. It also requires 18% less storage per pixel and uses only integer operations. Although many of the other methods offered lower execution times and storage requirements, their accuracy is insufficient for many applications.

Table 8.3 Algorithm performance on eBox test platform.

Algorithm	Time (ms/frame)	Rate (fps)	Storage (bytes/pixel)
Frame Differencing	7.6	131.96	3: packed RGB
Approximated Median	8.5	117.33	3: packed RGB
Median (SW)	69.2	14.45	12: 3 char × 4
Weighted Mean	26.8	37.28	3: packed RGB
Mean (SW)	28.2	35.49	12: 3 char × 4
MoG	273.6	3.65	88: 5 FP × 4 modes + 2 int
Multimodal Mean	43.9	22.78	72: (4 int + 2 char) × 4 cells

8.5.2 HP Pavilion Slimline Performance Results

In this section, we compare pixel-based background modeling techniques on a more powerful execution platform, an HP Pavilion Slimline S3220N PC. This platform includes greater computational throughput, more main memory, and floating point

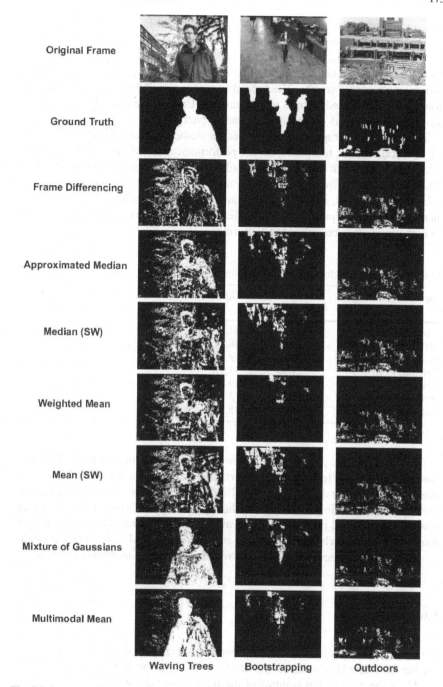

Fig. 8.5 Image quality comparison of backgrounding techniques.

support. This comparative analysis provides additional insight into algorithm demands and their performance on different embedded platforms.

In this comparison, two full frame (640×480) sequences are used to evaluate each backgrounding technique. The first is the outdoor sequence used previously with a length of 901 frames. The second sequence is a 750 frame (640×480) outdoor walkway outlined by trees on a sunny day. Under these real-world conditions, waving trees and shadows result in a dynamic background.

Table 8.4 lists average processing times per frame and average frame rates on the HP Pavilion Slimline test platform. The performance of MM on the HP platform is 4.23× faster than that of MoG, compared with a 6.2× improvement on the eBox. While the eBox improvement is partially due to lack of hardware supported floating point representations, it is clear that reducing overall algorithm complexity and a more compact data representation still offers a significant performance improvement on higher performance embedded platforms.

Table 8.4 Algorithm performance on HP Pavilion Slimline platform.

Algorithm	Time (ms/frame)	Rate (fps)
Frame differencing	17.29	57.83
Approximated median	20.77	48.16
Median (SW)	105.57	9.47
Weighted mean	27.84	35.91
Mean (SW)	33.49	29.85
MoG	269.33	3.71
Multimodal mean	63.64	15.71

Fig. 8.6 shows the performance on the HP Pavilion Slimline of the sliding window and multimodal techniques as the window size and number of modes, respectively, is successively doubled. The MoG and sliding window mean techniques have a uniform reduction in performance as the algorithm is scaled up. The sliding window median suffered the greatest performance impact because computing the median grows nonlinearly as the window size increases. MM consistently provides significant performance improvements over MoG across all numbers of modes.

8.6 Conclusion

This chapter compares several backgrounding techniques for time sensitive processing on embedded computing platforms. We have proposed a technique that combines the multimodal features of the mixture of Gaussians with simple pixel evaluation computations involving sums and averages. The multimodal mean method is able to achieve faster execution and lower storage requirements than mixture of Gaussians while providing comparable accuracy and output image quality. We show

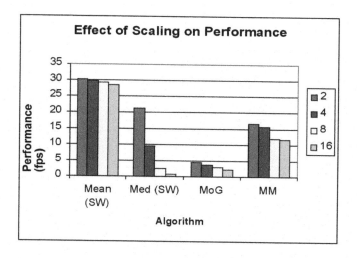

Fig. 8.6 Performance effect of successively doubling the window size or the number of modes.

that on embedded systems with limited storage and computation capabilities, multi-modal mean provides significant performance and storage improvements over mixture of Gaussians.

References

1. K. Appiah, and A. Hunter: A single-chip FPGA implementation of real-time adaptive background model. *IEEE International Conference on Field-Programmable Technology,* 95–102 (2005).
2. S. Cheung, and C. Kamath: Robust techniques for background subtraction in urban traffic video. *Video Communications and Image Processing,* SPIE Electronic Imaging, San Jose, Vol. 5308, 881–892 (2004).
3. DMP Electronics Inc.: *VESA PC eBox-2300 Users Manual.* (Available online, 2006), http://www.wdlsystems.com/downloads/manuals/1EBOX23_m.pdf.
4. S. Jabri, Z. Duric, H. Wechsler, and A. Rosenfeld: Detection and location of people in video images using adaptive fusion of color and edge information, *IEEE International Conference on Pattern Recognition,* Vol. 4, 627–630 (2000).
5. N. McFarlane and C. Schofield: Segmentation and tracking of piglets in images, *Machine Vision and Applications,* 8(3), 187–193 (1995).
6. M. Piccardi: Background subtraction techniques: a review. *IEEE International Conference on Systems, Man and Cybernetics,* Vol. 4, 3099–3104 (2004).
7. R. J. Radke, S. Andra, O. Al-Kofahi, and B. Roysam: Image change detection algorithms: A systemic survey, *IEEE Trans. on Image Processing,* 14(3), 294–307 (2005).
8. Silicon Integrated Systems Corp.: SiS55x Family Datasheet, Rev 0.9, 14 March 2002.
9. C. Stauffer and W. E. L. Grimson: Adaptive background mixture models for real-time tracking. *Computer Vision and Pattern Recognition,* 246–252 (1999).
10. K. Toyama, J. Krumm, B. Brummitt, and B. Meyers: Wallflower: principles and practices of background maintenance. *Proc. of ICCV,* 255–261 (1999).
11. C. R. Wren, A. Azarbayejani, T. Darell, and A. P. Pentland: Pfinder: real-time tracking of human body. *IEEE Transactions on Pattern Analysis and Machine Intelligence* 19(7), 780–785 (1997).

Chapter 9
Implementation Considerations for Automotive Vision Systems on a Fixed-Point DSP

Zoran Nikolić

Abstract In this chapter we evaluate numerical requirements for implementation of camera-based lateral position detection algorithms, such as lane keep assistant (LKA) and lane departure warning (LDW) on a fixed-point DSP. We first present methods that address the challenges and requirements of fixed-point design process. The flow proposed is targeted at converting C/C++ code with floating-point operations into C code with integer operations that can then be fed through the native C compiler for a fixed-point DSP. Advanced code optimization and an implementation by DSP-specific, fixed-point C code generation are introduced. We then demonstrate the conversion flow on tracking example (extended Kalman filter) using synthetically generated data, and we analyze trade-offs for algorithm implementation in fixed-point arithmetic. By using the techniques described in this chapter speed can be increased by a factor of up to 10 compared to floating-point emulation on fixed-point hardware.

9.1 Introduction

The design flow of computer vision algorithms usually begins with their implementation in floating-point on a PC or workstation. This abstraction from all implementation effects allows an exploration of the algorithm space. Memory, throughput, and word-length requirements may not be important issues for off-line implementation of the algorithms, but they can become critical issues for real-time implementations on embedded processors. The implementation of computer vision systems is faced with practical constraints because these algorithms usually need to run in real-time on fixed-point digital signal processors (DSPs) to reduce total hardware cost [2-4].

The first step in developing a camera-based steering assistance system is crafting algorithms to allow for the robust detection of lane boundaries. Several models for

Zoran Nikolić
Texas Instruments, Inc., Houston, TX, USA, e-mail: nikolicz@ti.com

177

lane boundaries have been proposed in the literature with a diversity of approaches
[5, 10, 15, 17]. Usually, the front end processing stages of the camera-based steering assistance systems involve pixel intensive calculations, such as noise filtering,
detecting edge points, grouping them as lines and selecting lane boundary lines.
The front end processing stages usually allow highly parallel execution and can be
completed in fixed-point arithmetic.

The final stage of steering assist algorithms often rely on floating-point arithmetic. In these systems, feature extraction and position tracking are often combined
into a closed loop feedback system in which the tracked lane position defines a priori
estimate of the location and orientation of the extracted features. The steering assistance algorithms require a road and vehicle model that retains accuracy for distances
of at least 30–40 m. This is required because a prediction of the vehicle trajectory at
least one second ahead of the vehicle is necessary in critical situations when driver
assistance systems are most useful.

The most common tracking technique used in lateral position detection systems
is extended Kalman filtering [10, 17]. The extended Kalman filter not only delivers
improved measurements of the run of the curve, but also a precise estimate of the
lateral position.

By implementing the algorithms in fixed-point, the correctness of the result is
compromised. Accuracy bounds for camera-based lateral position detection systems
must be determined in order to understand trade-offs of implementation in fixed-
point arithmetic. In other words, is a fast, but possibly inexact, system implementation in fixed-point arithmetic more acceptable than a slow but correct solution?

The design flow proposed in this chapter is targeted at converting C/C++ code
with floating-point operations into C code with integer operations that can then be
fed through the native C compiler for various DSPs.

Some published approaches for floating-point to fixed-point conversion use an
analytic approach for range and error estimation [11, 16], while others use a statistical approach [2, 3, 9].

The advantages of analytic techniques are that they do not require simulation
stimulus and can be faster. However, they tend to produce more conservative word-
length results. The advantage of statistical techniques is that they do not require a
range or error model. However, they often need long simulation time and tend to be
less accurate in determining word-lengths.

The semi-automated approach proposed in this section utilizes simulation-based
profiling to excite internal signals and obtain reliable dynamic range information [2].
During the simulation, the statistical information is collected for variables specified
for tracking. Those variables are usually the floating-point variables which are to be
converted to fixed-point.

The proposed design flow relies on the following main concepts:

- The range estimation software tool which semi-automatically transforms algorithms from C/C++ floating-point to a bit-true fixed-point representation that
  achieve maximum accuracy.
- Software tool support for generic fixed-point, data types. This allows modeling
  of the fixed-point behavior of the system on a PC.

- Seamless design flow from bit-true fixed-point simulation on a PC down to system implementation, generating optimized input for DSP compilers.

This chapter is organized as follows: the remainder of Section 9.1 gives an overview of floating-point and fixed-point design process. In Section 9.2 we give a brief overview of fixed-point arithmetic. In Section 9.3 we present the dynamic range estimation process: the quantization, bit true fixed-point simulation and tools for DSP specific optimization and porting of bit-true fixed-point algorithms to a fixed-point DSP. In Section 9.4 we evaluate numerical requirements for fixed-point implementation of camera-based lateral position detection algorithms, such as lane keep assistant and lane departure warning. The results are discussed and conclusions on performance of fixed-point implementation of camera based lateral position detection algorithms are drawn in Section 9.5.

9.1.1 Fixed-Point vs. Floating-Point Arithmetic Design Process

DSPs are divided into two broad categories: fixed-point and floating-point [18]. Computer Vision algorithms often rely on floating-point arithmetic and long word lengths for high precision, whereas digital hardware implementations of these algorithms need fixed-point representation to reduce total hardware costs. In general, the cutting-edge, fixed-point families tend to be fast, low power and low cost, while floating-point processors offer high precision and wide dynamic range.

Fig. 9.1 shows a chart about how DSP performance has increased over the last decade. The performance in this chart is characterized by number of multiply-accumulate (MAC) operations that can execute in parallel. The latest fixed-point DSP processors run at clock rates that are approximately three times higher and perform four times more 16×16 MAC operations in parallel than floating-point DSPs.

Therefore, there is considerable interest in making floating-point implementations of numerical algebra algorithms used in computer vision amenable to fixed-point implementation.

Often more than 50% of the implementation time is spent on the algorithmic transformation to the fixed-point level for complex designs once the floating-point model has been specified [2,11]. Design flow—in a case when the floating-point implementation needs to be mapped to fixed-point—is more complicated for several reasons:

- The quantization is generally highly dependent on the stimuli applied;
- It is difficult to find fixed-point system representation that optimally maps to system model developed in floating-point. Analytical methods for evaluating the fixed-point performance based on signal theory are only applicable for systems with a low complexity [2, 11]. Selecting optimum fixed-point representation is a nonlinear process, and exploration of the fixed-point design space cannot be done without extensive system simulation;

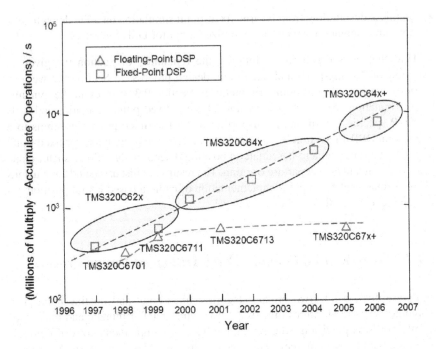

Fig. 9.1 DSP Performance trend.

- C/C++ does not support fixed-point formats. Modeling of a bit-true fixed-point system in C/C++ is difficult and slow.
- Due to sensitivity to quantization noise or high signal dynamics, some algorithms are difficult to implement in fixed-point. In these cases algorithmic alternatives need to be employed.

One approach to alleviate these problems when targeting fixed-point DSPs is to use floating-point emulation in a high level C/C++ language. However, this method severely sacrifices the execution speed because a floating-point operation is compiled into several fixed-point instructions. To solve these problems, a flow that converts a floating-point C/C++ algorithm into a fixed-point version is developed. A typical fixed-point design flow is depicted in Fig. 9.2.

9.1.2 Code Conversion

Conversion of a complete floating-point model to fixed-point can be time consuming, especially for complex systems. To speed up the porting process, only the most time consuming floating-point functions can be converted to fixed-point arithmetic. The system is divided into subsections and each subsection is benchmarked for

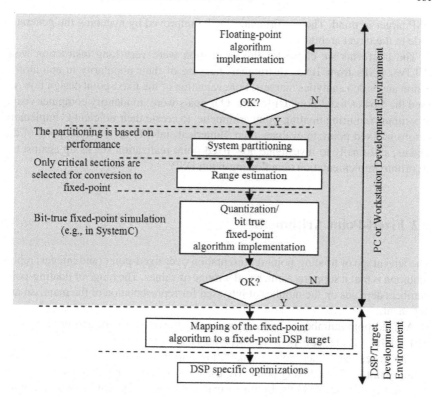

Fig. 9.2 Fixed-point design process.

performance. Based on the benchmark results functions critical to system performance are identified and only the critical floating-point functions are selected for conversion to fixed-point representation.

During the quantization process a bit-true, fixed-point system representation is built. The bit true fixed-point system model is run on a PC or a workstation. For efficient modeling of fixed-point bit-true system representation, language extensions implementing generic fixed-point data types are necessary. C/C++ does not support fixed-point data types and hence fixed-point modeling using pure ANSI C becomes a very tedious and error-prone task. Fixed-point language extensions implemented as libraries in C++ offer a high modeling efficiency [6, 7, 12]. The simulation speed of these libraries, on the other hand, is rather poor.

After validation on a PC or workstation, the quantized bit-true system is intended for implementation in software on a programmable fixed-point DSP. Here the bit-true system-level model developed during quantization serves as a "golden" reference for the target implementation which yields bit-by-bit the same results. To reach a high level of efficiency the designer has to keep the special requirements of the

DSP target in mind. The performance can be improved by matching the generated code to the target architecture.

The platforms we chose for this evaluation were very long instruction word (VLIW) DSPs from Texas Instruments because of their popularity in automotive vision and video analytics markets. For evaluation of the fixed-point design flow we used the C64x+ fixed-point CPU core. Our goals were: to identify computer vision algorithms requiring floating-point arithmetic, to create their efficient C implementations in fixed-point, to evaluate their numerical stability on the fixed-point of the C64x+, and finally to investigate how fixed-point realization stacks up against the algorithm implementation on a floating-point DSP.

9.2 Fixed-Point Arithmetic

The advantage of floating-point representation over fixed-point (and integer) representation is that it supports a much wider range of values. The range of floating-point numbers depends on the number of bits used for representation of the mantissa and exponent.

A fixed-point number consists of two parts: the integer part, and the fractional part, while '.' is the radix point that separates these two parts.

The generalized fixed-point format allows arbitrary binary-point location. The binary point is also called Q-point. We use the standard Q notation Qn where n is the number of fractional bits. In this format, the location of the binary point, or the integer word-length, is determined by the statistical magnitude, or range of signal not to cause overflows.

For a bit-true and implementation independent specification of a fixed-point operand, a triple is necessary: the *word length WL*, the *integer word length IWL*, and the *sign S*. For every fixed-point format, two of the three parameters WL, IWL, and FWL (fractional word length) are independent; the third parameter can always be calculated from the other two, $WL = IWL + FWL$.

9.3 Process of Dynamic Range Estimation

The proposed conversion flow involves the following steps: range estimation, bit true fixed-point simulation, and algorithm porting to a fixed-point DSP.

9.3.1 Dynamic Range Estimation

During conversion from floating-point to fixed-point, a range of selected variables is mapped from floating-point to fixed-point space. In this case, during the dynamic range estimation process, the word-length (WL) is kept constant (WL is constrained by the DSP architecture).

The floating-point simulation model is prepared for range estimation by changing the variable declaration from *float* to *ti_float*. The simulation model code must be compiled and linked with the overloaded operators of the *ti_float* class. The Microsoft Visual C++ compiler, version 6.0, is used throughout the floating-point and range estimation development.

The method is minimally intrusive to the original floating-point C/C++ code and has a uniform way of support for multidimensional arrays and pointers. The only modification required to the existing C/C++ code is marking the variables whose fixed-point behavior is to be examined with the range estimation directives. The range estimator then finds the statistics of internal signals throughout the floating-point simulation using real inputs and determines scaling parameters.

To minimize intrusion to the original floating-point C or C++ program for range estimation, the operator overloading characteristics of C++ are exploited. The new data class for tracing the signal statistics is named as *ti_float*. In order to prepare a range estimation model of a C or C++ digital signal processing program, it is only necessary to change the type of variables from *float* or *double* to *ti_float*, since the class in C++ is also a *type* of variable defined by users. The class not only computes the current value, but also keeps records of the variable in a linked list which is declared as its private static member. Thus, when the simulation is completed, the range of a variable declared as class is readily available from the records stored in the class.

Class *statistics* is used to keep track of the minimum, maximum, standard deviation, overflow, underflow and histogram of a floating-point variable associated with it. All instances of class *statistics* are stored in a linked-list class *VarList*. The linked list *VarList* is a static member of class *ti_float*. Every time a new variable is declared as a *ti_float*, a new object of class *statistics* is created. The new *statistics* object is linked to the last element in the linked list *VarList*, and associated with the variable. Statistics information for all floating-point variables declared as *ti_float* is tracked and recorded in the *VarList* linked list. By declaring linked list of *statistics* objects as a static member of class *ti_float* we achieved that every instance of the object *ti_float* has access to the list. This approach minimizes intrusion to the original floating-point C/C++ code. Structure of class *ti_float* is shown in Fig. 9.3.

Every time a variable, declared as *ti_float*, is assigned a value during simulation, in order to update the variable statistics, the *ti_float* class searches through the linked list *VarList* for the *statistics* object which was associated with the variable.

The declaration of a variable as *ti_float* also creates association between the variable name and function name. This association is used to differentiate between variables with the same names in different functions. Pointers and arrays, as frequently used in ANSI C, are supported as well.

Declaration syntax for *ti_float* is:

$$ti\_float\ <var\_name>(\text{``}<func\_name>\text{''},\text{``}<var\_name>\text{''});$$

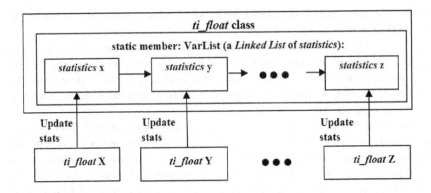

Fig. 9.3 *ti_float* class composition.

where *<var_name>* is name of floating-point variable designated for dynamic range tracking, and *<func_name>* is name of function where the variable is declared.

In the case where the dynamic range of the multidimensional array of *float* needs to be determined, the array declaration must be changed from:

$$float \ <var\_name>[<M>]\dots[<Z>];$$

to:

$$ti\_float \ <var\_name>[<M>]\dots[<Z>] =$$
$$= ti\_float("<func\_name>","<var\_name>", <M>*\dots*<Z>);$$

Please note that declaration of multi dimensional array of *ti_float* can be uniformly extended to any dimension. The declaration syntax keeps the same format for a one-, two-, three-, and *n*-dimensional array of *ti_float*. In the declaration, *<var_name>* is the name of the floating-point array selected for dynamic range tracking. The *<func_name>* is name of function where the array is declared. The third element in the declaration of the array of *ti_float* is size. Array size is defined by multiplying sizes of each array dimension.

In the case of multidimensional *ti_float* arrays only one *statistics* object is created to keep track of statistics information of the whole array. In other words, *ti_float* class keeps statistic information for array at array level and not for each array element. The product defined as the third element in the declaration defines the array size.

The *ti_float* class overloads arithmetic and relational operators. Hence, basic arithmetic operations such as addition, subtraction, multiplication, and division are conducted automatically for variables. This property is also applicable to relational operators, such as ==, >, <, >=, !=, and <=. Therefore, any *ti_float* instance can be compared with floating-point variables and constants. The contents, or private members, of a variable declared by the class are updated when the variable is assigned by one of the assignment operators, such as =, +=, -=, *=, and /=.

The dynamic range information is gathered during the simulation for each variable declared as *ti_float*. The statistical range of a variable is estimated by using histogram, standard deviation, minimum, and maximum value. In this case, a large floating-point dynamic range is mapped to one of 32 possible fixed-point formats. To identify the best fixed-point format the variable values are tracked by using a histogram with 32 bins. Each of these bins represents one Q-format. Every time during simulation the tracked floating-point variable is assigned a value, a corresponding Q-format representation of the value is calculated and the value is binned to a corresponding Q-point bin.

Finally, the integer word-lengths of all signals declared as *ti_float* are suggested (Q-point format in which the assigned value declared as *ti_float* can be represented with minimum IWL). The decision is made based on histogram data collected during simulation.

At the end of simulation, *ti_float* objects save collected statistics in a group of text files. Each text file corresponds to one function, and contains statistical information for variables declared as *ti_float* within that function [2].

9.3.2 Bit-True Fixed-Point Simulation

When the Q-point position is determined by the dynamic range estimation process, a fixed-point system simulation on a PC or workstation is required to validate if achieved fixed-point performance is satisfactory.

Since ANSI C or C++ offer no efficient support for fixed-point data types, it is not possible to easily carry the fixed-point simulation in pure ANSI C or C++.

The SystemC fixed-point data types, cast operators, and interpolator directives are utilized in proposed design flow [2, 7, 11]. Since ANSI C is a subset of SystemC, the additional fixed-point constructs can be used as bit-true annotations to dedicated operands of the original floating-point ANSI C file, resulting in a hybrid specification. This partially fixed-point code is used for simulation.

9.3.3 Customization of the Bit-True Fixed-Point Algorithm to a Fixed-Point DSP

In this study, we have chosen the TMS320DM6437™DSP with C64x+ fixed-point VLIW CPU and its C compiler as an implementation target [8].

Compiling the bit-true SystemC fixed-point model by using a target DSP compiler does not give optimum performance [2, 11]. The C64x+ DSP compilers support C++ language constructs, but compiling the fixed-point libraries for the DSP is not a viable alternative as the implementation of the generic data types makes extensive use of operator overloading, templates, and dynamic memory management.

This will render fixed-point operations rather inefficient compared to integer arithmetic performed on a DSP. Therefore, target-specific code generation is necessary.

The C64x+ IQmath library is a highly optimized mathematical function library for C/C++ programmers to seamlessly port the bit-true fixed-point algorithm into fixed-point code on the C64x+ family of DSP devices [6, 8]. The resulting system enables automated conversion of the most frequently used ANSI math libraries by replacing these calls with versions coded using portable fixed-point ANSI C.

The C code functions from IQmath library compile into efficient C64x+ assembly code. The IQmath functions are implemented by using C64x+ specific C language extensions (intrinsics) and compiler directives to restructure the off-the-shelf C code while maintaining functional equivalence to the original code [6].

Since the IQmath library functions are implemented in C, it is possible to recompile and run fixed-point target DSP code on a PC or workstation providing that DSP intrinsics library for the host is available.

9.4 Implementation Considerations for Single-Camera Steering Assistance Systems on a Fixed-Point DSP

In this section we evaluate numerical requirements for implementation of camera-based lateral position detection algorithms, such as lane keep assistant (LKA) and lane departure warning (LDW). We will determine the bound on the accuracy for a configuration typically used in camera-based steering assist applications. In turn, these bounds determine what steps must be made to achieve acceptable performance and the precision level required by tasks such as road modeling and road parameter tracking. We then demonstrate the conversion flow presented in the previous sections on tracking example (extended Kalman filter) using synthetically generated data, and we analyze trade-offs for algorithm implementation in fixed-point arithmetic [3].

9.4.1 System Considerations

The vision system described in this section is based on a single forward looking camera mounted between the rear-view mirror and the windshield. The system detects lane boundary lines and estimates road parameters by analyzing images taken by the onboard camera. The road parameters are used to warn a driver that the vehicle may be departing from a lane or assist the driver to keep to the center of a lane. In the case of LDW, a mechanism is designed to warn the driver when the vehicle begins to move out of its lane (unless a turn signal is on in that direction). The LKA system senses the vehicle leaving the lane and automatically pulls it back.

To optimize the speed performance of the algorithms, only compiler-driven optimization is used. In order to maintain portability and to keep simple mapping between the different stages of the float-to-fixed conversion flow, we did not change the original algorithms and the algorithm implementation is kept in C/C++.

To evaluate algorithm performance in fixed-point we used TMS320C6437 DSP (C64x+ CPU core).

9.4.1.1 Accuracy of the Camera System

Since we have only a single camera, we must estimate the range using perspective. Fig. 9.4 depicts the relationship between the camera and the plane of the road, together with a schematic diagram of the image plane coordinates $u = -y_c$ and $w = -z_c$.

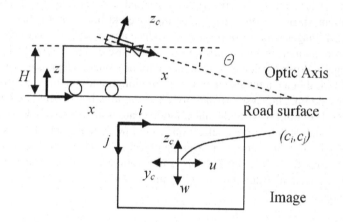

Fig. 9.4 Vehicle, road, and image coordinate systems. Road y-axis points into the page.

The relationship between u, w and ground plane coordinates x, y is:

$$x = \frac{-H\cos\theta - wH\sin\theta}{w\cos\theta + \sin\theta} \qquad y = -u(x\cos\theta + H\sin\theta) \qquad (9.1)$$

where the relationships between image plane coordinates u and w and pixel coordinates i and j are:

$$u = \frac{i - c_i}{f_i}p_i \qquad w = \frac{j - c_j}{f_j}p_j \qquad (9.2)$$

c_i and c_j is the pixel location at which the camera's optic axis intersects the image plane, p_i and p_j are pixel dimensions in i and j direction, respectively, and f_i and f_j are the effective focal lengths of the camera in the i and j directions, respectively. In (1), H and θ represent the height of the camera and pitch, respectively. Equations (1) and (2) require calibration of both extrinsic (H, θ) and intrinsic camera parameters

(f_i, f_j, c_i, c_j). The error Δx in range x for a stationary vehicle can be derived by using (1) and (2):

$$\Delta x = \frac{x^2 p_j}{H f_i (\cos\theta - w\sin\theta)^2} \Delta j \qquad (9.3)$$

The error increases as quadratic function of distance and percentage of error in depth $\Delta x / x$ increases linearly. The error Δy along y axis for a stationary vehicle can be derived from (1):

$$\Delta y = \frac{(-x\cos\theta - H\sin\theta)p_i}{f_i} \Delta i \qquad (9.4)$$

The error along y axis increases as linear function of distance.

The errors Δx and Δy are directly proportional to pixel size. By shrinking the pixel element, measurement error can be improved in both x and y directions. For example, an imager with 6 μm pixel will produce an error almost as twice as large as error from an imager with 3.6 μm pixel. In the case of a moving vehicle, motion blurs imagery. When motion is fast compared to the camera integration time, details become blurred in a captured frame. Linear motion includes both target movement (relative to the imaging system) and motion of the imaging system (stationary target). As a rule of thumb, when the linear motion causes an image shift less than 20% of the pixel size, it has minimal effect on system performance [1]. If v_x is average object velocity in x direction, v_y is average object velocity in y direction and Δt is integration time then target moves during integration time over distance $v_x \Delta t$ in x direction and $v_r \Delta t$ in y direction. In (i, j) image coordinates, considering (3), this corresponds to:

$$\Delta j = \frac{H f_j (\cos\theta - w\sin\theta)^2}{p_j x^2} v_x \Delta t \qquad \Delta i = \frac{f_j}{(-x\cos\theta - H\sin\theta)p_i} v_y \Delta t \qquad (9.5)$$

According to (9.5), error caused by linear motion affects moving objects close to the camera. In the case integration time Δt is 1 ms, a 7 mm lens camera is mounted at $H = 1.2$ m and object is moving at speed of 100 km/h, moving error can be neglected only for moving objects that are further than approximately 14 m from the camera. For high speeds and for long integration time, higher error is introduced and the error at short ranges can not be ignored. Imaging sensors with smaller pixel size are more sensitive to errors caused by moving objects.

Total error produced by the imager is the sum of stationary error (9.3), (9.4), and error caused by motion (9.5).

Based on this discussion, for an imager with 6 μm pixel, the number of fractional bits needed to represent distance from the camera is dictated by system accuracy at close range, as in formulas (9.3) and (9.4). Maximum operating range of the system dictates the number of required integer bits.

Based on the above discussion, motion blur is limiting accuracy to around 0.04 m at close range in cases when the vehicle is moving at high speeds. In the case of a slowly moving vehicle, motion blur can be neglected and camera accuracy for objects near to the imager becomes close to 0.003 m (dictated by (3)). Therefore, nine fractional bits are sufficient to describe this accuracy in cases when the motion blur can be neglected (for high vehicle speeds only five of nine fractional bits will be accurate). Typical operational range for these systems is 30–40 m; therefore, six integer bits are sufficient.

Clearly, range can be represented by using a fixed-point number with at least 15 bits (six binary digits should be reserved for integer part and nine bits should be dedicated for fractional part).

According to (9.4), lateral offset y requires approximately nine fractional bits at ranges close to the camera and only around four fractional bits at ranges of 50 m (assuming $H = 1.2$ m and imager with pixel size of 6 μm).

9.4.1.2 Vehicle and Road Modeling

Road modeling can be effective in increasing system performance by helping eliminate false positives via outlier removal. A simple parabolic road model incorporates position, angle, and curvature while approximating a clothoid model commonly used in the construction of highway roads [17]:

$$y(x,t) = y_0(t) + x(t)\tan\varepsilon(t) + \frac{C_0(t)}{2}x^2(t) \qquad (9.6)$$

In this equation, y is the lateral position of the road center with respect to the vehicle, and x the distance ahead, $\varepsilon(t)$ the bearing of the vehicle with respect to the center-line of the lane, and C_0 represents the curvature of the lane ahead of the vehicle. Usually, the steering assistance systems use a state vector (denoted at discrete time) that describes both the position of the vehicle and the geometry of the road ahead [17]:

$$s(t) = [y_0(t) \quad \tan\varepsilon(t) \quad C_0(t) \quad W(t) \quad \theta(t)]^T \qquad (9.7)$$

In (9.7) $W(t)$ represents the width of the lane and $\theta(t)$ the pitch of the camera to the road surface, which is assumed to be flat within the working range of our system.

The steering assistance system is designed to estimate parameters related to the road structure and the vehicle position in the lane. Based on observations from imaging sensors, road parameters are reconstructed. The coordinates of points on the lane boundary lines are used for estimating road parameters.

The most common estimation technique used in lateral position detection systems is extended Kalman filtering. The extended Kalman filter is a recursive observer that uses the actual measurements to correct the predicted state [17]. The vehicle dynamics are usually approximated using a bicycle model similar to that used in [17].

The extended Kalman filter usually calls for implementation in floating-point arithmetic. Since a majority of modern DSP processors are using fixed-point arithmetic to run this algorithm on an embedded target, one would either have to:

- Resort to floating-point emulation on a fixed-point DSP, or
- Convert the floating-point implementation to fixed-point arithmetic and port to a target DSP device.

A floating-point emulation approach severely sacrifices the execution speed. On the other hand, converting the complex algorithm from floating-point to fixed-point arithmetic by hand is a time-consuming task.

For fixed-point representation elements of the state vector $s(t)$ in (9.6) and (9.7) require at least nine fractional bits of precision when presented in fixed-point format (as discussed in the previous section).

9.5 Results

The conventional implementation of the Kalman filter—in terms of covariance matrices—is particularly sensitive to round-off errors. Although Kalman filtering has been called "ideally suited to digital computer implementation," the digital computer is not ideally suited to the task. Many methods have been developed for decreasing the sensitivity of the Kalman filter to round-off errors. The most successful approaches use alternative representation of covariance matrix of estimation uncertainty, in terms of symmetric products of triangular factors. Bierman's algorithm is one of the more stable implementations of the Kalman filter observational update [13, 14]. We used methodology described in this chapter to convert the Bierman's implementation of the extended Kalman filter from floating-point to fixed-point arithmetic.

Each cycle of the estimation process consist of two phases:

- *Time Update.* Using the model of the system behavior [17], the state vector estimated at time n is propagated to the next time step $n + 1$. With the measurement, the positions of the markings in the next time step can be estimated.
- *Observation Update Phase.* Depending on the predicted state and the actual measurements, a new state of the system is calculated such that the estimation error is minimized.

Test vector data used for the dynamic range estimation step was synthetically generated by using MATLAB [12]. Synthetically generated data is extremely useful for evaluating fixed-point implementation of the extended Kalman filter, since the location of all errors in the generated data is known. To construct the test vectors we used a clothoid road model and we generated test vectors by simulating a vehicle moving at various speeds down the road while we varied the road curvature parameters. To make the data more realistic, artificial noise is added to the test vectors.

During the simulation, the dynamic range of all floating-point variables in critical functions is tracked (Bierman observational update, Thronton time update and Jacobian matrix calculations).

After the optimum fixed-point format for each variable is found, bit true fixed-point simulation is performed in SystemC. Once numerical stability and accuracy is verified, the bit true fixed-point model is ported to the embedded platform using the IQmath (in our case, the fixed-point C64x+ CPU).

Performance numbers for two implementations of extended Kalman filter on fixed-point DSP are given in Table 9.1. Results in Table 9.1 assume 10-pixel observation vector (the number of lane boundary points used in the estimation).

Table 9.1 Floating-point emulation vs. fixed-point arithmetic on fixed-point C64x+ CPU.

C64x+ CPU cycles	Floating-point Emulation	Fixed-Point Arithmetic
Thornton time update	36,533	24,985
Bierman observation update	103,558	65,406
Jacobian matrix calculation	29,758	3,849

The maximum performance can be achieved only when inline function expansion along with maximum optimization and file level optimization compiler switches are used.

Execution time for two implementations of the extended Kalman filter on a C64x+ CPU core running at 500 MHz for different observation vector dimensions (number of lane boundary points) is shown in Fig. 9.5.

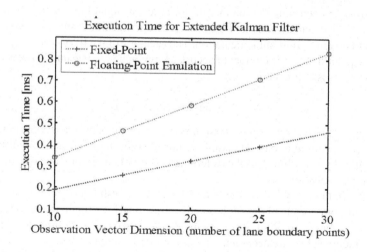

Fig. 9.5 Execution time of the extended Kalman filter on fixed-point C64x+ CPU running at 500 MHz.

The implementation of the Thornton time update and Bierman observation update functions in fixed-point arithmetic is around 1.5 times faster than implementations using floating-point emulation. Calculating the Jacobian in fixed-point arithmetic is about 7.7 times faster than implementation using floating-point emulation. Efficient IQmath implementations of trigonometric functions, and division and multiply operations contribute to a significant speed improvements when the Jacobian matrix is realized in fixed-point.

The main advantage of floating-point over fixed-point is its constant relative accuracy. The quantization error gets compounded through error propagation as more arithmetic operations are performed on approximated values. The error can grow with each arithmetic operation until the result no longer represents the true value. With floating-point data types, precision remains approximately constant over most of the dynamic range while with fixed-point types, in contrast, the signal-to-quantization noise ratio increases as the signal decreases in amplitude. To maintain high levels of precision, the signal must be kept within a certain range, large enough to maintain a high signal-to-quantization noise ratio, but small enough to remain within the dynamic range supported by the fixed-point data type. This provides motivation for defining optimal fixed-point data types for algorithm variables.

Fixed-point number formats use trade-off between dynamic range and accuracy [2]. In this implementation, 32-bit target DSP architecture forces trade-offs between dynamic range and precision. The 32-bits are divided to integer part (characterize dynamic range) and fractional part (define precision). To perform an arithmetic operation between two fixed-point numbers, they must be converted to same fixed-point format. Since WL of the DSP architecture is 32-bit long conversion between different fixed-point formats is associated with loss of accuracy.

The basic operations such as square root and division can be very sensitive to the operand noise [2].

In order to determine the number of accurate fractional bits for the fixed-point version of the extended Kalman filter, we compared tracking results between fixed-point and floating-point implementation. The accuracy of the fixed-point implementation is quantified by the number of accurate fractional bits. The number of accurate fractional bits is defined by:

$$N = \lceil -(\log_2 \max |f_{xp} - f_p|) \rceil$$

where $\max |f_{xp} - f_p|$ represents maximum absolute error between floating-point and fixed-point representations. The value obtained from the fixed-point algorithm is represented by f_{xp}, while f_p is the (reference) value obtained from the exact floating-point implementation.

Based on the input test vectors, the dynamic range estimation tool recommends $Q29$ fixed-point format (3 integer bits and 29 fractional bits) for elements of the state vector $s(t)$. Due to the algorithm implementation in fixed-point arithmetic, not all of the 29 fractional bits are accurate. The minimum required number of accurate fractional bits for correct system representation is estimated in previous sections. The number of accurate fractional bits for fixed-point implementation of the extended Kalman filter is presented in Table 9.2.

Table 9.2 Accuracy of state variables for the extended Kalman filter implementation in fixed-point arithmetic on a C64x+ CPU.

	$Y(t)$	$\tan\varepsilon(t)$	$C_0(t)$
Accurate fractional bits	19	23	27

Fixed-point implementation of the extended Kalman filter provides a higher number of accurate fractional bits than the minimum outlined in section discussing accuracy of the camera system (elements of the state vector $s(t)$ need to be represented with at least nine accurate fractional bits).

Therefore, implementation of the tracking algorithm in fixed-point arithmetic satisfies accuracy requirements outlined and offers significant improvements in calculation speed.

Further performance improvement of the fixed-point realization of the selected numerical algorithms can be achieved by hand-optimized implementation in assembly language. Since writing hand optimized assembly is a tedious and time-consuming task, this step is recommended only in cases when C compiler optimizations are not sufficient and an absolute maximum performance is required. The algorithm realization in C language offers portability and ease of maintenance, and these are typically lost in the case of hand-optimized assembly implementations.

9.6 Conclusions

The primary goal of this chapter was to address implementation aspects of the single-camera steering assist algorithms on fixed-point DSPs. The camera system accuracy bounds are used as guidelines for fixed-point implementation. Floating-point representation already approximates values and in this chapter we evaluated another approximation that is less accurate than floating-point, but provides for an increase in speed. Greater precision costs more computation time, so designers must consider the trade-off carefully. Speed for accuracy is an important trade-off and its applicability should be examined at each level that abstracts floating-point arithmetic.

The software tools presented in this chapter semi-automatically convert floating-point algorithms implemented in C/C+ to fixed-point algorithms that achieve maximum accuracy. We also compared performance between floating-point and fixed-point implementation of the extended Kalman filter in a computer model of a camera-based steering assist system. The algorithm considered here proved to be numerically stable in fixed-point arithmetic.

By implementation in fixed-point, a significant speed increase can be achieved compared to floating-point emulation. The high performance was achieved by using only compiler optimization techniques. It is possible to achieve even further performance improvement by careful analysis and code restructuring.

All phases of the fixed-point design flow discussed in the chapter are based on C/C++ language implementation, which makes it maintainable, readable, and applicable to a number of different platforms on which the flow can execute correctly and reliably.

References

1. G. C. Holst, *CCD Arrays Cameras and Displays,* SPIE Optical Engineering Press, 1996.
2. Z. Nikolić, H. T. Nguyen, and G. Frantz, Design and implementation of numerical linear algebra algorithms on fixed-point DSPs, *EURASIP Journal on Advances in Signal Processing,* 2007.
3. Z. Nikolić, Implementation considerations for single-camera steering assistance systems on a fixed-point DSP, *Proc. IEEE Intelligent Vehicles Symposium 2008,* Eindhoven, The Netherlands, June 2008.
4. B. Kisačanin, Examples of low-level computer vision on media processors. *Proc. IEEE CVPR, ECV Workshop,* 2005.
5. E. D. Dickmanns, A. Zapp, A curvature-based scheme for improving road vehicle guidance by computer vision. *Proceedings SPIE Conference on Mobile Robots,* Vol. 727, Oct. 1986.
6. C64x+ IQMath Library: A Virtual Floating-Point Engine, Module User's Guide, v2.1.1, Texas Instruments, 2007. Available: http://focus.ti.com/docs/toolsw/folders/print/sprc542.html.
7. IEEE Std 1666-2005 IEEE Standard SystemC Language Reference Manual, Available: http://standards.ieee.org/getieee/1666/download/1666-2005.pdf.
8. TMS320DM6437 Digital Media Processor Datasheet, Texas Instruments, Nov 2007, Available: http://focus.ti.com/docs/prod/folders/print/tms320dm6437.html.
9. S. Kim, K.-I. I. Kum, and W. Sung, Fixed-point optimization utility for C and C++ based digital signal processing programs, *IEEE Transactions on Circuits and Systems II: Analog and Digital Signal Processing,* vol. 45, no. 11, pp. 1455-1464, 1998.
10. E. D. Dickmanns and B.D. Mysliwetz, Recursive 3D road and relative ego-state recognition, *IEEE Transaction On Pattern Analysis and Machine Intelligence,* Vol. 14, No.2, February 1992.
11. M. Coors, H. Keding, O. Lúthje, and H. Meyr, Design and DSP implementation of fixed-point systems, *EURASIP Journal on Applied Signal Processing,* vol. 2002, no. 9, pp. 908-925, 2002.
12. "Matlab, the Language of Technical Computing," Function Reference, Version 7, The Mathworks 2006.
13. G. Bierman, Measurement updating using the U-D factorization, *14th Symposium on Adaptive Processes,* 1975 IEEE Conference, Volume: 14, pp. 337-346, Dec. 1975.
14. G. Bierman, C. Thornton, Numerical comparison of discrete Kalman filter algorithms: Orbit Determination case study, *15th Symposium on Adaptive Processes,* 1976 IEEE Conference, Volume: 15, pp. 859-872, Dec. 1976.
15. M. Bertozzi and A. Broggi, Real-time lane and obstacle detection on the gold system, *Proceedings of IEEE Intelligent Vehicles Symposium,* pp. 213-218, 1996.
16. C. Shi and R. W. Brodersen, Automated fixed-point data-type optimization tool for signal processing and communication systems, *Proceedings of 41st Annual Conference on Design Automation,* pp. 478-483, San Diego, Calif, June 2004.
17. A. Watanabe and M. Nishida, Lane detection for a steering assistance system, *Proceedings of the 2005 IEEE Intelligent Vehicles Symposium,* pp. 159-164, 2005.
18. G. Frantz and R. Simar, Comparing fixed- and floating-point DSPs," SPRY061, Texas Instruments, 2004. Available: http://focus.ti.com/lit/wp/spry061/spry061.pdf.

Chapter 10
Towards OpenVL: Improving Real-Time Performance of Computer Vision Applications

Changsong Shen, James J. Little, and Sidney Fels

Abstract Meeting constraints for real-time performance is a main issue for computer vision, especially for embedded computer vision systems. This chapter presents our progress on our open vision library (OpenVL), a novel software architecture to address efficiency through facilitating hardware acceleration, reusability, and scalability for computer vision systems. A logical image understanding pipeline is introduced to allow parallel processing. We also discuss progress on our middleware—vision library utility toolkit (VLUT)—that enables applications to operate transparently over a heterogeneous collection of hardware implementations. OpenVL works as a state machine, with an event-driven mechanism to provide users with application-level interaction. Various explicit or implicit synchronization and communication methods are supported among distributed processes in the logical pipelines. The intent of OpenVL is to allow users to quickly and easily recover useful information from multiple scenes, in a cross-platform, cross-language manner across various software environments and hardware platforms. To validate the critical underlying concepts of OpenVL, a human tracking system and a local positioning system are implemented and described. The novel architecture separates the specification of algorithmic details from the underlying implementation, allowing for different components to be implemented on an embedded system without recompiling code.

10.1 Introduction

Computer vision technology is profoundly changing a number of areas, such as human-computer interaction and robotics, through its interpretation of real-world scenes from two-dimensional projections. However, building computer vision

Changsong Shen, James J. Little, Sidney S. Fels
University of British Columbia, Vancouver, BC, Canada
e-mail: csshen@ece.ubc.ca, little@cs.ubc.ca, ssfels@ece.ubc.ca

systems remains difficult because of software engineering issues such as efficiency, reusability, and scalability. Especially when computer vision technology is applied in embedded systems, in which real-time performance is emphasized, these issues become critical. In a field with as rich a theoretical history as computer vision, software engineering issues, like system implementation, are often regarded as outside the mainstream and secondary to the pure theoretical research. Nevertheless, system implementations can dramatically promote the progress and mainstream applicability of a field, just like the success of OpenGL promoted the development of hardware acceleration coupled with significant theoretical progress in computer graphics.

In current computer vision, there are three main system implementation issues. The first issue is *efficiency*. Most video operations are computationally intensive tasks that are difficult to accomplish using traditional processors. For example, for a single camera with a sequence of 24-bit RGB color images at a typical resolution (640×480 pixels) and frame rate ($30\,fps$), the overall data volume to be processed is 27 MB/s. Moreover, even for a very low-level process such as edge detection, hundreds or even thousands of elementary operations per pixel are needed [7]. However, many computer vision applications, such as nearly all surveillance systems, require real-time performance, which means that the systems must interact with their environments under response-time constraints. Improving efficiency of the algorithms helps to meet these constraints.

The second issue is *reusability*. Hardware designers have developed various dedicated computer vision processing platforms [7, 9] to overcome the problem of intensive computation. However, these solutions have created another problem: heterogeneous hardware platforms have made it time-consuming and difficult (sometimes even impossible) for software developers to port their applications from one hardware platform to another.

The third issue is *scalability*. Recently, multi-camera systems have generated growing interest, especially because systems relying on a single video camera tend to restrict visual coverage. Moreover, significant decreases in camera prices have made multi-camera systems possible in practical applications. Thus, we need to provide mechanisms to maintain correspondence among separate but related video streams at the architectural level.

The open vision library (OpenVL) and its utility toolkits (VLUT) are designed to address efficiency, reusability and scalability to facilitate progress in computer vision. OpenVL, discussed in Section 10.3, provides an abstraction layer for applications developers to specify the image processing they want performed rather than how they want it performed. VLUT, discussed in Section 10.3.7, is created as a middleware layer to separate camera details, events management, and operating details from the specification of the image processing. By providing a hardware development middleware that supports different hardware architectures for acceleration, OpenVL allows code reuse without compromising performance. The novel software architecture separates the specification of algorithmic details from the underlying implementation, allowing for different components to be implemented on an embedded system without recompiling code. Further, when the embedded system's functionality changes, it is possible to change the drivers without changing the code, allowing application programmers to match the amount of embedded processing with the needs of their image processing application without rewriting any of their application code.

The next sections are organized as follows. Section 10.2 provides an overview of related work addressing the issues we mentioned above. In Section 10.3, we discuss our implementation of OpenVL and VLUT. Two example application designs are introduced in Section 10.4 as a proof of concept including how to implement them using OpenVL and VLUT. Conclusions and future works are briefly discussed in Section 10.5.

10.2 Related Work

In this section, we discuss previously published work that addresses the efficiency, reusability, and scalability issues. They are organized as follows. Section 10.2.1 discusses a widely used image processing library: OpenCV. In Section 10.2.2, we review the pipes and filters software architecture. OpenGL is also discussed in Section 10.2.3 as it provides part of the motivation behind our approach. Section 10.2.4 outlines related hardware architectures for parallel processing that are useful structures for implementing components of OpenVL.

10.2.1 OpenCV

The introduction of the OpenCV [5] is an important milestone addressing system implementation issues in computer vision. Currently it is probably the most widely used vision library for real-time extraction and processing of meaningful data from images.

The OpenCV library provides more than 500 functions whose performance can be enhanced on the Intel architecture. If available, the Intel integrated performance primitives (IPP) is used for lower-level operations for OpenCV. IPP provides a cross-platform interface to highly optimized low-level functions that perform image processing and computer vision primitive operations. IPP exists on multiple platforms including IA32, IA64, and StrongARM, and OpenCV can automatically benefit from using IPP on all of these platforms. When running applications using OpenCV, a built-in DLL switcher is called at run time to automatically detect the processor type and load the appropriate optimized DLL for that processor. If the processor type cannot be determined (or if the appropriate DLL is not available), an optimized C code DLL is used.

However, because OpenCV assumes essentially a sequential software architecture, the potential acceleration resources in computer vision are not fully exploited to improve performance. For example, many independent operations can run in parallel. The dependencies of operations are not explicitly specified in OpenCV, limiting hardware designers in fully utilizing possible speedup resources. Moreover, the OpenCV library does not provide an explicit capacity to support multi-camera streams, which limits the system scalability and puts the complexity for managing these solutions on the shoulders of application developers.

10.2.2 Pipes and Filters and Data-Flow Approaches

Compared to sequential software architecture, a pipes and filters architecture [14], which naturally supports parallel and distributed processing, is more appropriate for a system processing a stream of data. In the pipes and filters architecture, each component has a set of inputs and outputs. The components, termed *filters*, read streams of data as inputs and produce streams of data as outputs. The connectors, called *pipes*, serve as conduits for the streams, transmitting the output of one filter to the inputs of another. Fig. 10.1 illustrates this architecture.

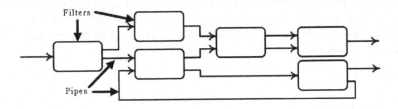

Fig. 10.1 Pipes and filters architecture. In the pipes and filters architecture, *filters* have a set of inputs and outputs. Each *pipe* implements the data flow between adjacent filters.

Jitter [6] is one example of an image library using a pipes and filters architecture. It abstracts all data as multidimensional matrices that behave as streams, so objects that process images can also process audio, volumetric data, 3D vertices, or any numerical information. Jitter's common representation simplifies the reinterpretation and transformation of media. DirectShow [12] and Khoros [10] also use pipes and filters as their underlying architecture model. The former is a library for streaming-media operations on the Microsoft Windows platform. The latter is an integrated software development environment with a collection of tools for image and digital signal processing.

The pipes and filters architecture has a number of features that make it attractive for some applications. First, this architecture allows the designer to understand the overall input/output behavior of a system as a simple composition of the behaviors of individual filters. Therefore, it is quite intuitive and relatively simple to describe, understand, and implement. It allows users to graphically create a block diagram of their applications and interactively control input, output, and system variables. Second, this architecture supports reuse: any two filters can be connected together, provided they agree on the data format being transmitted. Systems based on pipes and filters are easy to maintain and update: new filters can be added to existing systems and old filters can be replaced by improved ones. Third, the pipes and filters architecture provides an easy synchronization mechanism, because the filters do not share data with other filters. Fourth, because data-processing objects, i.e., filters, are independent, this architecture naturally supports parallel and distributed processing.

However, the general pipes and filters architecture has its own disadvantages. First, the pipes and filters architecture does not allow instructions from multiple loop iterations (or multiple calls to the same routine) to be issued simultaneously, as the simple data dependence model prevents it from differentiating between the different loop iterations (or each invocation of the routine).

Second, because filters are intended to be strictly independent entities (they do not share state information with other filters, and the only communication between filters occurs through the pipes), the pipes and filters architecture does not provide a mechanism for users to reconfigure the data flow routine in run time. This means that a pipes and filters architecture is typically not good at handling highly interactive applications that may have many branches in the data flow.

Third, each filter's output data must be copied to its downstream filter(s)' input, which can lead to massive and expensive data copying if care is not taken. Without modification, this architecture cannot efficiently broadcast data tokens or dispatch instruction tokens in a massively parallel system because of arbitrary filters' independence.

Our approach is a variation on the pipes and filters model with adjustments made to match some of the common structures found in computer vision algorithms.

10.2.3 OpenGL

The current situation in computer vision is very similar to the state of computer graphics over a decade ago. In 1992, SGI led a consortium to create OpenGL [8], an open source graphics library geared toward hardware acceleration. GLUT [8] was also successfully designed as its middleware to standardize applications' access to operating systems and hardware platforms.

In OpenGL, one of the foundations of real-time graphics is the graphics rendering pipeline. Graphics commands and data are distributed in a graphics rendering pipeline, which enables hardware designers to accelerate these common operations in each portion of the OpenGL pipeline to optimize performance. For example, all transformations of an object in OpenGL are performed using 4×4 matrices that describe translation, rotation, shear, and scaling. Multiple matrix operations use a matrix stack. Combinations of individual rotations and translations are accomplished by multiplying two or more matrices together. If an accelerated physical architecture is used to support 4×4 matrix operations, the throughput of the system is increased. Further, by supporting a logical pipeline representation of a chain of transformation operators that are based on these multiply operations, the application programmer has different perspectives upon which to program typical graphics algorithms that match concepts from the field. However, in the actual implementation, these operations can be premultiplied using a matrix stack, allowing significant increases in speed without impacting the logical structure that application coders are comfortable with.

Inspired by the success of OpenGL in promoting the development of hardware acceleration for computer graphics, we define and develop OpenVL for computer vision systems, bearing hardware acceleration, reusability, and scalability in mind. The intent of OpenVL is to allow users to *quickly* and *easily* recover useful information from *multiple* real dynamic scenes, and in a *portable* manner across various software environments and hardware platforms.

However, we cannot simply migrate the OpenGL architecture into computer vision, because the latter's processing is not exactly an inverse of computer graphics rendering. Moreover, OpenGL does not provide a mechanism for synchronization of multiple pipelines. Since multi-camera systems have generated significantly growing interest recently, we cannot ignore this issue.

10.2.4 Hardware Architecture for Parallel Processing

A variety of architectures have been developed for representing parallel processing. Flynn [3] classified them into three categories: (1) single instruction stream–multiple data stream (SIMD) (2) multiple instruction stream-single data stream (MISD) (3) multiple instruction stream–multiple data stream (MIMD). SIMD is well suited to low-level vision computing because many image processing operations in low-level are intrinsically parallel in the sense that the same rule must be applied to each of many data and the order in which the data are processed does not matter. Little et al. [11] implemented several computer vision algorithms using a set of primitive parallel operations on a SIMD parallel computer. SIMD is used in the graphics processing unit (GPU) on commodity video cards. However, SIMD is not particularly suitable for higher level processing where each operation involves lists and symbols rather than a small neighborhood and where we may wish to apply different operations to different part of the image. The flexibility of running different programs on each processing unit is provided by MIMD architecture. MISD, i.e., pipeline, can be employed to match the serial data inputs from camera to decrease the latency.

The use of hardware platforms with parallel processing is now generally accepted as necessary to support real-time image understanding applications [18]. Parallelism can be of several types: data, control, and flow. Data parallelism is the most common in computer vision. It arises from the nature of an image, a bidimensional regular data structure. Control parallelism involves processes that can be executed at the same time. The use of multiple cameras provides the potential source of control parallelism. Flow parallelism arises when an application can be decomposed into a set of serial operations working on a flow of similar data. The steady stream image data lends itself to pipelined parallelism.

OpenVL is intended to be cross-platform. Many hardware platforms are available that can be used to implement the OpenVL logical architecture. We anticipate that different drivers will be coupled with each implementation supplied by vendors to accelerate different components of the pipeline. Further, VLUT provides the interface to the different camera and hardware configurations that isolates applications from these details to increase reusability, much as OpenGL and GLUT work together. Some typical hardware platforms are: field-programmable gate arrays (FPGAs), digital signal processors (DSPs), digital media processors, GPUs, and various co-processor platforms.

GPUs, which are using a SIMD architecture, have evolved into extremely flexible and powerful processors. Since the GPU is built to process graphics operations that include pixel and vertex operations among others, it is particularly well suited to perform some computer vision algorithms very efficiently. For example, Yang and Pollefeys [19] implemented a stereo algorithm on an NVIDIA GeForce4 graphics card, whose performance is equivalent to the fastest commercial CPU implementations available.

The prototyping of the OpenVL hardware device on an Altera DE2 development board (using FPGA) is under development to illustrate how components of the OpenVL may be accelerated as a proof-of-concept for acceleration. We also plan to explore GPU and other co-processor architecture implementations of OpenVL.

10.3 A Novel Software Architecture for OpenVL

This section presents our novel software architecture—OpenVL to address the issues of *reusability*, *efficiency*, and *scalability* in the computer vision domain. It is a variation of the pipes and filters architecture, aiming at addressing the limitations of general pipes and filters while preserving its desirable properties by constraining it to typical image and vision processing algorithms.

10.3.1 Logical Pipeline

A general pipes and filters architecture cannot efficiently solve all of the dependencies found within an arbitrary topology of a large-scale parallel system. To address this problem, we introduce a logical pipeline to restrict the topologies of the filters into a linear sequence that are found in typical image processing tasks. This has two benefits: one, it provides a simple mental model for application developers for constructing models and, two, it provides a language model supporting a tractable description of image processing tasks that can be hardware accelerated.

10.3.1.1 Rationale for Logical Pipeline

Incorporating a logical pipeline into OpenVL makes hardware acceleration possible, because each stage can be implemented as a separate task and potentially executed in parallel with other stages. If hardware designers can provide a dedicated hardware platform to improve the performance of the common operations at each stage, the performance of the whole system can be significantly improved. Further, the structure of the pipeline itself can be used to develop dedicated hardware solutions to optimize the whole pipeline in addition to the individual components.

We differentiate between logical stages and physical stages. A logical stage has a certain task to perform, but does not specify the way that task is executed. A physical pipeline stage, on the other hand, is a specific implementation and is executed simultaneously with all the other pipeline stages. A given implementation may combine two logical stages into one physical pipeline stage, while it divides another, more time-consuming, logical stage into several physical pipeline stages, or even parallelizes it. From the perspective of an application programmer, the logical pipeline provides a clear conceptual model and language constructs to support descriptions of the processing that needs to be done. From the OpenVL implementers' perspective, the logical model provides the description needed to determine optimal ways to actually implement the operations.

10.3.1.2 OpenVL Logical Pipeline

The development of OpenVL is a large-scale project involving collaboration among researchers from various computer vision fields to assess which classes of processing tasks fit within the scope of OpenVL. In this chapter, we present human tracking as one class of algorithms that are planned to be within the scope of OpenVL and is our starting point for a proof-of-concept for OpenVL in general. We chose human tracking since it is one of the most active research areas in computer vision. Our example design implements all critical components of OpenVL to demonstrate the concepts behind it. We anticipate that if the proposed architecture can be applied to human tracking, it should be extensible to other classes of image and vision processing for other applications. We also use the class of multicapture single-image processing applications to define the OpenVL structure, however, these elements are not reported here.

Based on the reviews of human tracking algorithms in [1, 13], we propose an image understanding pipeline for human tracking.

For multiple video sources, multiple OpenVL pipelines would be created, as shown in Fig. 10.2. Operations in one pipeline can access data buffers of the same stage in other pipelines directly, suggesting that synchronization and communication mechanisms are implicit. Actual implementations to support this logical communication can use shared memory or other bus structures to provide differing price/performance levels as required.

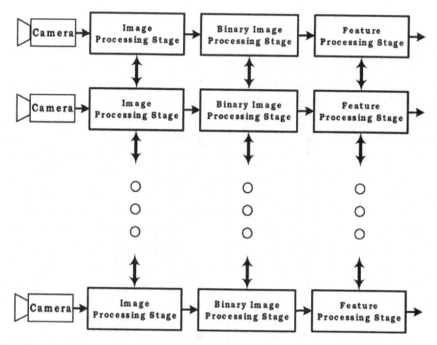

Fig. 10.2 OpenVL multiple logical image understanding pipeline. The pipeline is broken into several stages based on the type of data being processed. Each stage contains a set of data buffers and common operations, allowing for pipeline-based acceleration.

Fig. 10.3 shows a highlighted single logical pipeline. Based on the type of data representation being processed, this pipeline is broken into four primary stages: video capture, image processing, binary image processing and feature processing. Each stage can be divided further into substages. Pipelining reduces the cycle time of processing and hence increases processing throughput. As well, the granularity of the pipeline data flow may also be varied to include frames or subregions where the minimum size of the subregion is an OpenVL specification (i.e., nine pixels).

The input video data can be either from a physical camera using various ports, such as IEEE 1394 or USB, or from a "virtual camera" that loads video from files. Virtual camera concepts apply to offline analysis of video data or video editing applications, which also involve computationally intensive operations. In the image processing stage, the image buffer is used to store raw input and modified image data. This stage has several substages: color space transformation, image enhancement in the spatial domain, linear filtering, nonlinear filtering, geometrical transformation and temporal processing. In the binary image processing stage, the binary image buffer is used to store input and modified binary image data. This primary stage has two substages: morphological processing and nonlinear transformation. In the feature processing stage, a feature buffer is defined to store a feature values list. The content of the list is entirely dependent on the processing that took place at

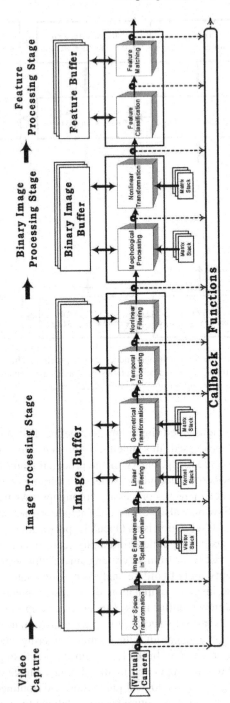

Fig. 10.3 OpenVL single logical image understanding pipeline.

Fig. 10.4 Parallel operations in OpenVL substages.

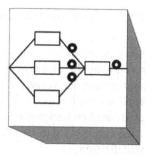

previous stages in the pipeline. This stage has two substages: feature classification and feature matching.

Fig. 10.4 gives an example collection of processes in a substage. Each substage contains a set of operations which can run in a parallel style when hardware implementation is supported, further improving optimized performance. For example, two edge detectors with different thresholds may run in parallel, and then an edge-linking process can connect the outputs.

Different approaches are possible to provide structures to address the link between the logical and physical layers to implement the various components of the logical pipeline. The following subsections provide some examples of these.

10.3.2 Stacks

The stack boxes in Fig. 10.3 represent a stack buffer that we propose to implement part of OpenVL's processing to optimize hardware acceleration by allowing preprocessing of operations. This approach is seen in OpenGL, for example, with the matrix stack for transformation operations. For image processing, convolution serves as an example that can use this approach. Convolution is a widely used operator in computer vision because any linear, shift-invariant operation can be expressed in terms of a convolution [4]. For example, both Gaussian filtering and edge detection use this operation. Because the convolution operation is associative, i.e.,

$$((f*g)*h)*\ldots = f*(g*h*\ldots)$$

where f is image data, $g, h, \ldots$ are filter kernels, we can improve the performance of the operation through the following means. First we can stack all of the filters and convolve them together, and then convolve the result with the image data. The resulting performance is much better compared with combinations of individual convolutions. Therefore, if physical architecture supports stacked convolution, system performance can be enhanced.

10.3.3 Event-Driven Mechanism

Since the pipes and filters architecture does not provide a mechanism for users to reconfigure the data flow routine in run time, it is not good at handling interactive applications. However, providing user interaction is important for computer vision applications. For example, different background segmentation techniques may be used based on background environments or the results of an image processing operation may be used to actuate some other process, such as some OpenGL process for visualization.

To support run-time interaction, an event management mechanism is introduced in VLUT (see Section 10.3.7) . Users employ event-handling and callback functions to perform application specific processing at appropriate points in the pipeline. Users can register interest in an event, such as when a feature stage has completed, by associating a procedure (i.e., callback function) with the event. The callback function is not invoked explicitly by the programmer. Instead, when the event occurs during OpenVL processing, the VLUT invokes all of the procedures that have been registered for that particular event. Thus an event announcement implicitly invokes the callback procedure to allow the application programmer to retrieve the result associated with the event.

In Fig. 10.3, a black circle represents a particular event happening. When an event happens, such as the arrival of a new image, convolution completion or erosion completion, the registered callback command will be triggered, giving the user control over data flow. For example, an application programmer may set up two callbacks: one to display an image as it comes in to the pipeline and another after the image processing stage is complete to see the effects visually.

Like OpenGL, using the event handling mechanism, OpenVL works as a state machine. We put into it various states that then remain in effect until we change them based on some events.

10.3.4 Data Buffers

One limitation in the general pipes and filters model is that each filter's output data must be copied to its downstream filter(s)'s input, which can lead to expensive data copying. To solve this problem, we introduce a data buffer concept, i.e., the buffer plane layers in Fig. 10.3. We abstract representations of common data structures from computer vision algorithms and store them in the data buffer. Because all processes in a stage can access data buffers belonging to that stage, data buffers are modeled as shared memory space in the logical architecture. This allows hardware designs to use *physical* shared memory as an option to avoid data copying as would be implied by a general pipes and filters architecture. Though, these designs need to ensure proper mutual exclusion and condition synchronization to realize this potential. In OpenVL, there are currently several primary data buffers: front, back, image, binary image, and feature.

10.3.5 Synchronization and Communication

In the OpenVL architecture, there are several kinds of synchronization and communication issues that we need to consider: (1) between camera and pipeline; (2) between processes in the same pipeline; (3) between processes in different pipelines; and (4) between user callback functions and the logical pipeline. We present each of them separately in the following sections.

10.3.5.1 Camera Capture and Processes in the Pipeline

The speeds of the camera capturing (writer) and processes in the pipeline (reader) may not be exactly the same. If a reader is faster than the writer, it will have to wait for additional data to arrive. Conversely, if the writer is faster than the readers, it may have to either drop data or disrupt the execution of the pipeline to deal with the new data. To deal with this in the logical pipeline we use a front and back buffer and configuration modes to establish which data handling policy to use. This may be implemented using a double buffer mechanism with mutual exclusion to allow for captured data to be stored in one buffer while the pipeline is processing the other.

10.3.5.2 Processes in the Same Pipeline

Because processes in the same pipeline can read or write a data buffer at the same time, mutual exclusion is needed to ensure that the data is shared consistently. In OpenVL, the mutual exclusion required is managed implicitly, thus, the implementation of OpenVL must ensure that buffers are protected to allow either one writer or multiple reader access exclusively.

10.3.5.3 Processes in Different Pipelines

In OpenVL, the logical architecture supports the notion that processes within a single stage of the pipeline have shared access to data buffers associated with that particular stage. This extends to all processes at the same stage in other pipelines as well. This provides a simple semantic mechanism for application developers. However, the actual implementation of this model may introduce significant delays if done sequentially, as data must be transferred explicitly between pipelines. However, hardware designers may also introduce special busses and/or shared memory segments that can handle multiple pipelines accessing these protected data spaces. Notice that data transfers between stages are not supported in the logical architecture directly, thus access to these must be done explicitly by the application programmer. An implementation may extend OpenVL by supporting these complicated transfers. However, as we anticipate their requirement is rare, we expect that most applications will not need the extra complexity and expense to support it.

10.3.5.4 Callback Functions and Processes in the Pipeline

Based on the relationships between callback functions and processes in the pipeline, we can categorize callback functions into three basic modes: fully synchronous callback, partial synchronous callback, and asynchronous callback as described below. A different synchronization mechanism is provided for each mode of callback functions as specified by the application developer in OpenVL. Callback functions may also run in a mixed mode, which is a combination of two or even three basic modes. In these cases, different synchronization mechanisms are used together. These mechanisms provide the OpenVL programmer flexible control for dealing with different types of timing constraints appropriate to their application. These modes are also designed to take into account different choices for optimizing hardware or software implementations of OpenVL.

Fully Synchronous Callback

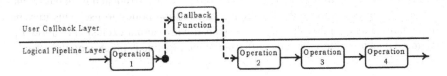

Fig. 10.5 Fully synchronous callback.

When the user needs to modify data using specific operations not provided in a given implementation of a pipeline, the callback function can be used to implement these operations. After the callback function finishes, results need to be joined back into the pipeline to gain accelerated performance. This is called fully synchronous callback mode, as shown in Fig. 10.5.

In this mode, the callback function works as a process in the pipeline. Therefore, synchronization in this case is also a multiple-writer and multiple-reader problem. Mutual exclusion, the same as that between processes in the same pipeline, should be provided by the OpenVL implementation.

Partial Synchronous Callback

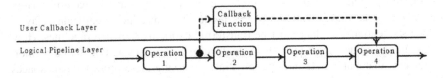

Fig. 10.6 Partial synchronous callback.

In this mode, the callback function provides the capacity for users to reconfigure the data-flow routine in run time. The unrelated processes, i.e., operations 2 and 3 in Fig. 10.6, can be run asynchronously with the callback function, while operations after these two operations need to synchronize with the callback function.

In this mode, mutual exclusion is needed to avoid the simultaneous use of the same data: operations' states, by the callback function and operations. Because this is a single-reader and single-writer problem, a simple synchronization mechanism, such as a binary semaphore mechanism, can be used to provide mutual exclusion.

Asynchronous Callback

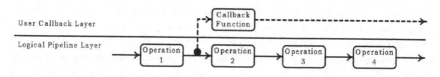

Fig. 10.7 Asynchronous callback.

In this mode, the callback function is employed by the user only to obtain intermediate results, as shown in Fig. 10.7. For example, the user needs the raw image from the camera for display. The callback function does not reconfigure the data-flow routine, and if all of the following operations do not need the results from the callback function.

Because callback functions are running asynchronously with processes in the pipeline, there is no need to let callback functions interfere with the operations. For example, this may be implemented with a bounded buffer to provide the synchronization between the callback function and the former process providing input to it. When the bounded buffer is full, there are two options for the producer, i.e., operation 1 in Fig. 10.7. The first option is to discard new input data. The second option is to store new data while the oldest data is discarded. There is only one option for reading when the bounded buffer is empty: the consumer, i.e., the callback function, has to wait.

10.3.6 Iteration

In Fig. 10.4, some operations require iteration with conditionals. Data-flow approaches have a difficult time representing semantics of iteration in a convenient way, however, this may be required given our current approach to OpenVL. Two issues need resolution: how iteration and conditional termination are expressed in the data-flow representation for OpenVL.

OpenVL provides two kinds of solutions to this issue. The first one is to provide a maximum fixed number of iterations. When the user needs more iterations, data continues being fed-back through a processing block for the given number of iterations. For the second, the application programmer specifies termination conditions

Fig. 10.8 Using device driver
and VLUT to mask hetero-
geneity.

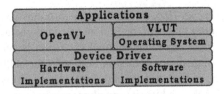

to stop the loop operation. For example, an erosion operation can be specified to run until there is only one pixel left. When this method is selected, some extra policies are provided to handle exceptions that may occur during the looping constructs. For example, an iteration operation may need to stop when it has exceeded some timeout parameter, or when some other conditions are met. The iteration mechanisms require language constructs such as *DoFor(n)* where *n* is the number of iterations, *DoUntil(cond, timeout)* where *cond* and *timeout* are termination conditions. However, these do not easily fit into a data-flow approach. We continue to develop convenience mechanisms to include these semantics into the logical architecture.

10.3.7 Isolating Layers to Mask Heterogeneity

Although the implementations of OpenVL may consist of a heterogeneous collection of operating systems and hardware platforms, the differences are masked by the fact that the applications use the VLUT and device driver layers to isolate the specific implementations, depicted in Fig. 10.8.

When there is hardware implementation to support processing, OpenVL calls the device driver to gain the benefit of hardware acceleration. Otherwise, a slower software implementation will be used. The VLUT layer is used to isolate the operating system, event management, hardware acceleration and cameras. Therefore, application developers cannot tell the difference between hardware and software implementations. The user will notice, however, that performance is significantly enhanced when hardware acceleration is available. Furthermore, the isolating layers make it possible for users to upgrade their applications to new OpenVL hardware, immediately taking advantage of their device's newly accelerated performance.

Moreover, individual calls can be either executed on dedicated hardware, run as software routines, or implemented as a combination of both dedicated hardware and software routines. Therefore, the isolating layers provide hardware designers with the flexibility to tailor a particular OpenVL implementation to meet their unique system cost, quality and performance objectives.

10.4 Example Application Designs

The development of real-time video analysis applications was a steering concern during development of the OpenVL software architecture. The applications presented here were used as testbeds for the implementation, testing and refinement of critical concepts in OpenVL. We first describe the procedure for implementing a computer vision application, and then two different human tracking systems are implemented to validate the critical underlying concepts of OpenVL and VLUT.

10.4.1 Procedure for Implementing Applications

The sequence of a typical OpenVL/VLUT program is illustrated in Fig. 10.9 (a):

(1) Use the VLUT function, *vlutInitializeCamera()*, to initialize the camera mode, including image resolution, color mode, geometries etc.

(2) Provide configuration of the OpenVL buffers including: which buffers are available, buffer resolutions, how many buffer planes and how many bits per pixel each buffer holds, etc., which will be used by the application. These are VLUT calls.

(3) Initialize OpenVL buffer values. The user may set initial values such as the convolution kernel values using OpenVL calls.

(4) Establish the OpenVL operation queues. The user sets the image understanding pipeline path to control data flow using OpenVL calls. These establish the state of the machine so that they are executed every cycle of the pipeline once the event manager enters its infinite main loop below (6).

(5) Register any callback functions with the event handler including the modes that the callback functions will operate in. Coupled to these are the actual callback functions that implement the desired application specific processing outside the OpenVL pipelines.

(6) The last call is to *vlutMainLoop()* to enter an infinite loop to manage events, run the pipelines and trigger callbacks.

10.4.2 Local Positioning System (LPS)

Location is one of the most important context information for surveillance systems. In [15], we have designed and implemented an LPS to locate the positions of objects in an indoor space. In our approach, the main idea is to use an infrared tag as an active transmitter, sending out a unique identification number to signal its presence to the system. There are five main steps in the pipeline of this system. The first step is noise removal. A Gaussian filter is applied to remove some noisy data. The second step is to use thresholding to get binary image data. The third step is to group bright spots, since the tag's bright spot is often captured as several small ones, we need to group them into one bright spot. The fourth step is to shrink this bright spot into

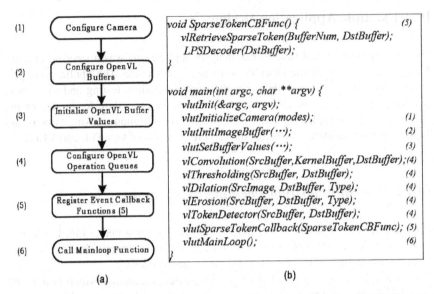

Fig. 10.9 In this figure, (a) shows the procedures to write a program using OpenVL. (b) illustrates a Local Positioning System pseudo-code using OpenVL.

one pixel so that only location information is stored. The final step is to decode the tag ID. The image processing operations in this local positioning system, such as filtering or morphological operations, are widely used in other video based surveillance systems. Moreover, these operations are some of the most time consuming ones among all image processing operations. Therefore, this local positioning system is a good choice to demonstrate OpenVL. We have reimplemented this simple local positioning system to demonstrate how OpenVL applications function and can be easily developed in a portable manner, and how they can be accelerated.

Fig. 10.9 (b) shows the concise code for implementing the local positioning system using OpenVL and VLUT. This code implements a Gaussian filter on input video data to remove noise, thresholds the result to find the bright spots in the image, dilates bright spots to group together close ones belonging to same tag, erodes each bright spot to one pixel bright spot, and finally generates a list of (x, y) locations where there is a bright spot. This list is passed into a registered callback function for the application specific code that decodes the tag IDs based on the pattern of blinking. If the OpenVL pipeline is implemented on a hardware device, this architecture not only reduces the computational load on the central CPU processor, but it also significantly reduces the amount of data that must be transferred between devices: a 99 KB (352×288) image reduces to a list of 5 to 50 points of 4 bytes (x, y) each, effectively reducing required data transfers by 500 to 5000 times.

```
void ThresholdCallback() {                                                     (5)
    vlGetBinaryImageBuf(BK_Data_Buffer);

    ... ...

    Communicate with other thread to display Background Subtraction results

    ... ...
}

void DistanceCallback() {                                                      (5)
    vlGetFeatureVectorBuf(Dis_Data_Buffer);

    ... ...

    Distance Calculation

    ... ...
}

void ViewAngleCallback() {                                                     (5)
    vlGetFeatureBuf(Angle_Data_Buffer);

    ... ...

    View Angle Calculation

    ... ...
}

void main(int argc, char **argv) {
    vlutInit(&argc, argv);
    vlutInitializeCamera(modes);                                               (1)
    vlutInitImageBuffer(···);                                                  (2)
    vlutSetBufferValues(···);                                                  (3)
    vlutSetBufferValues (VL_IMAGE_BUF_1, "/video/%d.pgm");                      (3)
    vlColorSpaceTransform(VL_RGB,VL_YUV);                                       (4)
    vlConvolution(SrcBuffer,KernelBuffer,DstBuffer);                           (4)

    // Background Subtraction
    vlGaussianModel(VL_IMAGE_BUF_1, 10, VL_UPDATE);                            (4)
    VL_THRESHOLD_VAL= 3;
    vlThreshold(VL_IMAGE_BUF_1,VL_THRESHOLD_VAL, VL_BINARY_IMAGE_BUF_1);        (4)

    // Calculate Distance
    vlFeatureMatrixMultiply(VL_FEATURE_BUF_2, FEATURE_MATRIX_1, VL_FEATURE_BUF_3);  (4)
    vlFeatureVectorSubtract(VL_FEATURE_BUF_2, VL_FEATURE_BUF_3, VL_FEATURE_BUF_4);  (4)
    vlFeatureVectorSquareroot(VL_FEATURE_BUF_4, VL_FEATURE_BUF_5);              (4)

    //Calculate ViewAngle
    vlEqualizeHist(VL_IMAGE_BUFFER_6, VL_IMAGE_BUFFER_7);                       (4)
    vlHaarDetectObjects(VL_IMAGE_BUFFER_7, cascade, storage, 1.1, 2, 0, 30, 30, VL_FEATURE_BUFFER_1);  (4)
    vlFeatureVectorScale(VL_FEATURE_BUFFER_1, scale, VL_FEATURE_BUFFER_2);      (4)

    // Register Events Callback Handles
    vlutCallback(VL_BINARY_IMAGE_BUFFER_1, ThresholdCallback);                 (5)
    vlutCallback(VL_FEATURE_BUFFER_5, DistanceCallback);                       (5)
    vlutCallback(VL_FEATURE_BUFFER_2, ViewAngleCallback);                      (5)
    vlutMainLoop();                                                            (6)
}
```

Fig. 10.10 This figure illustrates OpenVL pseudo-code for a human tracking system, which calculates the quality of view (QOV) and automatically selects the camera with the best QOV.

10.4.3 Human Tracking and Attribute Calculation

We have also implemented a more sophisticated human tracking and attribute calculation system using OpenVL and VLUT [16]. Initially, we use the method in [17] to calibrate cameras. A set of virtual 3D points is made by waving the laser pointer through the working volume. Its projections are found with subpixel precision and verified by a robust RANSAC analysis [2]. After calibration, we record a sequence of background images without a person in the scene. For each pixel in the background, we calculate the mean and variance of pixel intensity, resulting in a Gaussian distribution. To determine whether a pixel is in the foreground or a part of the background, its intensity is fit into the Gaussian model of the corresponding pixels. If image pixels are classified as background pixels, then these pixels are used to update background models. Instead of using a RGB color space, we use a YUV color space in our system to reduce shadows. The centroid and a distance map are obtained by applying distance transforms to the binary result image derived from the background subtraction process. Each value in the distance map corresponds to be the minimum distance to the background. From these, we calculate the distance between camera and the subject's centroid. Quality of view (QOV) calculations belong to an application layer; therefore, it is defined in user defined callback functions.

In this human tracking system, more complicated algorithms are used than the LPS. Nevertheless, the procedure for implementing this system using OpenVL is same as for LPS. Fig. 10.10 shows the concise code for implementing the human tracking system using OpenVL and VLUT.

10.5 Conclusion and Future Work

In this chapter, we presented a novel software architecture for OpenVL to promote hardware acceleration, reusability, and scalability in computer vision systems. The OpenVL API defined in this work is a starting point for a standardized interface that can work seamlessly on different software/hardware platforms. This chapter focused on the description of the logical architecture and provided some insight into techniques that may be used to implement it. The OpenVL API syntax and some of our architecture's critical concepts were demonstrated with two examples so far.

There are several directions we are currently pursuing. We plan to continue developing the OpenVL image understanding pipeline to cover other classes of computer vision algorithms and applications, and hopefully lead to its widespread adoption. We plan to develop models for control structures such as *iteration* and *conditionals* that are not part of a typical pipes and filters model but necessary for many computer vision applications. The prototyping of the OpenVL hardware device on FPGA and GPU are under development to illustrate how components of the OpenVL pipeline may be accelerated as a proof-of-concept for acceleration. We believe that the enhancement and adoption of OpenVL by a community of researchers will significantly improve the size and complexity of computer vision systems, since OpenVL enables easy and quick code development, independent of platform.

One issue in the current OpenVL design is that it is oriented towards the application programmer specifying *how* an image processing algorithm is implemented rather than *what* they want done. There are two problems with the *how* approach. One is that it is difficult to design implementations to accelerate algorithms as the details of the processes are already specified by the application leaving little freedom for optimization. Another reason is that nonimage processing experts may not know how particular algorithms work, but they do know what type of operations they want done. Thus, they are more focused on *what* needs to be done. Currently we are investigating the next generation of OpenVL to incorporate these semantics.

In summary, we have created our first version of an open vision library consisting of a logical pipeline coupled with a language model to support image processing applications that are reusable, scalable and can be accelerated by hardware by different vendors. We continue to expand and refine our pipeline to provide an open specification that can be implemented on different hardware and software platforms to support portable image processing applications.

10.6 Acknowledgements

This research is funded by the Natural Sciences and Engineering Research Council of Canada (NSERC), Bell University Labs, and the Institute for Robotics and Intelligent Systems (IRIS). We appreciate the inspiring ideas of Jim Clark, Jeremy Cooperstock, and Roel Vertegaal and the useful discussions with Steve Oldridge and Amir Afrah. Thanks to Craig Wilson for proofreading.

References

1. J. K. Aggarwal, Q. Cai (1999) Human motion analysis: A review. *Computer Vision and Image Understanding: CVIU* 73:428-440.
2. M. Fischler, R. Bolles (1987) Random sample consensus: a paradigm for model fitting with applications to image analysis and automated cartography. *Communications of the ACM* 24(6), 381-395.
3. Michael J. Flynn (1996) Very high speed computing systems. *Proc. IEEE.*
4. David A. Forsyth, Jean Ponce (2003) *Computer Vision: A Modern Approach,* Prentice Hall.
5. Intel Inc. (2001) Open Source Computer Vision Library: Reference Manual, Intel Corporation.
6. Jitter Tutorial (2006) version 1.6, *Cycling '74.*
7. J.M. Jolion, A. Rosenfeld (1994) *A Pyramid Framework for Early Vision,* Kluwer Academic.
8. Renate Kempf, Chris Frazier (1996) *OpenGL Reference Manual. The Official Reference Document for OpenGL,* Version 1.1, Addison Wesley Longman Inc.
9. Josef Kittler, Michael J. B. Duff (1985) *Image Processing System Architecture,* Research Studies Press.

10. K. Konstantinides and J. R. Rasure (1994) The Khoros software development environment for image and signal processing, *IEEE Transactions on Image Processing* 3:243-252.
11. James J. Little, G. E. Blelloch, T. A. Cass (1989) Algorithmic techniques for computer vision on a fine-grained parallel machine, *IEEE Transactions on Pattern Analysis and Machine Intelligence* 11:244-257.
12. DirectShow Reference (2007) MSDN.
13. Thomas B. Moeslund, Erik Granum (2001) A survey of computer vision-based human motion capture, *Computer Vision and Image Understanding: CVIU* 81:231-268.
14. Mary Shaw, David Garlan (1996) *Software Architecture: Perspectives on an Emerging Discipline,* Englewood Cliffs, NJ: Prentice Hall.
15. Changsong Shen, Sidney Fels, et. al (2005) RemoteEyes: A remote low-cost position sensing infrastructure for ubiquitous computing, *Transactions of Society of Instrument and Control Engineers* E-S-1:85-90.
16. Changsong Shen, Sidney Fels (2007) A multi-camera surveillance system that estimates quality-of-view measurement, *IEEE International Conference on Image Processing.*
17. T. Svoboda, D. Martinec, T. Pajdla (2005) A convenient multi-camera self-calibration for virtual environments, *Teleoperators and Virtual Environments* pp. 407-422.
18. Charles C. Weems (1991) Architectural requirements of image understanding with respect to parallel processing, *Proc. IEEE* 79:537-547.
19. Ruigang Yang, Marc Pollefeys (2003) Multi-resolution real-time stereo on commodity graphics hardware, *Proc. IEEE CVPR 2003.*

Part III
Looking Ahead

Chapter 11
Mobile Challenges for Embedded Computer Vision

Sek Chai

Abstract The mobile environment poses uniquely challenging constraints for designers of embedded computer vision systems. There are traditional issues such as size, weight, and power, which are readily evident. However, there are also other less tangible obstacles related to technology acceptance and business models that stand in the way of a successful product deployment. In this chapter, I describe these issues as well as other qualities desired in a mobile smart camera using computer vision algorithms to "see and understand" the scene. The target platform of discussion is the mobile handset, as this platform is poised to be the ubiquitous consumer device all around the world.

11.1 Introduction

Computer vision is a branch of computer science concerned with analyzing images to extract information about the environment. Much like the human visual system, embedded computer vision systems perform these same visual functions in a wide variety of products. They enable automation, speed, and precision for tasks that were previously manual.

Embedded smart cameras using computer vision algorithms are complex systems integrating an assortment of components such as lens, image sensors, processors, and memories. Designing such a system requires a team of experts with multidisciplinary knowledge ranging from optics to computer architecture in order to deliver products that run the algorithms. Unlike today's imaging applications that involve well-understood algorithms for image finishing and compression, computer vision algorithms embody elements of perception and intelligence that can require processing power in the range of supercomputers.

Sek Chai
Motorola Labs, Schaumburg, IL, USA, e-mail: sek.chai@motorola.com

In embedded portable devices such as mobile camera phones, digital cameras, and camcorders, the elevated performance has to be delivered with limited size, weight, and power. These constraints directly correlate to the performance of the smart camera because size, weight, and power limit the type of optics, lighting, and processor that can be integrated. The main task for designers would therefore involve the selection of the best components for the smart camera while meeting these technical constraints.

In addition to technical challenges, embedded smart cameras face other intangible barriers in deployment. The barriers range from the very basic issues such as user acceptance of new technology to the more complicated issues such as having a good business model for the application. It is important to note that these factors play a major, if not principal, role in determining whether a consumer product using computer vision algorithms can be deployed successfully.

This chapter describes these challenges—both technical constraints and intangible barriers—in more detail. The goal is to motivate future designers by delineating issues that may arise. It is not intended as a cookbook or checklist because such an approach would more likely produce unsuccessful results for the readers. The overall focus of this chapter revolves around mobile handsets as the choice for an embedded system to integrate computer vision algorithms. While there have been numerous articles and books on the design of mobile handsets, the application that runs on it, and the wireless network it uses for communication, there is no comprehensive article about the use of computer vision on this platform.

The growth of the digital imaging industry is driven primarily by mobile handsets with embedded cameras, that is, camera-phones. First introduced in 2000, sales of camera phones have since surpassed sales of both film and digital cameras, and the entire digital imaging market continues to accelerate [1]. Today, imaging applications on camera phones involve the capturing, processing, and transmission of visual content on wireless mobile devices for images. In the next-generation camera-phones, these applications will demand higher resolution (multiple megapixels), better image quality through image finishing, and faster frame rates (video quality at 30 frames per second). Furthermore, designers will look towards new product features based on computer vision algorithms, much akin to those in smart cameras [2,3] in order to improve sales. The leading marketable feature, pixel resolution, has lost its momentum as consumers are already becoming satisfied with the quality of an image of several megapixels.

Section 11.2 provides an overview of applications. In Section 11.3, technology constraints for the mobile environment are discussed. Intangible obstacles are covered in Section 11.4. Finally, Section 11.5 concludes with future directions for mobile embedded computer vision systems.

11.2 In Search of the Killer Applications

This section briefly describes imaging applications in mobile handsets in order to highlight the computation and memory access characteristics. The aim is to show both computational and memory requirements for these applications. It motivates the designer to consider parallel processing elements and efficient memory access in order to manage applications for embedded computer vision.

Today's mobile imaging applications include color interpolation, white balance, gamma correction, and compression/decompression. For the sub megapixel resolutions such as VGA-sized images (640×480), these functions can be easily handled by off-the-shelf imaging DSPs (digital signal processors) with performance ranging up to 500 MOPs (million operations per seconds). Next-generation mobile imaging applications will be the same but for higher-resolution images and video frame rates. Furthermore, computer vision algorithms will be used to enable smart camera features. These next-generation applications will demand more resolution and smart camera features that can exceed more than twice the performance of an imaging DSP [2,3].

11.2.1 Image Finishing

Image finishing consists of a series of processing steps to render raw sensor data into images pleasing to the human eye [4]. They consist of a variety of algorithms that include: color interpolation, white balance, gamma correction, and compression. Virtually all mobile imaging devices implement these algorithms either in image sensor companion chips or in application processors.

Color interpolation is used to convert a single sensor's output from a mosaic of colored pixels into a full-color image. The mosaic is typically organized in such a way that images are captured in an interlaced RGB (red, green, blue) pattern. The process involves finding the correct color value for the missing pixel located among several other pixels. The algorithm includes filtering operations over a range of 3×3 to 5×5 tiles for the three RGB color planes.

White balance and gamma correction are steps to tune the image pixel data to match the intended color range. For example, a white color should be visually white, with RGB colors saturated for their range of values. However, the image sensor does not necessarily produce ideal color ranges due to ambient noise, temperature, and dark currents [5]. Processing is needed to redistribute and scale the energy content of the RGB values. The algorithms typically include 3×3 matrix multiplications of pixel data with a filter and look-up-tables (LUT) to map the result to a new non-linear color space.

Finally, compression standards such as JPEG [6], include steps to convert the RGB color space into a YCbCr color space with luminance (Y), red chrominance (Cr), and blue chrominance (Cb), before the compression procedure. The compression algorithm involves block comparisons, typically 8×8, and LUT to encode the image data. Memory access patterns are 2D blocks based on the filter tile sizes (3×3 or 5×5 for color interpolation and 8×8 for JPEG compression).

11.2.2 Video Codec

MPEG compression standards [7] are widely used in digital video encoding products such as digital camcorders. Video messaging and two-way video conferencing are already available in camera phones today, but popular demand for such services takes time to foster. Wider-bandwidth networks, driven by content providers' eagerness to create a new market in mobile devices, will enable new applications such as video-on-demand and mobile TV broadcast. Content from home entertainment systems can be seamlessly shown on mobile devices, enabling user access in addition to mobility.

In general, the encoding process begins with preprocessing, which may include format conversion to convert the image into YCbCr color space and resizing to a desired image size. Motion estimation, 2D DCT, quantization, and entropy coding are the next stages in the coding process. For a CIF-sized video (352×240), the encoding process requires more than 1000 MOPs, which is beyond the capabilities of today's single embedded scalar processors [8]. The decoding processing follows a simpler inverse procedure and requires only 200 MOPs (easily achievable in scalar processors). Memory access patterns are based on macro-block and DCT filter sizes, which are typically 8×8 over the entire image.

11.2.3 Computer Vision

Smart cameras use computer vision algorithms to "see and understand" the scene. The "see" portion uses computer vision algorithms to segment, classify, and identify objects; the "understand" portion includes more complex learning algorithms to model and track objects. There are already application examples in security, entertainment, safety, and transportation, but not all of these applications apply to camera-phones. In general, these applications have the following abilities: to extract features and structures from images, and to derive semantic meaning in the form of metadata through a series of pattern-matching operations.

Computer vision algorithms identify objects in a scene, and consequently produce one region of an image that has more importance than other regions of the image. For example, in body gesture recognition [3], the region of the video image that includes portions of the hand (a region of interest, or ROI) may be studied to find the hand posture over a series of frames. A video image may also be processed to track different parts of the body. Information about detected objects is stored in data structure with fields containing features and location. Each object lies in a different region of the captured images which must be processed simultaneously to find the overall effect of the body gesture. Memory access patterns are dependent on object size in the image, ranging from a few hundred to thousands of pixels in order to have enough resolution for feature detection. Furthermore, the object moves in subsequent frames, which corresponds to fetching a "moving" block of pixels from memory. That is, the memory access patterns would shift in memory addresses as the tracked object moves in a series of captured image frames.

11.2.4 Example Applications

While there are mobile imaging applications using aspects of computer vision, none has risen to a "killer app" status. Early example applications include business card readers [9] and aids for the visually impaired [10]. To be considered a "killer app," the application must be so compelling that consumers will find it absolutely necessary to have the feature. Such an application would surpass all of its competitive alternatives in consumer demand and popularity.

An application area that is growing in importance is image editing and manipulation. As users take more pictures using their camera phone, they also want to edit the captured images to improve its presentation. For example, users may want to change the contrast and brightness, or simply crop away portions of the image. Rather than performing these edits on a computer, whereby pictures must be downloaded beforehand, users can do so directly on their camera phone. This capability would enable user experiences that improve the spontaneity of photo-taking and sharing them at the same instant. Without this feature, many users may not even bother because the download process is too cumbersome.

In many cases, the editing process can be enhanced and automated by using computer vision algorithms to understand objects in the image. For example, object and face detection can simplify photo album creation by properly labeling photos as they are taken. Cropping and framing can be done to properly center the image on a face. Furthermore, panoramic images can be created by stitching together multiple images taken from different viewpoints. There are now companies that are marketing and licensing niche intellectual property and software with these features [11].

In addition to image editing, another application area is user interaction enhancements, whereby mobile handset users can attain a better experience in using the device because of an embedded camera running computer vision algorithms. These applications deal with supplementing or completely augmenting the way user interacts with the device. In addition to picture-taking, the camera's role is extended to input devices such as keyboards, joysticks, or touch screens. Computer vision algorithms enable the camera to function as a visual sensor to detect body and hand gestures [3,12].

A good example that illustrates this capability is map reading, where users would need to scroll quickly to different map regions or zoom into different areas [13]. Instead of repeatedly pressing keypads to perform the scroll and zoom, a smart camera application would track the user's face in relation to the onboard camera.

The effect is a fluid and intuitive movement of the displayed map region, resulting in a shorter time to complete the task of map reading.

Videogames are also examples where repetitive key presses can be replaced with object tracking using computer vision. Camera-based toys, such as the Sony EyeToy^{TM}, are a good example of the use of motion tracking and color recognition to effect game control [14]. Although promising, today's video games on mobile handsets lags behind such handhelds as the Sony PSP^{TM}and Nintendo DS^{TM}, due to the stark difference in processing power. Furthermore, the difficulty in advertising and delivering mobile games are some of the biggest reasons behind the growth in mobile gaming [15].

There are many other application areas that would benefit from the use of computer vision. They range from security (e.g., face detection), surveillance (e.g., person tracking), marketing/advertising (visual search) to health monitoring. While there are no killer apps to date, future designers should be encouraged, as the field looks promising and primed for future success.

11.3 Technology Constraints

This section describes some of the technical issues in mobile computer vision systems. The aim is to show both the traditional issues with embedded system design, and also issues specific to integrating computer vision applications in mobile handsets.

11.3.1 The Mobile Handset

Few consumer products match mobile handsets in the level of application integration. Mobile handsets not only make phone calls, but also take pictures and play music. They serve as a personal digital assistant (PDA), a game platform, a text-messaging system, and a television unit. Each generation of mobile handset brings new features as designers jockey for market position. Designers must meet the pressure of lowering the bill of materials (BOM) in order to deliver low product average selling price (ASP). This challenge comes amongst the increasingly growing set of features in a single product. This "feature creep" aspect is driven by both consumer demand and marketing.

Ever since the inception of the mobile handset in 1973, there has been continuous momentum to combine useful features for the consumer. Fig. 11.1 shows the timeline of key mobile phone introduction that intertwines with those of the digital camera timelines to bring us camera phones. The smart camera timeline has evolved from robotics, such as the Mars Exploration Rovers [16], to consumer products such as the Sony EyeToy^{TM}[14]. In the not too distant future, the mobile handset timeline might intersect with the smart camera timeline, producing an integrated product using computer vision algorithms.

Additional features must be balanced with device usability. It is important to note that people may not always value an overly high-featured product. In a series of studies measuring what people value in selecting a product and later after using the product, users have been found to prefer a much simpler device [17]. The research has concluded that "even the tech-savvy suffered from this 'feature fatigue' effect." When considering smart camera functionality in mobile handsets, computer vision applications should be designed to improve device usability and not add to "feature fatigue."

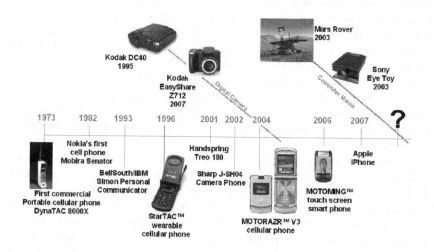

Fig. 11.1 Mobile handset timeline intersects digital camera and computer vision timelines.

In addition to application integration, the mobile handset is a marvel of component integration. The basic parts are comprised of the following: a small microphone, a speaker, an LCD display, a keypad, antenna, battery. There are also chips to convert signals from analog to digital and vice versa. The heart of the phone is the application processor that handles the housekeeping and user interface. A digital signal processor (DSP) handles the signal processing for RF (radio frequency) amplifiers that transmit and receive signals through the antenna.

Great efforts have been made to integrate these components to single-chip solutions in order to reduce area on the circuit board, power dissipation, and overall system cost. Semiconductor vendors now offer application processor with DSPs as well as on-chip memory [18,19]. A graphical processing unit (GPU) [20] is used to display application content to the user. The reader is referred to [21] for more details about the mobile handset. The camera module for the mobile handset comes in an integrated module with lens, image sensor, and companion chips. The companion chips are signal processing chips programmed with software to perform image finishing and compression. The finished image is transferred directly to the application processor for storage and further processing.

11.3.2 Computing Platform

Computer vision algorithms can reside in many different computing platforms on the mobile handset: application processor, DSP, GPU, camera-module companion chips. It is not unusual for existing applications to consume all of the processing horsepower in all of these computing platforms at once. For example, in an application such as video teleconferencing, the application processor may be running video codecs (coding and decoding of video streams), the DSP may be handling video transmission and reception, the GPU is rendering the image, and the camera-module companion chip is finishing the captured image.

In order to consider computer vision algorithms, the designer should consider how it would be integrated into the overall user experience. For example, in an operating scenario where a normal voice call is being made, the application processor may be lightly loaded, making it suitable to run other applications. In another example where the user is browsing the web, the camera-module companion chip may be lightly loaded or not used at all. It is important to make the computer vision application run seamlessly alongside existing applications. Otherwise, user acceptance would be low when the overall user experience suffers.

Today, the application processor would be the most acceptable computing platform to run the computer vision application as mobile handset makers are opening this platform to third-party software developers [22,23]. The GPU, DSP, or camera-module companion chip usually contains firmware that is not accessible to the public. Most third-party software is written in Java [24], with some support for native level drivers. Software libraries and application programmer interface (API) are made available in software developers kit (SDK). In most cases, software developers are given access to a frame buffer containing the image captured by the camera module. There is little to no support for designers to specify parameters in the camera module such as frame rate and exposure time [5]. This means that current computer vision applications are usually relegated to use image sensor settings that are optimized for picture taking. In the future, when the computing and camera module are part of an open platform, designers will have more flexibility to program and control the components.

It is also not uncharacteristic to consider extra processing hardware specifically for running computer vision algorithms. The hardware can come as a separate chipset or in the form of hardware accelerators in the application processor. There is already precedence: in the gaming application, graphics are accelerated on the GPU (a chip specifically made for that purpose) [25]; in video playback applications, DFT hardware engines [18,19] accelerate portions of video codecs. In addition, specialized streaming processors [26] and low-power FPGA/CPLD [27,28] have been proposed for computer vision, but integration of an extra computing platform for computer vision would add cost and increase ASP. It can only be justified when there is a compelling application, or "killer app," that consumer demands.

11.3.3 Memory

In addition to computational horsepower needed by the computer vision algorithms, the designer should also consider memory bandwidth and memory allocation during early stages of the design process. These items are often considered as a design afterthought, which may cause the application to run slower than expected. This could result in poor device usability.

Section 11.2 of this chapter already provides some example memory access patterns for different applications such as image finishing, codecs, and computer vision. While still image processing consumes a small amount of bandwidth and allocated memory, video can be considerably demanding on today's memory subsystem. At the other end of the spectrum, memory subsystem design for computer vision algorithms can be extremely challenging because of the extra number of processing steps required to detect and classify objects.

There is promising research in memory controller designs to improve the memory bandwidth issues for streaming data [29]. Because computer vision data have predictable access patterns such as streaming data, the transfer of data from external memory to processor can be made more efficient. In [30], stream buffers are used to separate stream data from cached data because stream data have low temporal locality and can trash cache contents. In [31], a stream memory controller prefetches and buffers stream data from memory by dynamically reordering the accesses. In [32], data from sparse DRAM locations are prefetched and assembled as a contiguous cache line using shadow addresses (memory ranges not backed by DRAM). With a stream memory controller, system performance becomes dependent on average memory subsystem's bandwidth with less sensitivity to peak latency to access a data element. The total bus traffic is reduced and large caches are not necessary.

11.3.4 Power Consumption

Power dissipation is an important consumer metric for mobile handsets as it dictates the usage time (talk time, Internet use time, video playback time, audio playback time, etc.) and standby time. It is obvious that the longer the usage and standby time, the more desirable the device. At the same time, there is an opportunity to reduce the size and weight of the battery to achieve the same usage and standby time.

Mobile handsets have low-power consumption while operating (much less than desktop and laptops), and an almost negligible standby power when the device is not in use. This is evident in the drive for low power designs in the application processors [18,19,33]. Consequently, designers should pay attention to the energy budget in the battery and not expect a computer vision algorithm to run continuously. To save power, for example, designers may consider turning off the camera module when it is not needed or lowering the frame rate when the desired performance is not needed.

11.3.5 Cost and Performance

Mobile handsets can be separated into three categories[1]: low-cost, mid-tier, and smart phones. The lower-end phones are low-cost, high-volume devices with little to no features, except the ability to make phone calls. These low-cost phones may not even include a camera. The mid-tier phones are mid-range in prices with standard features such as a megapixel camera. They may be targeted toward the teens and tweens, and may have a music player for music enthusiasts.

Smart phones offer advanced capabilities much like a portable computer. Example smart phones include Nokia N95^{TM}, Apple IPhone^{TM}, RIM Blackberry^{TM}, and Motorola Q^{TM}. These phones are decked out with features such as PDA functions, large displays, and high-resolution (multi-megapixel) camera. They are targeted to the tech-savvy and also the business professionals, that is, those who can afford the premium cost. New computer vision applications are likely to first appear in smart phones. These mobile handsets have higher performance computing platform that can handle the extra application load. Furthermore, the better cameras provide better resolution and higher quality images for computer vision algorithms.

11.3.6 Image Sensor

The image sensors in today's mobile handset are primarily CMOS (complementary metal oxide semiconductor) image sensors. In comparison to CCD (charged-coupled devices), they have risen in quality and lowered in price in recent years [1], making them a good fit for the price-conscious mobile handset market. The resolution of an image sensor determines the amount of information that can be captured from a single shot. The higher the resolution, the more details at edges and the sharper the image in digital zooming.

Pixel resolution has been the leading marketable feature for camera phone sales. It is losing its momentum as most consumers are satisfied with the quality of an

---

[1] The categorizations and descriptions are generalizations to simplify discussions in this chapter. DynaTAC^{TM}, StarTAC^{TM}, Motorola Razr^{TM}, MotoMing^{TM}, and Motorola Q^{TM} are trademarks of Motorola Inc. Other product names are the property of their respective owners.

image at several megapixels. At those resolutions, the picture looks crisp, especially for spontaneous and casual snapshots. For archival or printing purposes, higher resolution may be desired.

As a result of market demand, semiconductor manufacturers have been optimizing image sensor designs for the mobile handset market. The large number of pixels in a single chip has been enabled by reducing individual pixel size. This is done to improve yield and cost of the imager. However, the sensitivity of each pixel is reduced because there is less area in each pixel to collect light. The dynamic range is also lessened because the pixel is collecting a smaller amount of light over time. That is, the saturation capacity of each pixel is reduced. To compensate, cameras increase the shutter speed to allow a smaller amount of light at one time, but produce images with less depth of field. This is equivalent to reducing the camera aperture. Finally, smaller pixels may be more subjective to dark noise, which is measurement of the variation in the number of electrons that are thermally generated within the imager [5]. Computer vision algorithms must then counteract the image sensor that is optimized for picture taking in a mobile handset. This may mean additional filters and processing stages to compensate for image sensors with smaller pixels.

There is ongoing research to develop better, more responsive image sensors [34]. These new approaches may enable or facilitate how computer vision algorithms are designed. For example, the image sensor may provide means to extract depth information [35], thereby reducing processing steps in the algorithm. Designers should also pay attention to image sensor research that is applied to other industries. Image sensors for the automotive and surveillance industry are typically more light-sensitive, have higher dynamic range, and are able to tolerate varying temperature ranges.

11.3.7 Illumination and Optics

Illumination and optics play a significant role in the camera operation and computer vision algorithm performance. Without sufficient illumination, the object of interest cannot be detected by the camera; without good optics, the object of interest may be blurred and difficult to detect. Extra processing steps may be required for image segmentation. This section will offer a cursory treatment of the subject area as a comprehensive discussion is beyond the scope of this chapter or book. The reader is directed to other texts for details on the theory and definitions of the terms related to measurement of light [36,37].

Designers should ask if additional lighting sources are needed in order for the application to work properly. The mobile handset offers only limited choices of active illumination. There may be an LED (light emitting diode) lighting source that is pulsed to provide constant light intensity while image is being captured. In higher-end camera phones, there may be a xenon strobe to illuminate the subject. There is also a battery drain issue to keep the illumination active. Designers should understand these issues when developing their algorithm because lighting sources in a laboratory setting are well placed and the subject is adequately lit.

Most camera modules use lenses with short, fixed focal lengths. The focal length is the distance between the optical center of the lens to the image sensor where the image is focused. A short focal length means that the camera is set up for wide area shots rather than a deep one. In most cases, it is best to keep the subject within three to four feet of the camera. While there are options for movable optical lens for autofocus and other features, the added cost and weight make these options unsuitable for the mobile handset market.

There is active research aimed at producing new lens products for camera phones. For example, Varioptic's liquid-based lens offer variable focal lengths by changing the curvature of the liquid material in their lens without any moving parts [38]. Other approaches include hybrid lenses that bend and refocus light through a series of small mirrors within the lens [39].

11.4 Intangible Obstacles

This section describes some of the less technical issues in mobile computer vision systems. These issues are "intangible" because they deal with human psychology, measurability, and business models. The aim of this section is to show how such issues can influence the productization of computer vision applications in mobile handsets. It brings to light that even the best technical solution may not produce a successful product if these intangible obstacles are not addressed.

11.4.1 User Perception and Attitudes Towards Computer Vision

Computer vision is new technology that is being applied in many consumer products. Even though there has been very recent news about the success of computer vision [16,40], most mobile handset users do not understand the technical details behind the application. They are more likely to perceive difficulties in performing a task that is augmented with computer vision.

Users consider computer vision applications as technological, and therefore they will scrutinize it more than other additive technologies that offer incremental improvements. Unlike the task of making a voice call, which users already consider routine, they may find the interaction within computer vision application foreign and consequently difficult. Designers should pay attention to the following items:

- *Reliability:* The application should consistently produce accurate results as advertised. That is, if the application is supposed to detect a certain object, it should be able to do so all the time.
- *Responsiveness:* The application should complete its tasks within a reasonable amount of time. For example, users expect to take snapshots every few seconds.

Extra delay introduced with computer vision algorithms would be considered an annoyance.

- *Intuitiveness:* The application should present an interaction that is simple and natural. That is, the computer vision algorithm should not impose requirements, such as body gestures, that are unnatural or produce unnecessary fatigue.

Furthermore, users will have an innate desire to maintain privacy and security of their information. When users realize that computer vision applications have the ability to see and understand images captured from their camera, there is an immediate negative reaction towards the product feature. For safety- and security-related applications, such as fingerprint detection and face detection, users may relax their concerns. However, for other tasks, designers will have to face the challenge of adverse user attitudes.

Usability studies to explore the user interaction would be necessary to tune the application such that it becomes easier to use. "Once a technology becomes commonplace, people tend not to think of it as technological" [41]. At that point in time, user perception and attitudes of the usefulness of computer vision applications would have changed.

11.4.2 Measurability and Standardization

There is a lack of methods to measure the general effectiveness of computer vision implementations. Comparisons should include metrics that are quantitative and objective to produce results that are unbiased and repeatable.

There are existing standards to compare algorithms within certain applications. In face recognition systems, for example, there are ratings for successfully identifying a face (recognition rate) as well as incorrectly matching a face (false positives and false negatives). There is a database of facial images to standardize the evaluation system [42]. There is other existing research that attempts to standardize the performance of computer vision algorithms (i.e., how well it performs). In [43], testing procedures, metrics, and data are provided to standardize algorithm testing methodology. Furthermore, insights into algorithm design and its affect of implementation are provided.

What is needed are application benchmarks that can be used to determine the performance of computing platforms (i.e., how well it runs). Similar to MediaBench [44] and MineBench [45], these benchmarks would be useful to compare different embedded hardware solutions for computer vision. The suite should be constructed from a unique set of algorithms with prioritization based on how often that algorithm is used.

Discussions on measurability will eventually lead to discussions on standardization. There is a basic need to standardize the algorithm and application interface so that designers can easily integrate a number of different algorithmic parts to form a processing chain. The interface can be as simple as a parameter list for a C-function call, or an elaborate protocol definition to define detectable objects. Open Source effort such as OpenCV [46-48] is a good example that would lead to standardization. This standardization effort may follow precedence from SMIA (standard mobile imaging architecture) [49,50] where there is a joint effort among 500 organizations to standardize the components in imaging modules, starting from sensors to housing and optics.

11.4.3 Business Models

It is important for designers of computer vision applications on mobile handsets to consider innovative business models when introducing the technology. As presented earlier in this chapter, there is a number of technical challenges that need to be resolved before productization. Even though computer vision can be a major technology disrupter [51] or a killer application to today's applications, business leaders may still find it risky. Technical issues must be resolved before they would consider it feasible for integration into a mobile handset. There may not be enough incentives to introduce computer vision applications in light of the technical challenges.

Designers often conceive new applications for technology's sake. In these applications, computer vision is only a fancy feature among many other gadgets or faddish technology of the time. For example, a gaming application using computer vision for tracking is nice, but is it absolutely necessary, especially with more accurate sensors? In most likelihood, users would not find the computer vision solution compelling because of user perception issues, described earlier in this chapter, and "feature fatigue" [17].

To lower such barriers, computer vision designers may want to avoid gadget-centric applications. Designers should consider a holistic approach in developing the application by including other components in the mobile handset and network. Computer vision algorithms can interact with the audio system, GPS navigation, web browsers, network servers, advertisement, and so on. Only with such integration with existing mobile handset infrastructure can designers realize the potential of computer vision. Only then can designers consider proper business models that can justify for computer vision applications' place in a mobile handset.

11.5 Future Direction

While this chapter has proposed several aspects of measuring effectiveness of a computer vision implementation with metrics such as reliability, responsiveness, and intuitiveness, this list is not complete and it lacks a proper rating scale. Designers of computer vision algorithms should consider the psychological aspects that influence the acceptance of the technology. With understanding of how users effectively use computer vision features in a mobile handset and what motivates them to continue using the feature, designers can make inroads into having the technology as a commonplace feature set.

Furthermore, we should consider the sociological impact of pervasive computer vision technology in our everyday lives. This statement is not necessarily a call to monitor and examine every aspect of the technology in our society. Instead, it is an opinion for designers to consider computer vision applications that have great social impact. Technology such as computer vision can be applied to improve daily lives by making routine tasks faster and safer. We should seek to utilize mobile technology to improve the way to communicate and educate [52] ourselves.

This chapter started with the notion that the design of computer vision applications is complex and requires a team of experts with multidisciplinary skills. A range of issues, both technical and less technical, are then discussed along with insights into the implications of the computer vision algorithm operation. It would be evident that the mobile environment offers even more restrictive and unique challenges. Design teams would expand to consider usability and business aspects that would make a successful product deployment.

Despite these issues, some discussed here in this chapter and undoubtedly new ones to come, the prospects of mobile computer vision applications are excellent. Challenges can be overcome with properly directed research, and applications would arrive as momentum builds with this technology.

References

1. Brian O'Rourke, "CCDs & CMOS: Zooming in on the image sensor market," In-Stat Report IN030702MI, September 2003.
2. D. S. Wills, J. M. Baker, Jr., H. H. Cat, S. M. Chai, L. Codrescu, J. Cruz-Rivera, J. C. Eble, A. Gentile, M. A. Hopper, W. S. Lacy, A. López-Lagunas, P. May, S. Smith, and T. Taha, "Processing architecture for smart pixel systems," *IEEE J. Select Topics Quantum Electron,* v. 2, no 1, pp. 24-34, 1996.
3. Wayne Wolf, Burak Ozer, Tiehan Lv, "Smart cameras as embedded systems," *IEEE Computer,* September 2002, pp. 48-53
4. J. Adams, K. Parulski, and K. Spaulding, "Color processing in digital cameras," *IEEE Micro,* no. 18, pp. 20-30, 1998.
5. Andrew Wilson, "Understanding camera performance specs," *Vision Systems Design,* vol 12, no 7, July 2007, pp. 39-45.
6. Gregory K. Wallace, "The JPEG still picture compression standard," *Communications of the ACM,* v. 34, no. 4, April 1991, pp.30-44.
7. Didier Le Gall, "MPEG: a video compression standard for multimedia applications," *Communications of the ACM,* Special issue on digital multimedia systems, v. 34, no. 4, April 1991, pp. 46-58.
8. Vasudev Bhaskaran, Konstantinos Konstantinides, *Image and Video Compression Standards,* 2nd edition, Kluwer Academic Press, 1997.
9. Xi-Ping Luo, Jun Li, Li-Xin Zhen, "Design and implementation of a card reader based on built-in camera," *Proceedings of the 17th International Conference on Pattern Recognition,* v. 1, 23-26 Aug. 2004, pp. 417-420.
10. J. Coughlan, R. Manduchi, "Color targets: fiducials to help visually impaired people find their way by camera phone," *EURASIP Journal on Image and Video Processing,* special issue on image and video processing for disability, v. 2007, article ID 96357, 2007.

11. Scalado AB, Lund, Sweden, "Scalado heralds the dawn of a 'new age' for mobile imaging at the Mobile World Congress in Barcelona," press release, www.scalado.com/m4n.

12. Eyal de Lara, Maria Ebling, "New products: motion-sensing cell phones," *IEEE Pervasive Computing,* v 6, no 3, July-Sept. 2007, pp.15-17.

13. M.Sohn, G. Lee, "ISeeU: Camera-based user interface for a handheld computer," *Mobile-HCI'05,* Sept 2005, pp. 299-302.

14. Sony Computer Entertainment, Inc., Sony Eye Toy, www.eyetoy.com.

15. Kris Graft, "Analysis: history of cell-phone gaming," *Business Week,* January 22, 2006.

16. Y. Cheng, M.W. Maimone, L. Matthies, "Visual odometry on the Mars exploration rovers – a tool to ensure accurate driving and science imaging," *IEEE Robotics & Automation Magazine,* v. 13, no. 2, June 2006, pp. 54-62.

17. Roland T. Rust, Debora V. Thompson, RebeccaW. Hamilton, "Defeating feature fatigue," *Harvard Business Review,* Feb 1, 2006.

18. D. Talla, J. Gobton, "Using DaVinci technology for digital video devices," *Computer,* v. 40, no.10, Oct. 2007, pp. 53-61.

19. Max Baron, "Freescale's MXC voted best: the crown goes to Freescale's MXC91321 chip," *Microprocessor Report,* January 30, 2006, pp. 1-3.

20. Tomas Akenine-Müller, Jacob Strüm, "Graphics for the masses: a hardware rasterization architecture for mobile phones," *ACM Transactions on Graphics (TOG),* v. 22, no 3, July 2003, pp. 801-808.

21. Pei Zheng, Lionel Ni, Lionel M. Ni, *Smart Phone and Next-Generation Mobile Computing,* Elsevier Science & Technology Books, December 2005.

22. Alan Zeichick, "Look Ma, no wires," *NetNews,* v. 11, no. 4, December 2007, pp. 5-8.

23. Richard Harrison, Mark Shackman, *Symbian OS C++ for Mobile Phones,* Symbian Press, Wiley, 2007.

24. Tommi Mikkonen, *Programming Mobile Devices: An Introduction for Practitioners,* Wiley, 2007.

25. J. Owens et al., "A survey of general-purpose computation on graphics hardware," *Proc. Eurographics,* 2005, pp. 21-51.

26. S. M. Chai, et al., "Streaming processors for next-generation mobile imaging applications," *IEEE Communications Magazine,* Circuits for Communication Series, vol 43, no 12, Dec 2005, pp. 81-89.

27. M. Cummings, S.Haruyama, "FPGA in the software radio," *IEEE Communications,* v. 37, no. 2, Feb 1999, pp. 108-112.

28. T. Tuan, S. Kao, A. Rahman, S. Das, S. Trimberger, "A 90-nm low-power FPGA for battery-powered applications," *Proceedings of the 2006 ACM/SIGDA 14th International Symposium on Field-Programmable Gate Arrays,* Monterey, California, 2006, pp. 3-11.

29. A. López-Lagunas, S. M. Chai, "Memory bandwidth optimization through stream descriptors," *ACM SIGARCH Computer Architecture Newsletter,* vol 34, no 1, pp. 57-64, March 2006.

30. S. Palacharla, R.E. Kessler, "Evaluating stream buffers as a secondary cache replacement," *Proceedings of the 21st Annual International Symposium on Computer Architecture,* pp. 24-33, April 1994.

31. S. A. McKee, et. al., "Dynamic access ordering for streamed computations," *IEEE Transactions on Computers,* Vol. 49, No. 11, November 2000.

32. L. Zhang, Z. Fang, M. Parker, B. K. Mathew, L. Schaelicke, J. B. Carter, W. C. Hsieh, S. A. McKee, "The impulse memory controller," *IEEE Transactions on Computers,* pp. 1117-1132, Nov 2001.

33. A. Bellaouar, M. I. Elmasry, *Low-Power Digital VLSI Design: Circuits and Systems,* Springer, June 30, 1995.

34. W. Bidermann, A. El Gamal, S. Ewedemi, J. Reyneri, H. Tian, D. Wile, D. Yang, "A 0.18 /spl mu/m high dynamic range NTSC/PAL imaging system-on-chip with embedded DRAM frame buffer," *IEEE International Solid-State Circuits Conference,* v.1, 2003, pp. 212-488.

35. S. B. Gokturk, H. Yalcin, C. Bamji, "A time-of-flight depth sensor - system description, issues and solutions," *Computer Vision and Pattern Recognition Workshop,* June 2004, p. 35.

36. Eugene Hecht. *Optics* (4th ed.). Pearson Education. 2001.
37. N. Paragios, Y. Chen, and O. Faugeras, eds., *The Handbook of Mathematical Models in Computer Vision,* Springer, 2005.
38. B. Berge, "Liquid lens technology: principle of electrowetting based lenses and applications to imaging," *Proc. IEEE International Conference on Micro Electro Mechanical Systems,* 2005.
39. E. J. Tremblay, R. A. Stack, R. L. Morrison, and J. E. Ford, "Ultrathin cameras using annular folded optics," *Applied Optics,* Vol. 46, Issue 4, pp. 463-471.
40. Martin Buehler, Karl Iagnemma, and Sanjiv Singh, *The 2005 DARPA Grand Challenge: The Great Robot Race,* Springer, 2007.
41. C. Lankshear, I. Snyder, *Teachers and Technoliteracy: Managing Literacy, Technology and Learning in Schools,* St. Leonards, NSW, Australia: Allen & Unwin, 2000.
42. P. J. Phillips, M. Hyeonjoon, S.A. Rizvi, and P.J. Rauss, "The FERET evaluation methodology for face-recognition algorithms" *IEEE Transactions on Pattern Analysis and Machine Intelligence,* v. 22, no. 10, Oct. 2000, pp. 1090-1104.
43. P. Courtney, N. A. Thacker, "Performance Characterization in Computer Vision." In *Imaging and Vision Systems,* Jacques Blanc-Talon and Dan Popescu (Eds.), NOVA Science Books, 2001.
44. Chunho Lee, Miodrag Potkonjak, William H. Mangione-Smith, "MediaBench: a tool for evaluating and synthesizing multimedia and communicatons systems," *Proceedings of the 30th annual ACM/IEEE International Symposium on Microarchitecture,* 1997, pp. 330-335.
45. R. Narayanan, B. Ozisikyilmaz, J. Zambreno, G. Memik, A. Choudhary, "MineBench: A benchmark suite for data mining workloads," *2006 IEEE International Symposium on Workload Characterization,* Oct. 2006, pp. 182-188.
46. OpenCV. http://www.intel.com/research/mrl/research/opencv/
47. Gary Bradski, Adrian Kaehler, *Learning OpenCV: Computer Vision with the OpenCV Library,* O'Reilly Media, Inc., 2008.
48. Petri Honkamaa, Jani Jäppinen, Charles Woodward, "A lightweight approach for augmented reality on camera phones using 2D images to simulate 3D," *Proceedings of the 6th International Conference on Mobile and Ubiquitous Multimedia,* vol. 284, Oulu, Finland, 2007, pp. 155-159.
49. SMIA: Standard Mobile Imaging Architecture, http://www.smia-forum.org.
50. Lee Nelson, "Solving the Problems of Mobile Imaging," *Advanced Imaging,* vol 22, no 4, April 2007, pp. 10-13.
51. Clayton M. Christensen, *The Innovator's Dilemma: The Revolutionary Book that Will Change the Way You Do Business,* Collins, 2003.
52. David Metcalf, *M-Learning: Mobile E-Learning,* HRD Press, Inc., January 2006.

Chapter 12
Challenges in Video Analytics

Nikhil Gagvani

Abstract Video analytics technology has matured and found application in a variety of fields over the past decade. This chapter discusses the current state-of-the-art, and describes challenges for future video analytics implementations. Current applications and markets for video analytics are described in the context of a processing pipeline. Application-specific challenges are described with potential solutions to those challenges. This chapter also lists some implementation considerations for embedded video analytics and concludes with future and emerging applications of video analytics.

12.1 Introduction

Video analytics is an industry term for the automated extraction of information from video for a variety of purposes. It is a combination of imaging, computer vision, pattern analysis, and machine intelligence applied to real-world problems. Its utility spans several industry segments including video surveillance, retail, and transportation. Video analytics is distinct from machine vision or machine inspection and is similar to automotive vision. Some applications of analytics include the detection of suspicious objects and activities for offering better security, in license plate recognition and traffic analysis for intelligent transportation systems, and in customer counting and queue management for retail applications.

The past decade has seen the maturation of algorithms and the adoption of analytics solutions in these markets. Analytics has progressed from research labs, with algorithms running on powerful workstations and PCs to current real-time embedded implementations on consumer-grade embedded processors. At the same time, the range of applications for analytics has also grown, with current trends indicating

Nikhil Gagvani
Cernium Corporation, Reston, VA, USA, e-mail: ngagvani@cernium.com

continued growth in the capabilities of this technology, its installed base, and its continued application to new markets.

This chapter provides an overview of current video analytics technology and its applications, introduces a processing framework amenable to embedded implementations, and describes possible future applications for embedded video analytics. There are several challenges to wider adoption of video analytics. These challenges are not just technical or scientific in nature. Practical, mass market adoption of vision and learning technologies demand economically viable, and robust implementations. Analytics is poised to enter a new era of expansion that will push applications into the mainstream and into regular use. Solutions to the challenges presented here will be critical to that expansion.

Section 12.2 provides an overview of applications. In Section 12.3, we describe the building blocks of a video analytics system with technical challenges for each block. The issues faced by embedded implementations of analytics are covered in Section 12.4, followed by a discussion of new problem areas and future applications in Section 12.5.

12.2 Current Technology and Applications

Video analytics in its most general form is concerned with visual scene understanding from a sequence of pictures in temporal order. In a manner similar to web analytics, which attempts to derive intelligence from web logs, video analytics treats video as a data source with the goal of extracting meaningful information. The output of video analytics is generally quantitative and structured information that summarizes some aspect related to the content of video. Therefore, it is also called video content analysis (VCA) or video intelligence.

Techniques in video analytics draw from multiple disciplines, with the goal of scene understanding. In most instances, video analytics does not have a cognition aspect, and is not expected to act or respond autonomously; it is, however, expected to adapt and learn. Video analytics is also distinct from machine vision used in the context of visual inspection. The difference is in the range of conditions, both environmental and illumination, and the relatively unconstrained camera setup that must be handled by analytics. For instance, video analytics systems employed for video surveillance are expected to work uninterrupted in real-world illumination over multiple seasons and weather conditions using a wide range of camera and lens combinations. Analytics applications also frequently run in unattended or unmanned settings without a human in the loop, with little or no intervention or control available for tuning. This poses a challenge to techniques and algorithms in that they need to adapt and learn over extremely long periods of time.

Applications of video analytics vary in the type of analysis and in the level of performance and robustness expected. Economic and computational considerations also impact the choice and complexity of algorithms employed. Comparison of video analytics implementations is therefore challenging. Further, comparisons that are done with short video clips are typically not representative of continuous operation, required of embedded systems. The selection and tuning of algorithms to fit a given need must be based on objective criteria with metrics selected to qualify performance on realistic long duration video.

Analytics implementations are generally evaluated based on some well-accepted metrics. The PETS [10] workshops have attempted to formalize these to a great extent. For instance, frame-based metrics are used to determine the accuracy of analytics on individual frames of a video sequence, without taking into account the preservation of identity of the object over its lifespan. Algorithms can then be objectively measured based on the measurement of true and false positives and negatives against ground truth data. For this purpose, the following definitions allow practical evaluation of alternate techniques.

1. **True Positive (TP).** The number of frames where output from the system and ground truth agree on the presence and location of one or more objects.
2. **False Positive (FP).** The number of frames where the system reports at least one object, while ground truth has no object, or where the location of system results do not intersect results from ground truth data.
3. **True Negative (TN).** The number of frames where output from the system and ground truth agree on the absence of any object.
4. **False Negative (FN).** The number of frames where ground truth contains at least one object while the system does not report any object, or reports objects that do not intersect ground truth objects.

Additionally, TF is the total number of frames in the sequence.

Bashir et al. [2] describe several metrics to measure tracking performance, based on these definitions. Some examples include:

$$\text{Detection Rate} = \frac{TP}{TP+FN} \qquad (12.1)$$

$$\text{False Alarm Rate, } FAR = \frac{FP}{TP+FP} \qquad (12.2)$$

$$\text{Specificity} = \frac{TN}{FP+TN} \qquad (12.3)$$

$$\text{Accuracy} = \frac{TP+TN}{TF} \qquad (12.4)$$

Embedded applications that incorporate video analytics must meet several requirements. Devices incorporating video analytics are generally deployed in environments where they are expected to work continuously with little or no human intervention. Computational, memory, and power resources available in these environments are limited compared to those available on general-purpose computing platforms. Some technical and operational requirements for a pragmatic solution are listed below.

1. **High Detection Rate.** It is desirable that practical applications correctly detect a high number of objects. For this purpose, true positives need to be maximized while minimizing false negatives.
2. **Low FAR.** A high detection rate may be achieved by increasing the sensitivity or reducing the detection threshold; however this generally results in an unacceptable number of false alarms, which can reduce confidence in the system to the extent that it is not used. Therefore, false positives must be kept to a minimum while maintaining a high number of true positives.
3. **Small Footprint.** Practical implementations need to be cost effective. Computational cycles and memory usage must be minimized in embedded applications of analytics.
4. **Ease of Setup and Use.** Mass market products and applications need to run predictably. End users are not expected to have a high degree of technical expertise, or the inclination to continue tuning algorithms to achieve desired objectives. Therefore, algorithms must adapt to changing conditions, and be able to run *out of the box* in a variety of situations.

A goal for video analytics implementations should be a very high detection rate, while minimizing false alarms, with low memory footprint and *plug and play* operation by the average user. These goals are often conflicting, and the algorithm designer or product developer needs to make tradeoffs that best fit the intended use and market.

Currently, analytics technology is commercially used in three major market segments: surveillance, retail and transportation. The following sections describe applications and challenges in these market segments. For a detailed discussion of markets and applications, the reader is referred to Chapter 3.

12.2.1 Video Surveillance

Various techniques are employed for automated and often unattended video surveillance. Video analytics is implemented as firmware in a variety of embedded devices including cameras, digital video recorders, video processors, and servers. Techniques are used to detect, classify, track and report the motion and activities of people and vehicles. Video analytics for surveillance provides a personnel-multiplier effect, by analyzing hundreds and even thousands of video feeds. It reduces the manpower burden for monitoring and searching through surveillance video. It is used both for real-time monitoring and forensic processing. Current implementations such as Cernium's *Perceptrak* [7] can reliably detect and report a variety of behaviors such as

- single or multiple people
- single or multiple vehicles
- walking, running, loitering, or fallen people
- stopped or speeding vehicles

- abandoned objects or removed objects
- wrong way motion

Video input can be either in the visible spectrum or from infrared (IR) or thermal imagers. Typical challenges faced by analytics for surveillance applications include robustness to illumination and environmental effects and variations in these conditions. These applications are expected to work continuously without modification in natural or artificial lighting, in sunny and cloudy weather, over multiple seasons that can include rain, snow, fog, and moving water. Further, the goal of video surveillance is to cover a large area with a minimum number of cameras; hence wide fields of view are common, which results in a very low number of pixels on target; it is not uncommon to have less than 1000 pixels for a person in surveillance video.

While commercial systems that apply analytics for video surveillance are currently available and deployed, significant challenges remain. Primarily, these challenges can be summarized in the ability of vision algorithms to run unattended and operate effectively in a variety of environmental and illumination conditions. Such challenges are particularly significant in outdoor environments and in mixed indoor-outdoor environments such as parking garages. For instance, a person moving through a parking garage, as shown in Fig. 12.1, appears from deep shadow (top), and successively walks into bright sunlight (center, bottom). The contrast between the person and the background varies greatly across this span, which poses a challenge for correct segmentation and detection. Additional challenges are discussed in Section 12.5.

12.2.2 Retail

Applications of analytics in retail environments provide marketing information and can result in increased operational efficiency. Analytics can automatically count the number of people entering or leaving a store, and compute statistics of store occupancy over time. It can provide information about the number of people waiting to be served, and the wait time. These are used to estimate the number of lanes/counters that should be manned.

Further, traffic patterns in various sections of a store can be measured to understand buying habits, control inventory, and gauge the success of promotions. Customer dwell time in front of signage or product advertisements can provide clues for marketing purposes. It can also potentially be used to detect shop-lifting. Integration with *point-of-sale (POS)* systems can be used to correlate purchases with payment and prevent losses, in the event that items are removed without payment.

The challenges for retail applications are somewhat different from those for surveillance. Retail environments are typically indoor, and have controlled artificial lighting and hence clutter from illumination and environmental effects is not a major challenge. On the other hand, while surveillance environments tend to have limited occlusion, and a single or a few interacting entities, retail environments are subject to occlusions in crowded aisles, multiple interacting persons, shopping carts and

Fig. 12.1 A person walking across the scene moves from deep shadow to bright sunlight over a few frames. This can cause challenges for segmentation and tracking.

other mobile and fixed furniture. Accurate tracking is a greater challenge in retail environments, while segmentation presents a bigger challenge in video surveillance.

Cameras in retail environments tend to be ceiling-mounted looking vertically downwards. Algorithms employed for person detection and tracking use head-candidate selection [13] techniques because the head and shoulders tend to be the un-occluded and visible parts of persons in the scene. However, this poses a challenge for constructing and maintaining an online appearance model for each individual in the store, due to limited visibility of clothing and other distinguishing features.

Fig. 12.2a shows the count of people walking through a corridor using a ceiling-mounted camera. The count on the left indicates the number of people that have walked in the right-to-left direction. The count on the right indicates the number of people that have walked in the left-to-right direction.

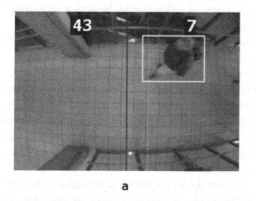

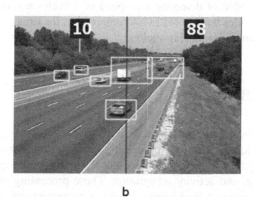

Fig. 12.2 Automated counting of (a) people and (b) vehicles. Bidirectional counts are shown based on movement from left-to-right or right-to-left.

12.2.3 Transportation

The applications of analytics in transportation stem from both security and operational requirements. These applications vary widely, from automated license plate recognition (ALPR) systems, to traffic enforcement cameras.

Vision systems are also employed for vehicle counting, toll collection, and highway monitoring for disabled vehicles. Wrong way detection or zone violation is employed for security in airports, perimeter protection in marine terminals, and to detect people and objects on railroad tracks. Environments span both indoor and outdoor installations.

Fig. 12.2b shows an application of vehicle counting on a highway. Vehicles going in either direction are counted and reported. Note that such applications must deal with occlusions from other vehicles.

Traffic enforcement cameras must be able to detect conditions such as running a red light, wrong way motion, and illegal turns. They must work in outdoor settings, continuously under adverse weather conditions. Furthermore, such cameras are mounted on poles close to the lights, and are subject to significant motion due to wind. Detection techniques must be robust to these conditions. Additionally, video of fast-moving traffic can exhibit significant motion blur which must be factored out prior to analysis. A further requirement for enforcement cameras is the need for evidence-quality video and storage. Watermarking techniques are employed for this purpose to detect tampering.

An example of video analytics for traffic surveillance is described in [3]. A smart camera using a CMOS imager is described with an embedded DSP for analytics. This camera is capable of detecting the speed of vehicles and detecting stopped cars. It further provides built-in MPEG-4 compression for streaming video over an IP network to a central monitoring station.

12.3 Building Blocks

Most video analytics applications use a series of processing steps, composed of well-known techniques. A generic processing pipeline is shown in Fig. 12.3. The processing steps are shown as rectangular blocks, which include segmentation, classification, tracking, and activity recognition. These processing blocks depend on models that can include a background model, a camera model, one or more appearance models, motion models, and shape models. These models are generally updated over time, with learning and adaptation being done over a series of frames. As frames progress through these processing steps, intermediate output results are produced which are shown in the bubbles in the top row of Fig. 12.3. Analytics applications in specific domains may not employ all these steps, or may not apply them strictly in the order specified. Multiple trackers or classifiers may run in parallel or run optionally based on the results of upstream processes. These steps are described in detail below.

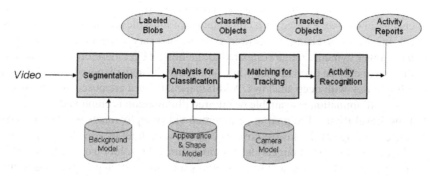

Fig. 12.3 Video analytics processing pipeline.

12.3.1 Segmentation

Segmentation is the process of separating foreground objects from the background. Pixels are grouped into either background pixels or foreground pixels. Foreground pixels are further grouped into blobs, each of which is generally a connected set. In real-world video, extraneous or spurious foreground pixels may be detected due to the presence of environmental and illumination influences, called clutter. Therefore, a clutter removal step is necessary to eliminate foreground blobs due to rain, snow, wind, water, shadows, reflections, and so on. Background separation generally assumes a static camera; however, for pan-tilt cameras, the background may change.

The output of segmentation is a set of labeled blobs, each blob corresponding to a unique object. There has been a lot of work on background subtraction [16]. While this is a well-researched problem, significant challenges remain.

Challenges in segmentation are particularly relevant because errors in this step can adversely impact downstream processing. Some challenges encountered in real-world video are listed below.

1. **Clutter:** Clutter refers to changes in the scene owing to environmental and illumination effects. While background statistics may be used to eliminate periodic motion due to waves, rain, etc., illumination effects are harder to eliminate especially if they are of a localized and transient nature. For instance, reflections and glare that appear instantaneously and move through the scene may be detected as foreground blobs. Headlights sweeping across the scene illuminate a portion of the scene including objects such as parked cars. This can result in an apparent motion of the parked car, again causing incorrect foreground detection. There is a balance between clutter removal and detection rate; more clutter can be removed at the expense of a lower detection rate. This tradeoff is dependent on the application.
2. **Contrast:** The contrast in the scene can vary significantly based on the time of day, season, ambient lighting, and camera gain logic. Most commercial cameras incorporate automatic gain control (AGC), auto-iris, and automatic white balance

(AWB). The perceived change in the video output may be greater than the actual change in the scene based on a combination of multiple adjustments in the camera. In addition to changes over time, contrast may vary across the scene. Imagers have lower dynamic range compared to the human eye; therefore some parts of the image may be overexposed while others may be underexposed, especially on a bright day with deep shadows. Additional challenges are posed at night when limited illumination is available or infrared illumination is employed.

3. **Low Resolution:** The goal in commercial video deployments is often to maximize coverage at the lowest cost. Therefore, wide field of view lenses are employed, yielding small targets and extremely limited resolution on the target. This may not provide a sufficient set of features for consistent and correct segmentation, or for discrimination against clutter.

4. **Compression Artifacts:** Video is rapidly transitioning from analog to digital over Internet Protocol (IP) networks. Some form of lossy compression such as MJPEG or MPEG-4 is employed to compress video prior to transmission over a network. This causes loss of high-frequency information, and introduces artifacts such as "ringing," and blockiness. Further, these artifacts do not change smoothly over time, introducing discrete changes in the scene. These changes can also be perceived as foreground, causing incorrect segmentation.

General solutions to these challenges will greatly expand and enhance the applications of video analytics in current and new markets.

12.3.2 Classification and Recognition

After segmented blobs corresponding to unique objects have been separated from the background, classification techniques can be used to assign a class label such as *person, vehicle,* or *animal.* Classification techniques vary widely in their approach and outcome. Techniques described by [19] use a supervised learning approach based on a set of features for each blob. Dalal and Triggs [8] describe a detection scheme for humans in video sequences that combine appearance and flow, and generalize very well to moving backgrounds and work in the presence of camera motion. Brown [4] describes a technique for view-independent person and vehicle classification. A key aspect of classification is the selection of features that persist over multiple frames and are discriminative for purposes of classification. SIFT [14] has been shown to provide these properties.

Recognition attempts to identify a specific instance rather than a general category as is done in classification. For instance, license plate recognition can specifically identify a unique vehicle by looking up the number in a database of registered vehicles. Recognition works well only where the set of unique instances is small, as in the numbers and letters present in a license plate. Face recognition continues to be a well-researched topic [25], although it is not typically within the realm of video analytics. Video analytics applications are required to work in unconstrained illumination conditions with little control over camera position and view. Current ALPR and face recognition systems need tight control over these parameters. As recognition techniques improve to allow a variety of operational scenarios, these will be assimilated into video analytics systems.

While classification works well in separating people from vehicles, multiclass classification remains a challenge. As the number of valid classes increase, the training burden grows, in addition to the runtime computational costs. Practical and optimized multiclass classifiers running on embedded platforms continue to pose a challenge as well. Segmentation errors resulting from clutter and low resolution also make it challenging to extract coherent features for purposes of classification.

12.3.3 Tracking

Tracking is the problem of establishing correspondence between blobs over successive frames of video. These correspondences can be used for scene interpretation and behavior or activity recognition.

There are various methods for tracking that are based on motion coherence, appearance, and shape models. A good survey of tracking techniques is provided in [23]. Tracking suffers from several challenges. As objects move through the scene, they change their pose and orientation with respect to the camera, and can look different over multiple frames. The same features may not be visible in each frame, which makes it difficult to establish correspondences. Further, people moving in the scene exhibit articulated motion, which can significantly change the shape of the blob.

Another challenge in tracking occurs due to occlusions. These occlusions can be due to:

1. Background Occludes Foreground: In this case, pixels from the background occlude foreground pixels, either partially or fully. An example of such occlusion is a person walking behind a tree and re-appearing. Tree pixels would be considered background; hence for one or more frames, foreground pixels are occluded by background pixels.
2. Foreground Occludes Foreground (different objects): In this case, two distinct and separate foreground objects occlude one another. In this case, front-back relationships may be difficult to establish, especially for articulated objects. An example of this would be a person stepping out from the car, with the car door ajar, and in front of the person, the person being in front of the car.
3. Foreground Self-Occludes: Articulated objects can have parts that occlude one another. This is very common when people walk, and their swinging arms may occlude the torso.

An important issue in tracking is the ability to identify multiple, relatively invariant features on each blob. For correspondence, at least a few common feature locations must be visible over successive frames. This is only possible if segmentation is accurate, and there is sufficient resolution for the tracked blob. Errors in segmentation may cause the track to be lost periodically; therefore it is important to be able to re-acquire the track.

12.3.4 Behavior and Activity Recognition

After foreground objects have been segmented, classified, and tracked, the motion and behavior of these objects can be described in the context of the scene. Furthermore, the behavior of other objects in the scene relative to a given object can also be analyzed. Activity recognition can be done at various levels. At a high-level, activities can be described based on the gross dynamics of the object. Track trajectories and ground plane models are very useful for such analysis. Examples of high level activities include a loitering person, a fallen person, or a slow-moving vehicle.

Additional part-based analysis may be done at increasing levels of granularity. For instance, part-based analysis of articulated objects may be done based on a kinematic model. Such analysis can provide information on activities such as jumping, crouching, reaching, and bending. These typically require an unoccluded view of the object at a reasonably high resolution. Motion capture techniques that use marker-based joint extraction are not generally suitable for video analytics; however, kinematic models of human motion derived from motion capture may be used for activity recognition. Finally, gesture recognition techniques can report on the detailed movements of the hands and fingers and can be used to qualify activities such as grasping, pointing, and waving. Aggarwal and Cai [1] provide a review of techniques for human motion analysis. Moeslund et al. [15] have done a comprehensive review of techniques for human activity analysis and recognition.

Fig. 12.4 summarizes the processing pipeline. An example is shown where a person walks into the scene and falls down. After segmentation, two blobs are extracted and labeled, shown as white blobs. The blob on the top is classified as clutter. The blob at the bottom is classified as a person. Further, the person blob is tracked through the scene. This track is indicated by the trajectory tail. Behavior analysis results in a message being generated and displayed on an operator console that a person has fallen down.

12.4 Embedded Implementations

Part II of this book describes several techniques for embedded implementations of computer vision algorithms. Typically, processing and memory tradeoffs need to be considered for real-time implementation. Additionally, given the variety of algorithms available for video analytics, consideration ought to be given to balancing the processing pipeline.

Digital signal processors and FPGAs now have accelerated support for basic image processing functions such as color conversion, convolution and filtering, and

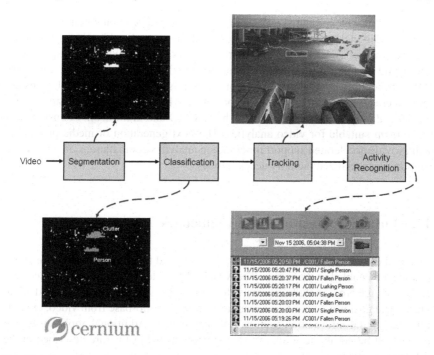

Fig. 12.4 Example of fallen person detection. The output from each step is shown visually. The final result is generally displayed as a text message alerting an operator about a fallen person.

histogram equalization. Advanced computer vision techniques for background modeling, feature and edge extraction, or tracking are uncommon and need to be programmed or implemented manually. The OpenCV library provides a commonly used set of computer vision algorithms with platform specific optimizations for Intel processors.

At this time, hardware support for machine learning techniques is not easily available. Basic matrix operations are available in some architectures; however accelerated support for techniques such as mean-shift [22] and support vector machines [6] is lacking.

Cache architectures exploit spatial and temporal coherence, and work well for linear arrays. However, images are stored in memory in row-major or column-major format, and linear pre-fetching techniques do not work well with subimage blocks that are $N \times M$ pixels. Pre-fetch algorithms and cache implementations need to reflect memory access patterns specific to images. Block DMA operations that can transfer subimages can avoid a lot of address calculations allowing the processor to work on image processing tasks.

Specifically, a practical analytics system may employ specific additional processing based on the content of the scene. For instance, in a scene with multiple objects or targets, an advanced tracker may be employed to deal with occlusions and merge/split interactions. This tracker might depend on local appearance features [9] which may not be computed every frame, but would be computed on demand, requiring additional processing cycles. This results in unpredictable processor loading on a per-frame basis. Embedded system designers need to budget for peak loading and would design a system that includes the time for feature computation in every frame. Since this computation may not be exercised unless severe occlusions are encountered, such budgeting for peak loads would be wasteful of processing cycles.

General purpose processors already have SIMD and multimedia extensions that make them suitable for video analytics. The next generation of media processors will provide accelerated support for common analytics computations, in addition to supporting specialized memory access modes.

12.5 Future Applications and Challenges

The field of video analytics is expanding rapidly, and there are several applications that can be enabled in the future. The VACE [12] series of programs included several challenge areas including news video, meetings, surveillance video, and aerial video. The goal was to create a semantic, searchable info-base from video, exploiting multimodal information such as text and speech. Additional applications can be enabled based on the solution to some open problems that are described in the following sections.

12.5.1 Moving Cameras

Current embedded analytics are mostly computed on static scenes with fixed cameras, and are based on the concept of background subtraction. Moving cameras that are either hand-held or vehicle-mounted must separate camera motion from object motion. Various techniques have been proposed for estimation of camera motion [24]. These techniques are computationally intensive and may require working memory that has been beyond the scope of most commercially viable embedded processors. However, advances in automotive vision and aerial surveillance have resulted in FPGA or ASIC implementations that can work with moving cameras. The Acadia Vision Processor [18] allows real-time mosaicing or frame-to-frame camera motion computation on a single video channel.

Vehicle-mounted cameras for surveillance and operational purposes are common in law enforcement and public transit. These views exhibit significant parallax, and affine transformation models cannot be used to estimate frame-to-frame motion accurately. Feature tracking and homography computations have been shown to work in these cases although they are still limited in the range of camera motion and the duration for which accurate tracking may be done. Accurate tracking over several minutes and hours from a vehicle or aircraft-mounted camera remains an open problem. This challenge is further compounded by the limitations of embedded systems.

With the easy availability of low-cost CMOS imagers, stereo vision systems are being developed that can mitigate several issues with cameras mounted on moving vehicles. Woodfill et al. [21] describe an embedded stereoscopic vision system that performs background modeling and stereo correlation from a pair of imagers in real-time. This can reduce issues with clutter and occlusion, and can aid in segmentation by incorporating depth information.

12.5.2 Multi-Camera Tracking

Tracking an object in a single view is achieved using methods described in Section 12.3. However, applications in surveillance, retail, and transportation can benefit from track association across views and cameras. For instance, for surveillance it may be important to track the motion of people and vehicles over a large region that has multiple cameras. Retail environments tend to have multiple nonoverlapping cameras. In order to track customer activities and behavior, it is important to be able to correlate the same customer across multiple views. This requires an online discriminative model to be constructed for re-acquisition and association of the person between views.

Active tracking systems employ pan-tilt-zoom (PTZ) cameras that can simultaneously detect and track objects, while controlling the motion of the camera to keep a subject centered in the view. These systems are challenged by occlusion and clutter as well. Camera motion needs to be factored out while the pan-tilt unit is in motion. Scale ambiguities from zooming can cause difficulty with target tracking. For busy scenes with multiple targets, the tracker may occasionally jump between targets, causing erratic motion of the pan-tilt head, or track switching.

Multi-camera tracking may be done with overlapping cameras or nonoverlapping cameras. In the case of overlapping cameras the tracked object must be correlated across different views. Each view may see a different portion of the target. Camera calibration can aid with such tracking. Calibration-free association of objects across overlapping but widely differing viewpoints remains challenging. This is further complicated if the scene has multiple objects that may be occluding or passing one another.

Multi-camera tracking across nonoverlapping cameras requires the construction of a fingerprint or signature for each object that is being tracked. Such systems may have the flexibility of providing similar views of the object; therefore, similar features would be visible from each camera. However, finding discriminative features among objects of a single class is challenging. Shan et al. [17] describe a technique to track vehicles from roughly overhead nonoverlapping views and show good results over a set of 200 vehicles captured at different times of the day.

Multi-camera tracking and association over nonoverlapping, uncalibrated cameras with different viewpoints remains an active area of research. An additional challenge occurs if multiple classes of objects, such as persons and vehicles need to be tracked simultaneously.

Embedded applications of multi-camera tracking remain challenging. Typically, the processing for each camera is done on a co-located processor. This information needs to be communicated in near real-time over networks to participating cameras. Current network latencies cannot allow such information to be communicated and processed within a frame time and methods to handle delayed tracking information must be employed. Further, there may not be a central node which has the state from all cameras, and not all cameras may see the same object. Identification of peer cameras in the potentially visible set, especially with uncalibrated cameras creates additional challenges.

12.5.3 Smart Cameras

In [20], Wolf describes an embedded smart camera that incorporates a 32-bit VLIW media processor. Both low-level and high-level processing functions are implemented in the camera such as region extraction, ellipse fitting, and graph matching. Discrete hidden Markov models are used to detect human actions and gestures based on motions of body parts. Current-generation video analytics for surveillance is embedded in smart cameras using digital signal processors. Cernium's Edge library allows multiple channels of video to be analyzed on a single Texas Instruments TMS320DM6446 SoC.

As processors get faster, and video-specific acceleration blocks become available, smart megapixel cameras will be possible. Megapixel imagers offer unprecedented resolution, which can allow gesture recognition and much better fidelity for advanced activity recognition. However, they also result in added clutter motion, which must be removed and factored out.

Mobile smart phones increasingly have video capabilities. Coupled with faster processors incorporating multimedia acceleration blocks, video analytics on a mobile phone is becoming a reality. Chapter 11 of this book describes various applications and challenges for vision on mobile platforms. In [5] Bruns et al. describe a recognition application for museums that is reported to have an accuracy over 95% for over 150 objects. Instead of solving a multiclass recognition problem, a two-layer neural network is used on a small subset of objects. This subset is identified based on localization of the camera. Vision applications running on the phone have also been used for sign recognition.

12.5.4 Scene Understanding

Current applications of video analytics build upon computer vision and pattern recognition technologies, and are able to "perceive" changes and interpret them to report discrete events. This is primarily based on the analysis of foreground pixels and their motion. Background pixels provide context that can be exploited to gain a semantic understanding of the scene.

As a video analytics system observes the scene, and classifies and tracks people and vehicles, it can infer the 3D characteristics of background objects. Scene geometry estimation can be done with uncalibrated cameras, if certain simplifying assumptions can be made such as the presence of a ground plane where pedestrians and vehicles are detected. Further, output from tracking can indicate background objects that cause occlusions. Such front-back relationships between background objects can provide cues for depth estimation.

Recent work by Hoiem [11] uses a statistical framework that simultaneously infers object identity, surface orientation and camera viewpoint using a single uncalibrated image. A key challenge for such approaches is reliable segmentation and localization of foreground objects. Additionally, a scene model that is representative of the content in the scene must be constructed online. Robust online scene modeling and maintenance over long periods of time continues to be a challenge.

Future applications based on scene understanding will be able to address the problem of converting video to text. A narrative of a video sequence provided in natural language would mimic a human observer. It is conceivable that such a system could surpass human abilities in specific scenarios.

12.5.5 Search and Retrieval

The combination of inexpensive video cameras, efficient compression technology and affordable storage solutions has resulted in increasingly larger amounts of video data being stored and archived. In surveillance, it is common to find hundreds of video streams being stored for weeks or months.

With video driving a large portion of growth in Internet traffic and usage, analytics applications to organize, analyze, interpret, index and retrieve video will be required. We envision a future where high-level semantic queries for video will be used to retrieve video segments from an enormous corpus of video content with highly relevant results. The user experience would be similar to text searching on the web today. The volume of video content generated will far exceed the capability of offline algorithms to analyze it. Therefore, online video analytics algorithms that compute rich metadata using streaming video will be required.

Current techniques for video indexing and retrieval depend on the computation of features such as color histograms, texture, shape, and geometry. *Query-by-content* and *query-by-example* systems require a user to submit an exemplary image, the result of which is a set of similar images. Natural language queries continue to be a challenge. Further, most systems address image retrieval, and do not directly exploit the temporal nature of video. Video queries that describe entire activities such as *"find me all people that climb on a bus and have a blue backpack"* require semantic analysis of the scene, and feature descriptors that span multiple frames of a video sequence.

12.5.6 Vision for an Analytics-Powered Future

Over the next decade, we expect that video analytics will go mainstream and will be a part of our daily lives. Video sensors will be ubiquitous, embedded in everything including buildings, appliances, automobiles, furniture and possibly clothing. Embedded analytics and communication stacks in these sensors will enable them to collaborate to achieve specific tasks autonomously. The intelligence embedded in these networks of sensors will allow them to be tasked to "watch" and "react" autonomously. Intelligent traffic systems will achieve flow control by adaptively routing traffic around hotspots. Analytics-driven sensors embedded in automobiles will automatically interpret traffic signs, and alert the driver to speed limits, or possibly regulate speed. Analytics sensors embedded in clothing will be context aware, and will alert a person to activities occurring outside the human field-of-view; the equivalent of having unblinking eyes behind your head!

The human-machine interface that enables natural interaction with these capabilities will be critical to the adoption and use of analytics. The best interfaces are those that are transparent and enable users to focus on the task, rather than on learning the interface. Widespread usage will dictate that analytics not be obtrusive; rather, it would be best for end users to not realize the presence of machine intelligence. For social acceptance, it will be critical to address privacy issues with video. Embedded analytics in which the sensors interpret video at its source, and only forward key metadata instead of images, will mitigate concerns about privacy.

Applications of video analytics will extend beyond current markets in surveillance, retail, and transportation. Most consumer video today consists of broadcast, film and sports content which has a very wide variety of scene characteristics and subject motion. We imagine a future where a user will be able to pose a high-level query to retrieve a specific moment in a game, or search for a specific type of scene in a film either through natural language or by presenting examples of similar scenes. These applications will run on increasingly faster embedded processors, which will be capable of running for extended periods using very low power, and will be able to communicate with their surroundings.

12.6 Summary

Video analytics is currently used in several products and applications. The availability of embedded video processors, combined with embedded codecs and network stacks is making it possible to design and develop smart cameras, video servers and digital video recorders. We expect the use of analytics to grow rapidly over the next decade, and become ubiquitous by being embedded in devices such as mobile phones. The range of capabilities will also expand to include both fixed and moving cameras, networks of cameras that work cooperatively and provide a higher level of scene understanding that will approach or even exceed human perception in some cases.

Several challenges remain to be solved prior to widespread adoption of analytics in our daily lives. The primary challenge is in the ability of analytics to run unattended over extremely long periods of time spanning years without degradation in detection rate or increase in false alarm rates. Additional challenges result from the limited ability of classifiers to work unsupervised, and be able to discriminate reliably among tens or hundreds of classes of objects.

We expect advances in processor architectures and acceleration blocks dedicated to image processing and vision to be available in the coming years. These advances, combined with software stacks that make it easy to program and use these blocks will be critical to fostering the development of new embedded vision algorithms. A joint effort between academic institutions, national and international research initiatives, and industry groups will be critical to the continued success and growth of video analytics.

References

1. J. Aggarwal and Q. Cai. Human motion analysis: A review. *Computer Vision and Image Understanding*, 73:428–440, 1999.
2. F. Bashir and F. Porikli. Performance evaluation of object detection and tracking systems. *IEEE Int. Workshop on Performance Evaluation of Tracking and Surveillance (PETS)*, 2006.
3. M. Bramberger, J. Brunner, B. Rinner, and H. Schwabach. Real-time video analysis on an embedded smart camera for traffic surveillance. *Real-Time and Embedded Technology and Applications Symposium, 2004. Proceedings. RTAS 2004. 10th IEEE*, pages 174–181, 25–28 May 2004.
4. Lisa M. Brown. View-independent vehicle/person classification. *Proceedins of the ACM 2nd International Workshop on Video Surveillance and Sensor Networks*, pages 114–123, New York, 2004.
5. Erich Bruns, Benjamnin Brombach, Thomas Zeidler, and Oliver Bimber. Enabling mobile phones to support large-scale museum guidance. *IEEE MultiMedia*, 14(2):16–25, 2007.
6. O. Chapelle, P. Haffner, and V. Vapnik. Svms for histogram-based image classification. *IEEE Transactions on Neural Networks: Special Issue on Support Vectors*, 1999.
7. Cernium Corporation. *Perceptrak User Guide*. Reston VA, 2006.
8. Navneet Dalal and Bill Triggs. Histogram of oriented gradients for human detection. *IEEE Conference on Computer Vision and Pattern Recognition*, volume 1, pages 886–893, San Diego, June 2005.
9. Gianfranco Doretto and Stefano Soatto. Dynamic shape and appearance models. *IEEE Transactions on Pattern Analysis and Machine Intelligence*, 28(12):2006–2019, 2006.
10. J.M. Ferryman. Performance evaluation of tracking and surveillance. *IEEE Int. Workshops on Performance Evaluation of Tracking and Surveillance (PETS)*, 2000–2007.
11. Derek Hoiem, Alexei A. Efros, and Martial Hebert. Putting objects in perspective. *Proc. IEEE CVPR Conference*, 02:2137–2144, 2006.
12. R. Kasturi, D. Goldgof, P. Soundararajan, V. Manohar, M. Boonstra, V. Korzhova, J. Zhang, R. Bowers, and J. Garofolo. Framework for performance evaluation of face, text, and vehicle detection and tracking in video: Data, metrics, and protocol. *IEEE Transactions on Pattern Analysis and Machine Intelligence*, March 2008.
13. Alex Leykin. *Visual Human Tracking and Group Activity Analysis: A Video Mining System for Retail Marketing*. PhD thesis, Indiana University, Devember 2007.
14. David G. Lowe. Distinctive image features from scale-invariant keypoints. *International Journal of Computer Vision*, 60(2):91–110, November 2004.

15. T.B. Moeslund, A. Hilton, and V. Kruger. A survey of advances in vision-based human motion capture and analysis. *Computer Vision and Image Understanding*, 103(2-3):90–126, November 2006.

16. R.J. Radke, S. Andra, O. Al-Kofahi, and B. Roysam. Image change detection algorithms: a systematic survey. *IEEE Transactions on Image Processing*, 14(3):294–307, March 2005.

17. Ying Shan, Harpreet S. Sawhney, and Rakesh (Teddy) Kumar. Unsupervised learning of discriminative edge measures for vehicle matching between nonoverlapping cameras. *IEEE Conference on Computer Vision and Pattern Recognition*, volume 1, pages 894–901, Los Alamitos, CA, 2005. IEEE Computer Society.

18. G. van der Wal, M. Hansen, and M. Piacentino. The Acadia vision processor. *Proc. Fifth IEEE International Workshop on Computer Architectures for Machine Perception*, pages 31–40, 2000.

19. Paul Viola and Michael Jones. Rapid object detection using a boosted cascade of simple features. *Proceedings IEEE Conf. on Computer Vision and Pattern Recognition*, 2001.

20. W. Wolf, B. Ozer, and T. Lv. Smart cameras as embedded systems. *Computer*, 35(9):48–53, Sep 2002.

21. John Iselin Woodfill, Ron Buck, Dave Jurasek, Gaile Gordon, and Terrance Brown. 3D vision: Developing an embedded stereo-vision system. *Computer*, 40(5):106–108, 2007.

22. Changjiang Yang, Ramani Duraiswami, and Larry Davis. Efficient mean-shift tracking via a new similarity measure. *IEEE Conference on Computer Vision and Pattern Recognition*, volume 1, pages 176–183, San Diego, June 2005.

23. Alper Yilmaz, Omar Javed, and Mubarak Shah. Object tracking: A survey. *ACM Computing Surveys*, 38(4), December 2006.

24. Tong Zhang and Carlo Tomasi. Fast, robust, and consistent camera motion estimation. *Computer Vision and Pattern Recognition*, 01:1164, 1999.

25. W. Zhao, R. Chellappa, P. J. Phillips, and A. Rosenfeld. Face recognition: A literature survey. *ACM Comput. Surv.*, 35(4):399–458, 2003.

Chapter 13
Challenges of Embedded Computer Vision in Automotive Safety Systems

Yan Zhang, Arnab S. Dhua, Stephen J. Kiselewich, and William A. Bauson

Abstract Vision-based automotive safety systems have received considerable attention over the past decade. Such systems have advantages compared to those based on other types of sensors such as radar, because of the availability of low-cost and high-resolution cameras and abundant information contained in video images. However, various technical challenges exist in such systems. One of the most prominent challenges lies in running sophisticated computer vision algorithms on low-cost embedded systems at frame rate. This chapter discusses these challenges through vehicle detection and classification in a collision warning system.

13.1 Computer Vision in Automotive Safety Applications

Many automotive safety systems that used to rely on radar, laser, ultrasound, or other types of sensors now have their counterparts using cameras. The availability of low-cost and high-resolution cameras on the market and the abundant information contained in video images make such vision-based systems appealing. Computer vision techniques have been widely used in camera-based automotive safety systems including occupant sensing, lane-departure warning and collision warning. Sophisticated algorithms are essential to address a large variety of complex situations on the road and surrounding areas. For example, in a collision warning system, vehicles of different shape and color, highly cluttered background, and various illumination and weather conditions all create challenges to such camera-based safety systems and the associated computer vision algorithms. Nevertheless, these sophisticated computer vision algorithms impose a high demand on the low-cost embedded hardware when the end system needs to run at frame rate.

Yan Zhang, Arnab S. Dhua, Stephen J. Kiselewich, and William A. Bauson
Delphi Electronics & Safety, Kokomo, IN, USA

Corresponding author e-mail: yan.zhang@delphi.com

This chapter discusses the challenges of embedded computer vision systems in camera-based automotive safety systems through vehicle detection and classification in collision warning. Section 13.2 provides a literature review on camera-based vehicle detection methods. Section 13.3 presents the edge- and symmetry-based vehicle cueing approach. Section 13.4 describes the feature extraction methods. Section 13.5 presents the vehicle classification approach. Section 13.6 presents the vehicle classification experiments. Section 13.7 summarizes our vehicle detection approach and concludes the chapter.

13.2 Literature Review

Collision warning is an important part of the automotive safety systems. Such warning systems based on active sensors including laser range sensors or radars have shown promising results. However, active sensors have several drawbacks including low data acquisition speed, low resolution, and high costs. On the other hand, vision-based warning systems have attracted more interest in the past decade because of the extensive information contained in images, the fast camera data acquisition, and the affordable cost of high-resolution cameras. Some collision warning systems use both radar and cameras to take advantages of both active and passive sensors.

Collision warning systems in general include forward vehicle collision warning, blind spot detection, lane departure warning, intersection collision warning, and pedestrian detection. This chapter is concerned with vehicle detection and classification. Such systems usually start with the region-of-interest (ROI) detection of possible vehicles in an image. This step is also called vehicle cueing. A subsequent vehicle classification step further classifies the detected objects into vehicles and nonvehicles.

The detection of ROIs is straightforward in radar-vision fused systems [1, 2]. In such systems, the radar cueing information along with the camera calibration parameters can locate the potential vehicles in an image. The ROI detection in vision-only systems is more complicated. Vehicle characteristics such as edges, corners, symmetries, under-vehicle shadows, and rear tail lights have often been employed to determine the ROI. Zielke et al. [3] presented two symmetry detection methods based on image intensity information and local orientation for rear-end vehicle recognition. Matthews et al. [4] proposed the use of principal component analysis and a multilayered perceptron classifier. Sun et al. [5, 6] described wavelets and Gabor features and a support vector machine (SVM) classifier. They demonstrated the superiority of the SVM to a two-layer, feed-forward neural network classifier trained using back propagation. Betke et al. [7] presented a hard real-time vehicle detection and tracking system in which they used a correlation-based image tracker to track recognized vehicles. Most recently, Avidan [8] described a support vector tracking scheme that integrated an SVM classifier into an optical flow–based image tracker. They constructed support vector pyramids in a coarse-to-fine scheme to handle large motions between consecutive video frames. Zhang et al. [9] proposed Legendre moments and Gabor filters along with an SVM classifier for vehicle classification.

13.3 Vehicle Cueing

This section focuses on developing a system that detects regions of interest (ROI's) in an input image that are highly likely to be vehicles. This system is designed to replace radar-based cueing that was found to have some limitations: mainly the imprecisely located regions of interest and the presence of a large number of false positives (incorrect detections). We use the term cueing to indicate that this is a preliminary step in the detection process and does not result in the final detected vehicle regions. The final regions are detected after a full appearance-based classification and this process is described in later sections of this chapter.

In this section we use the scene perspective geometry constraints to greatly reduce the search and computation requirements, to yield a fast and accurate cueing system. We also use edge, symmetry and entropy information, which have been proven in the literature to be some of the most reliable indicators of vehicle presence. This section also proposes a method to determine the symmetry value in an image region. Further, we propose the use of a neural network system to help in selecting regions of interest from the list of symmetrical regions. This neural network system acts as a detector and is designed to use features that can be computed rapidly, much faster than the typical features used in a full-fledged appearance-based classification system. Finally a vehicle bounding box refinement algorithm is presented that lets us position more accurate bounding boxes around the vehicles. A summary of all the steps in the algorithm is shown is Fig. 13.1. We can see that three of the stages actually discard some false regions, thus giving the algorithm a cascade structure. Each of the stages is described in detail in the following subsections.

We know from projective geometry that as a vehicle is further away from us, it appears smaller too. Also as a vehicle is further away along an approximately horizontal road, it appears progressively higher in an image of the road scene. We use these two known geometry constraints to greatly reduce the search requirements when looking for a vehicle in an input image. We look for the widest vehicles regions starting at the bottom of the image. As we go up the image we look for progressively smaller vehicle regions. The knowledge of the expected vehicle width as we move from the bottom of the image towards the top is what lets us significantly reduce our computation requirements.

The first step is to estimate this relationship between the vehicle width and the image row given the specifications of the camera and its mounting position in the host vehicle. We used manually labeled vehicles from video sequences taken with the same camera setup to obtain this relationship. As we can see in Fig. 13.2, this relationship is almost a straight line. Thus, given the image row in which we are currently searching for a vehicle, we know the expected width of the vehicle in the image. Of course, this is only an expected width; the actual width will vary based on

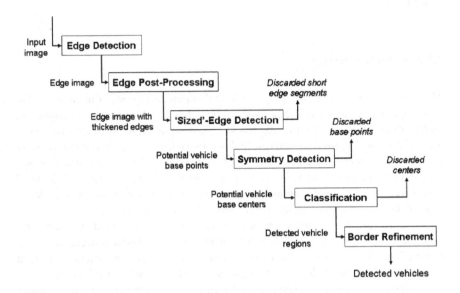

Fig. 13.1 Summary of the algorithm steps. Notice how the system has a cascade structure.

the different classes of vehicles (cars, minivans, trucks, etc.). As a side note, if the camera calibration information (intrinsic and extrinsic parameters) is available, then the relation can be calculated directly without requiring use of manually labeled vehicle regions.

13.3.1 Cueing Step 1: Edge Detection and Processing

Armed with this relationship between the vehicle vertical location and its expected width we proceed to the first step of the algorithm. The first step is standard edge detection on the input image; our requirement was to obtain as many useful edges of the vehicle as possible. The system has been implemented with the Canny edge detector; however it is possible to use any of the standard edge detectors that can detect the important edges of a vehicle, especially the bottom edge. A point to note is that while the Canny edge detector usually provides the best edge map it is also the most computationally expensive. The edge map is then post-processed to get rid of some slant edges and very long horizontal edges that may lead to false detections. The slant edge removal is performed on some subregions of the image using the Hough transform (subregions are shown in Fig. 13.3).

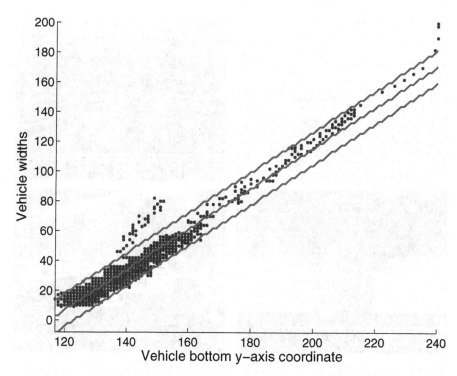

Fig. 13.2 This is a plot of the vehicle width vs. the y-coordinate of the bottom of the vehicle. We can see that the relation between the two variables is almost a straight line. Thus given a particular image row we know the expected width of a vehicle present in the image with that row as the bottom row of the vehicle.

Since we are looking for vehicles on a row by row basis we need to make the method robust to vehicle edges that are not perfectly horizontal. We do this by thickening only the horizontal edges, thus making the approach robust to small deviations from the horizontal. The process of obtaining and processing the edges is shown in Fig. 13.3.

13.3.2 Cueing Step 2: Sized-Edge detection

The next step of the approach makes the first use of the expected width information. We process the thickened edge map obtained in the previous step in a row-by-row manner starting at the bottom row. We convolve each row with a sized-edge filter, tuned to the expected vehicle width at that row. The operation and output of the sized-edge detector is depicted in Fig. 13.4. The sized-edge detector returns true for those portions of the edge row that can have an edge segment of at least the required width centered on them. The sized-edge filter is robust to the presence of missing

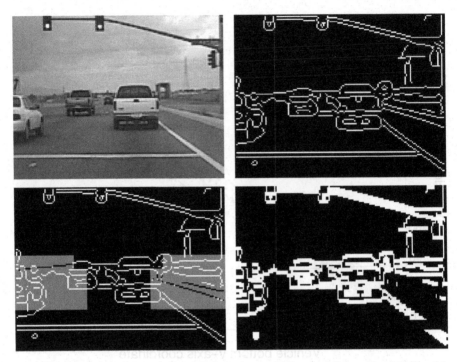

Fig. 13.3 [Left to right, top to bottom] (a) Input image. (b) Result of Canny edge detection. (c) Result after slanted edge removal is performed in the regions colored in gray. The edges marked in black have been deleted. (d) Edge dilation and long edge removal. Note the long horizontal edges image removed from the lower part of the image.

pixels as shown in Fig 13.4. The sized-edge filter kernel is simply a constant edge segment of the required width, normalized to sum to 1. We can see the output of the sized-edge detector on the whole image in Fig. 13.5. The output of the sized-edge detector is all those locations that have the potential to be the center pixel of a vehicle based on the location of the remaining edge pixels on that row.

13.3.3 Cueing Step 3: Symmetry Detection

The next step of the algorithm is to evaluate which of the points in the center locations satisfy the symmetry criterion. This processing is also performed using the expected width and starting at the bottom row of the image and going up. Earlier work in the literature has also used symmetry, but the symmetry has been evaluated at various widths and at all locations, which is very time consuming. We process the symmetry computation only at the expected width, reducing computation requirements. The sets of connected points returned by the sized-edge detector and the expected width are passed to the novel symmetry detector. The symmetry detector

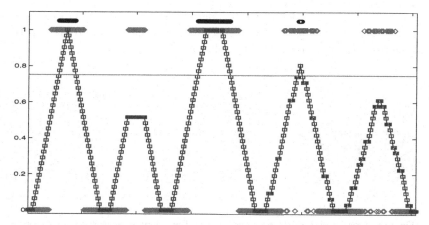

Fig. 13.4 This figure shows the result of applying the sized-edge detector to an example edge image row. The points (marked with a diamond symbol) at a y-axis value of 1 represent edge pixels, and the points (marked with a diamond) at a y-axis value of 0 represent absence of edge pixels. The points (marked with a square) are the raw output of the sized-edge filter. The horizontal line is the tolerance threshold at 75%. The points (marked with a circle) at the top of the figure represent the output of the sized-edge detector. Centered at each of these output points an edge segment of width within the required tolerance was found. The method is robust to presence of missing pixels as shown in the last two edge segments. The last segment had far too many missing pixels, thus bringing its output below threshold.

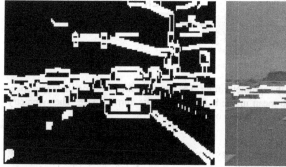

Fig. 13.5 On the left is the post-processed edge image, and on the right we can see the output of the sized-edge detector overlaid on the input image. All the points that have edge segments of the expected width centered around them are marked in white.

is implemented as a 2-dimensional filter. The symmetry detector does not work directly on the input image, but on a high pass filtered version of the input image. For efficiency considerations, this high pass filtered image is actually created by subtracting a smoothed version of the input image form the input image itself as shown in Fig. 13.6. This method was chosen because a smoothed version of the image is already created during the edge detection. The symmetry filter kernel is not a constant kernel but varies from region to region. The kernel is actually the mirror image of the image region under the filter window. The filtering process is shown in Fig. 13.7. The output of the symmetry filter is normalized so that a perfectly symmetrical region has a symmetry value of 1.0.

IMAGE   -   Smooth (IMAGE)   =   Zero-Mean IMAGE

Fig. 13.6 Creation of the high-pass filtered image. The rightmost image also has the property that every subregion within that image has a mean pixel value that tends to 0.

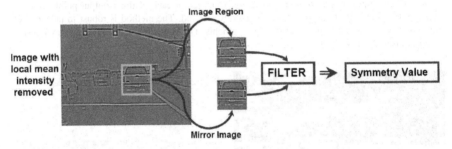

Fig. 13.7 The implementation of the symmetry filter. The specified image region (having a specified width) cropped from the zero-mean image is filtered with its mirror image. The symmetry values are normalized to have a maximum value of 1.

An example of the output from the symmetry detector is shown in Fig. 13.8. Nonmaximal suppression of the output of the symmetry detector yields the regions of significant symmetry. The output of the symmetry detector applied on every row of the edge image is shown in Fig. 13.9. The dark pixels within the white segments show the regions where significant symmetry is present. Each of these dark pixels represents a potential vehicle region that needs to be classified. Each region to be classified is picked by marking a rectangular region with a dark pixel as the center of the base of the rectangular region. The width of the rectangular region is dictated by the expected width at that image row. The height is obtained from the width by using a default aspect ratio. The default aspect ratio is chosen to be that of a standard car, so that it represents a region that would be common to most categories of vehicles, had they been present at that location.

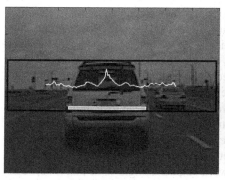
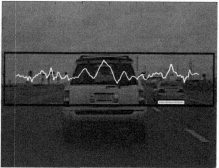

Fig. 13.8 The black rectangle indicates the region under consideration. The light bar (along the lower edge of the rectangle) indicates the width at which the symmetry is being evaluated. The light-colored plot is the output of the symmetry detector. In the image on the left, the symmetry is being evaluated at a large width and only one region has a symmetry at that width, as is also reflected in the output of the symmetry detector. In the image on the right there are multiple symmetries at the smaller width.

Fig. 13.9 [Left image] Output of the sized-edge detector. [Right image] Output of the symmetry detector is overlaid as dark points over the white line segments. The symmetry detector is evaluated using the expected width at each of the horizontal sized-edge (white point) segments. The dark points are obtained after nonmaximal suppression of the output of the symmetry detector.

13.3.4 Cueing Step 4: Classification

The regions centered on the dark pixels obtained in the previous step (see Fig. 13.9) are now classified into valid/invalid regions of interest based on simple summarizing features. The reasons for performing a simple classification are three-fold: (1) There are many regions and full-fledged appearance based classification would be very time consuming. (2) Full-fledged classification requires precise alignment of the input region with the training regions, whereas the summarizing features that we use do not require a precise alignment. This also saves us time because we are not required to perform a local search before the classification. (3) Performing a less-detailed classification at this stage, mainly to remove the false positives, makes the system act as a cascade of classifiers. At this step there are more regions to classify; we would like to perform a fast classification to reduce the number of regions that are sent to the next stage of the classification.

As mentioned before, we use features for classification that do not require that the regions be aligned. The features used for classification are the symmetry of the region, the entropy of the region, the edge density of the region, and various combinations of the ratio of horizontal, vertical edges to the total number of edge pixels. A total of 10 feature values are used for the classification and the neural network used is a feed-forward neural network with two hidden layers of size 17 and 5 neurons, respectively. The neural network size parameters were selected using five-fold cross-validation. The neural network outputs a single value that is between 0 and 1 inclusive. This continuous value between 0 and 1 is then separated into three different output classes: (1) strong ROI, (2) weak ROI, (3) not an ROI. The only difference between the strong and weak region of interest classes is that for a weak ROI, processing of image regions above the detected ROI is continued; while for a strong ROI class further processing is discontinued.

13.3.5 Cueing Step 5: Vehicle Border Refinement

As mentioned before, the region chosen for the classification is based on the expected width and a default aspect ratio; therefore it may not exactly fit the actual vehicle present in the region. This does not affect the classification because of the type of the features used for the classification. But before this region of interest is sent to the next stage of classification (outside of the cueing system) we need to make sure that the border of the region is as accurate as possible. Appearance-based classifiers used in the later stages of the system would be sensitive to the exact border region.

The border refinement is performed on all the regions classified as strong or weak ROIs. Each such region is evaluated with slight changes in widths, vertical locations and using different aspect ratios (from a predefined set of aspect ratios). The values of symmetry and entropy of the candidate regions are used to discriminate between the regions; the best vehicle region has the highest symmetry and lowest entropy. The default regions that were classified and the final placement of the borders for an input image frame are shown in Fig. 13.10.

13.3.6 Timing Issues

In transferring an algorithm to an embedded platform, one of the main issues is the speed of execution on the embedded platform. As mentioned earlier in this section, we use projective geometry constraints to reduce our search requirements during the implementation of the sized-edge and symmetry detectors. Another good way to

Fig. 13.10 [Left image] Shows examples of the default vehicle regions that are used for classification. The default vehicle regions are obtained by placing a box centrally over each of the dark points in Fig. 13.9. The boxes placed use the expected width at that row as their width and get their height using a default aspect ratio (that of a car). [Right image] Shows the final bounding boxes after refinement. Note the improvement in accuracy of the bounding boxes.

speed up the execution is to run the algorithm on a subsampled version of the input image. Since the cueing algorithm uses features that are reasonably independent of the size of the input image it is a good candidate for running at different scales, without requiring modification. Table 13.1 gives a summary of the time taken for the different steps of the cueing algorithm when run at different resolutions. These runs were performed on a PC running at 2.4 GHz. The reported times are the total times taken by the various parts of the cueing algorithm when processing a full frame. These values were obtained by averaging over multiple frames.

Table 13.1 Time taken for the various cueing steps. Average times for the various steps over a full frame.

Resolution	320×240	160×120
Step	**Time**	**Time**
Edge detection	6 ms	1 ms
Edge post-processing	3 ms	<1 ms
Slant edge removal	5 ms	2 ms
Sized-edge detection	11 ms	1 ms
Symmetry detection	9 ms	<1 ms
Features and classification	11 ms	3 ms

13.4 Feature Extraction

A second-stage classifier is necessary to further remove the false positives detected by the previous cueing. Image features facilitate classification and it is important that the features are both representative and discriminative. We evaluate five types of features that represent both structural and textural information of objects including over-complete Haar wavelets, edge-based density and symmetry features, Legendre moments, edge orientation histograms, and Gabor features.

13.4.1 Over-Complete Haar Wavelets

The over-complete Haar wavelets transform defines a square window as a mask in which pixels have values of -1 and $+1$. The size of the window and the sign of the pixels correspond to the scale and the orientation of the wavelet transform, respectively. The over-complete wavelet transform shifts the window across the target image and convolves with the underlying image to obtain a set of dense wavelet features. The shift distance is often set to be a fraction of the window size in order to achieve an over-complete (dense) image representation. We have found that a shift distance equal to one-fourth or half of the window size yielded the best results while maintaining a moderate dimension of wavelet features. As pointed out in [10], the over-complete Haar wavelets are a denser representation than the standard Haar wavelets, and are more appropriate for object classification tasks. These over-complete Haar wavelets are essentially very similar to the rectangular features described in [22] except that the rectangular features were calculated also from three-rectangle regions and therefore have a much higher dimension.

For our application involving 40×40 images of vehicles and nonvehicles, we have used the over-complete Haar wavelets templates at four scales–32×32, 16×16, 8×8, and 4×4, and in three orientations—horizontal, vertical, and diagonal. For scales 32×32 and 16×16, we have shifted the window by 8 and 4 pixels, respectively, i.e., $1/4$ of the width/length of the window. For scales 8×8 and the 4×4 scale, we have shifted the window by 4 and 2 pixels, respectively, i.e., one-half of the width/length of the window. As a result, we have obtained a total of 2109 over-complete Haar wavelet features for a 40×40 image.

Figs. 13.11 and 13.12 depict the grayscale coded wavelet maps in three orientations and three resolutions for a vehicle and a nonvehicle. The dark to bright pixels correspond to small to large wavelet values. The first row in these figures is at resolution 16×16, the second row for 8×8, and the third row at 4×4. The first column is vertical wavelet map, the second is horizontal wavelet map, and the third is diagonal wavelet map. While the wavelet map of the vehicle shown in Fig. 13.11 clearly captures the horizontal edges and the contour of the vehicle, the wavelet map of the nonvehicle shown in Fig. 13.12 lacks this characteristic. These visualized wavelet maps indicate that the over-complete Haar wavelets are capable of representing the shape of vehicles in multiple resolutions.

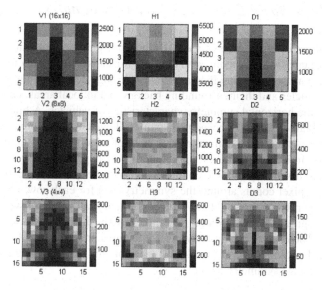

Fig. 13.11 Grayscale coded wavelets maps for a vehicle.

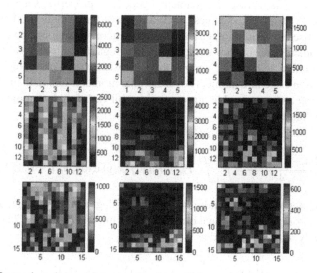

Fig. 13.12 Grayscale coded wavelets maps for a nonvehicle.

13.4.2 Edge-Based Density and Symmetry Features

The edge-based density and symmetry features are simple to compute, yet are very effective when being used along with the Haar wavelets as shown in our earlier work on occupant and vehicle classification [9]. While edge density captures the contrast between vehicles and their surrounding background in local areas, edge symmetry represents the horizontal symmetry characteristics of vehicles. A binary edge map has been obtained from a Sobel edge operator followed by an adaptive thresholding. Edge density is therefore defined as the count of edge pixels in subregions of the edge map. More details can be found in our earlier paper [11]. For edge symmetry features, we assume the middle column as the symmetry axis and extract the ratio of the edge pixel counts around the symmetry axis for each row. Only the ratios that are larger than a threshold are kept as symmetry ratios. These symmetry ratios are further grouped and summed into three evenly divided regions column- and row-wise. The edge density and symmetry features are calculated from horizontal and vertical edge maps, respectively. We therefore have obtained a total of 24 edge density and edge symmetry features.

13.4.3 Legendre Moments

Geometric moments represent fundamental geometric properties such as area, centroid, moments of inertia, skewness, and kurtosis of a distribution. Moments have been widely used in various image analysis and pattern recognition applications. Orthogonal moments are superior to the others with regard to information redundancy and representation ability [12]. Among the most widely used orthogonal moments, we have chosen Legendre moments over Zernike moments due to their lower computational cost and comparable representation ability. Legendre moments of order $(m+n)$ are defined as [12]

$$\lambda_{mn} = \frac{(2m+1)(2n+1)}{4} \int_{-1}^{1} \int_{-1}^{1} P_m(x)P_n(y)f(x,y)\,dxdy, \ m,n = 0,1,2,\ldots \quad (13.1)$$

where $P_m(x)$ denotes the Legendre polynomial of degree m. The Legendre polynomials form a complete orthogonal basis set on the interval of $[-1,1]$. The mth-order Legendre polynomial is defined as

$$P_m(x) = \frac{1}{2^m m!} \frac{d^m}{dx^m} (x^2 - 1)^m, \ x \in [-1,1] \quad (13.2)$$

and can be computed from lower-order polynomials recursively as

$$P_m(x) = \frac{(2m-1)xP_{m-1}(x) - (m-1)P_{m-2}(x)}{m} \quad (13.3)$$

In the image coordinate system where $i, j \in [0, N-1]$, Legendre moments have the following discrete approximation as

$$\lambda_{mn} = \frac{(2m+1)(2n+1)}{N^2} \sum_{i=0}^{N-1} \sum_{j=0}^{N-1} P_m\left(\frac{2i-N+1}{N-1}\right) \times P_n\left(\frac{2j-N+1}{N-1}\right) f(i,j) \quad (13.4)$$

The selection of an appropriate order of the moments has been a nontrivial and application-dependent task. Higher-order moments represent the distribution more accurately at a higher computational cost. On the other hand, the higher-order moments are more susceptible to noises and outliers than their lower-order companions. The survey in [12] has indicated that the literature has often chosen the appropriate moments order heuristically. In this work, we have chosen up to the 6th-order Legendre moments empirically and obtained a set of 140 moments features from both the entire image and its four quadrants.

13.4.4 Edge Orientation Histogram

Edge orientation histogram (EOH) was first proposed by Freeman et al. [14] for hand gesture recognition. EOH has received considerable attention since Lowe [15] successfully used it to encode local salient points for general image matching and object recognition. More recently, EOH has been applied to face detection [13] and human detection [16] and has demonstrated superior performance. EOH is an attractive feature because of its invariance to local geometric and photometric transformations. We adapted the definition of R-HOG (rectangular histogram of gradients) in [16] and adjusted the parameters for 40×40 images in our application. Specifically, each cell contains 8×8 pixels and each block contains 2×2 cells. The EOH features are extracted from overlapping blocks that shift by eight pixels in x and y directions. We have chosen six histogram bins empirically for the $0° - 360°$ orientation range. Therefore, we have obtained a total of 384 EOH features for each image. Fig. 13.13 depicts the EOH features extracted from the gradient orientation of each pixel.

13.4.5 Gabor Filter

Gabor filters have been successfully used in texture analysis and image classification [17, 18]. A 2D Gabor filter acts as a local band-pass filter with certain optimal joint localization properties in both the spatial and the spatial frequency domain [19]. Typically, an image is filtered with a set of Gabor filters in several preferred orientations and spatial frequencies that appropriately cover the spatial frequency domain of the image. The statistical characteristics are then extracted from the Gabor filtered image set for texture analysis, segmentation, and classification. A 2D Gabor

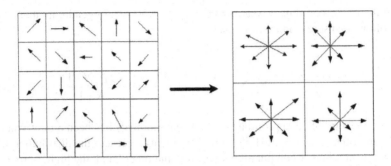

Fig. 13.13 The edge orientation histogram extracted from cells.

filter function is defined as a Gaussian function modulated by an oriented complex sinusoidal signal. In particular, a 2D Gabor filter $g(x,y)$ and its Fourier transform $G(u,v)$ are defined as

$$g(x,y) = \frac{1}{2\pi\sigma_x\sigma_y} \exp\left[-\frac{1}{2}\left(\frac{x'^2}{\sigma_x^2} + \frac{y'^2}{\sigma_y^2}\right)\right] \exp\left[j2\pi Wx'\right] \quad \text{and} \qquad (13.5)$$

$$G(u,v) = \exp\left[-\frac{1}{2}\left(\frac{(u-W)^2}{\sigma_u^2} + \frac{v^2}{\sigma_v^2}\right)\right], \qquad (13.6)$$

where W is the center frequency, $\sigma_u = \frac{1}{2\pi\sigma_x}$, $\sigma_v = \frac{1}{2\pi\sigma_y}$ denote scales in the frequency domain, and

$$x' = x\cos\theta + y\sin\theta, \quad y' = -x\sin\theta + y\cos\theta, \qquad (13.7)$$

where $\theta = n\pi/N$ represents the filter orientation. Parameter N is the total number of the orientations, and $n = 0, 1, \ldots, N-1$.

Fig. 13.14 shows a set of single-scale and four-direction Gabor filters in the spatial domain encoded in 40×40 grayscale images. The four orientations are $0°, 45°, 90°$, and $135°$. The scale parameters σ_x and σ_y are three pixels. The center frequency W is 0.18.

Fig. 13.15 shows Gabor filtered images for a vehicle and a nonvehicle. The orientation of the filter is zero degrees. The other parameters of the filter are the same as those used in Fig. 13.14. Fig. 13.15(b) and Fig. 13.15(d) demonstrate that the $0°$-Gabor filter has captured the characteristics that vehicles have more horizontal features than nonvehicles. These examples illustrate that the Gabor feature is capable of distinguishing vehicles from nonvehicles.

We have used a Gabor filter design strategy similar to [17] to reduce the redundant information in the filtered images. In particular, we have chosen four orientations as $0°, 45°, 90°, 135°$, two scales as 3×3 and 6×6 pixels, and the center frequency $W = 0.18$ and $W = 0.09$ for the two scales, respectively. Our Gabor filter

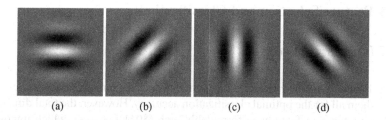

(a) (b) (c) (d)

Fig. 13.14 Examples of Gabor filters in the spatial domain with four orientations of $\theta = 0°, 45°, 90°$, and $135°$. The scale parameters $\sigma_x = \sigma_y = 3$ pixels, and the center frequency $W = 0.18$. (a) $\theta = 0°$, (b) $\theta = 45°$, (c) $\theta = 90°$, and (d) $\theta = 135°$.

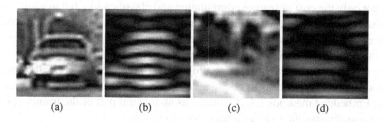

(a) (b) (c) (d)

Fig. 13.15 Examples of Gabor-filtered vehicle and nonvehicle images. The scale parameters $\sigma_x = \sigma_y = 3$ pixels, and the center frequency $W = 0.18$. The orientation is $\theta = 0°$. (a) A vehicle image, (b) Gabor filtered (a), (c) a nonvehicle image, and (d) Gabor filtered (c).

set therefore consists of eight filters. We partition each Gabor filtered 40×40 image into 16 overlapping 16×16 subregions for redundant local texture characteristics. We then compute three types of texture features including mean (μ), standard deviation (σ), and skewness (k) from each filtered subregion. The Gabor feature set therefore consists of a total of $8 \times 16 \times 3 = 384$ features as

$$f = \{\mu_{11}\sigma_{11}k_{11}, \mu_{12}\sigma_{12}k_{12}, \ldots, \mu_{8,16}\sigma_{8,16}k_{8,16}\}, \tag{13.8}$$

where μ_{mn}, σ_{mn}, and k_{mn} represent the mean, standard deviation, and skewness, respectively for the mth Gabor filter and the nth subregion.

13.5 Feature Selection and Classification

13.5.1 Feature Selection

As each type of feature represents different image characteristics, it seems desirable to use them all for the optimal classification accuracy. However, the total dimension of the five types of features is formidably high (3041 features), which imposes a high computation cost to both feature computation and classification. This is widely known as the "curse of dimensionality." Feature selection is defined as selecting a subset of features from the original set of candidate features that are in some sense the most important in determining an accurate classification. This procedure can reduce not only the cost of feature computation and classification, but in some cases it can also result in better classification accuracy due to finite sample size effects [20]. Feature selection approaches usually fall into three categories: wrappers, filters, and embedded methods [21]. Wrappers utilize a specific learning machine as a black box to score subsets of variables according to their predictive power. Filter methods select subsets of variables as a pre-processing step, independently of the chosen predictor. Embedded methods select features as an integral part of the training process and are usually specific to a particular type of classifier.

We have used two embedded methods in our research that we have found to be very effective. The first method involves the use of the See5 system [23], which is designed to construct decision trees. Identifying those features that appear near the top of the tree provides one way to select important features for a specific application. The second method is to use a variant of the AdaBoost algorithm proposed by Viola and Jones [22]. This algorithm constructs a sequence of very simple decision trees, each of which involves a single feature and a single threshold value. Each of the simple decision trees yields the lowest possible classification error for a given set of example image data. During the training process, weights associated with each training pattern are adjusted in order to increase or decrease the emphasis placed on that pattern, and the final decision is calculated by summing the outputs of the weak classifiers and comparing the value obtained to a threshold. Identifying the feature used at each step of the algorithm provides another means for selecting the most important features. Both See5 feature selection and AdaBoost feature selection produce reasonable results. Generally, however, we prefer the AdaBoost feature selection method because a smaller number of AdaBoost-selected features appears to yield the same classifier performance as a larger number of See5-selected features.

13.5.2 Vehicle Classification Using Support Vector Machines

Support vector machines (SVMs) map the training data in the input space nonlinearly into a higher-dimensional feature space via function Φ, and construct a separating hyperplane with the maximum margin there [24]. The kernel function K integrates the mapping and the computation of the hyperplane into one step, and avoids explicitly deriving the mapping function Φ, which in many cases is a nontrivial task. Fig. 13.16 illustrates the essential SVM principle, which turns a complicated nonlinear decision boundary into a simpler linear hyperplane.

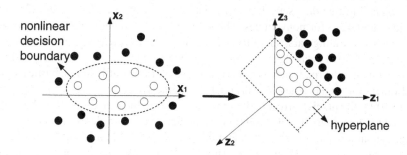

Fig. 13.16 A SVM classification example. A monomial function maps the samples in the input 2D space (x_1, x_2) to the 3D feature space (z_1, z_2, z_3) via $(x_1^2, \sqrt{2}x_1x_2, x_2^2)$. The nonlinear decision boundary in the input space corresponds to the linear hyperplane in the mapped feature space.

For a set of l samples $(x_i, y_i), i = 1, 2, \ldots, l, y_i \in \{-1, +1\}$ from two classes, the hyperplane decision function is defined as

$$f(x) = \text{sgn} \left(\sum_{i=1}^{l} y_i \alpha_i \cdot K(x, x_i) + b \right), \qquad (13.9)$$

where $K(x, x_i)$ is the kernel function. The parameters α_i and b are obtained by solving the dual quadric optimization problem [24] in seeking the hyperplane with the maximum margin. A pattern x_i corresponding to the nonzero α_i is a support vector for the hyperplane. The most widely used kernel functions include Gaussian RBF (radial basis function), polynomial, and sigmoidal function. Although different kernels lead to different learning machines, they tend to yield similar classification accuracy and largely overlapping support vectors. We have chosen the Gaussian RBF kernel due to its simple parameter selection and high performance reported in the literature. The Gaussian RBF kernel function is defined as

$$K(x, x_i) = \exp \left(-\gamma \|x - x_i\|^2 \right), \quad \gamma > 0. \qquad (13.10)$$

13.6 Experiments

Forward collision warning is mainly concerned with the detection of rear and
slightly skewed views of vehicles. We have collected videos for such vehicles using
a monochrome camera during a three-month period to include various weather and
lighting conditions including fog, rain, overcast, and strong sunshine. We have manually cropped individual vehicle and nonvehicle images from the videos to form the
training and testing data sets. The entire data set consists of 6482 images, 2269 for
vehicles and 4213 for nonvehicles. The vehicle data set includes three major types
of vehicles including cars, small trucks and SUVs, and large trucks in various colors and up to 70 m away from the camera. The nonvehicle data set contains various
objects on/near the road such as road signs, road barriers, traffic lights, bushes, trees
and vegetation, and bridges. The original size of the images varies from 10×10 pixels to 200×200 pixels corresponding to a 2 m-wide vehicle at 15 to 70 m. We have
resized the images to 40×40 pixels corresponding to a 2 m-wide vehicle 50 m away
from the camera and linearly stretched the image contrast to account for illumination changes. Figs. 13.17 and 13.18 show such example images for vehicles and
nonvehicles, respectively.

Fig. 13.17 Examples of vehicle images used in the experiments.

The five types of features form a total of 3041 features for each 40×40 image
in the training set. Our feature selection step selected 86 most distinguishable features and removed the redundancy in the feature set. Fig. 13.19 shows the selected

Fig. 13.18 Examples of nonvehicle images used in the experiments.

over-complete Haar wavelet features in a vehicle image in our experiments. A five-fold cross-validation classification using SVM yielded a classification accuracy of 98.49%.

Fig. 13.19 Selected features in a vehicle image.

Table 13.2 shows the computation time of each type of features for a 40×40 image on a 1.8GHz PC. The entire collision warning system consisting of cueing and classification runs at 15 fps on the 1.8 GHz PC. When being converted to an embedded board, such complex algorithms impose a high demand to both speed and memory requirements of the embedded board. Several major companies in the processor field have been actively working on developing designated high-speed processors for computer vision techniques. Considering the 2-dimensional nature of the images and the convolution operations involved in most computer vision algorithms, a parallel processor may be able to increase the computation speed significantly.

Table 13.2 Computation time of feature extraction (ms)

Feature	Edge	L Moments	Wavelets	EOH	Gabor
Time	0.23	0.82	1.13	0.58	4.24

13.7 Conclusion

This chapter described a camera-based vehicle detection approach for forward collision warning in automotive safety. The approach consists of vehicle cueing, feature extraction, and classification. Many other object detection tasks such as pedestrian detection in pre-crash sensing share the similar approach. On one hand, sophisticated computer vision algorithms are essential to address a large variety of complex situations on the road and surrounding areas. Nevertheless, such sophisticated computer vision algorithms impose a high demand in both speed and memory requirements on the ordinary low-cost embedded hardware when the end system needs to run at frame rate. Using constraints such as the projective geometry constraints used in this chapter; or running the algorithm (or parts of the algorithm) at lower resolutions, one can achieve adequate frame rates even on embedded hardware. With the aid of designated special-purpose processors, the possibility of running such camera-based automotive safety systems at video-frame rates is very promising.

References

1. A. Gern, U. Franke, P. Levi: Robust vehicle tracking fusing radar and vision. *Proc. Int'l Conf. Multisensor Fusion and Integration for Intelligent Systems,* 323–328 (2001).
2. B. Steus and C. Laurgeau and L. Salesse and D. Wautier: Fade: a vehicle detection and tracking system featuring monocular color vision and radar fusion. *Proc. IEEE Intell. Veh. Symposium,* 632–639 (2002).
3. T. Zielke, M. Brauckmann, W. V. Seelen: Intensity and edge-based symmetry detection with an application to car-following. *CVGIP: Image Understanding,* 58(2), 177–190 (1993).
4. N.D. Matthews, P.E. An, D. Charnley, C. J. Harris: Vehicle detection and recognition in greyscale imagery. *Control Engineering Practice,* 4, 474–479 (1996).
5. Z. Sun, G. Bebis, R. Miller: On-road vehicle detection using Gabor filters and support vector machines. *Proc. Int'l Conf. on Digital Signal Processing,* 2, 1019–1022 (2002).
6. Z. Sun, G. Bebis, R. Miller: Improving the performance of on-road vehicle detection by combining Gabor and wavelet features. *Proc. IEEE Int'l Conf. Intelligent Transportation Systems,* 130–135 (2002).
7. M. Betke, E. Haritaglu, L. Davis: Multiple vehicle detection and tracking in hard real time. *Proc. IEEE Intell. Veh. Symposium,* 2, 351–356 (2006).

8. S. Avidan: Support vector tracking. *IEEE Trans. Pattern Anal. Machine Intell.*, 26(8), 1064–1072 (2004).

9. Y. Zhang, S. J. Kiselewich, W. A. Bauson: Legendre and Gabor moments for vehicle recognition in forward collision warning. *Proc. IEEE Int'l Conf. Intelligent Transportation Systems*, 1185–1190 (2006).

10. M. Oren, C. Papageorgiou, P. Sinha, E. Osuna, T. Poggio: Pedestrian detection using wavelet templates. *Proc. IEEE Int'l Conf. Computer Vision and Pattern Recognition*, 193–199 (1997).

11. Y. Zhang, S. J. Kiselewich, W. A. Bauson: A monocular vision-based occupant classification approach for smart airbag deployment. *Proc. IEEE Intell. Veh. Symposium*, 632–637 (2005).

12. C. Teh, R. T. Chin: On image analysis by the methods of moments. *IEEE Trans. Pattern Anal. Machine Intell.*, 10(4), 496–513 (1988).

13. K. Levi, Y. Weiss: Learning object detection from a small number of examples: the importance of good features. *Proc. IEEE Int'l Conf. Computer Vision and Pattern Recognition*, 2, 53–60 (2004).

14. W. T. Freeman, M. Roth: Orientation histograms for hand gesture recognition. *Proc. IEEE Int'l Workshop Automatic Face and Gesture Recognition*, 296–301 (1995).

15. D. G. Lowe: Distinctive image features from scale-invariant keypoints. *Int'l Journal of Computer Vision*, 60(2), 91–110 (2004).

16. N. Dalal, B. Triggs: Histograms of oriented gradients for human detection. *Proc. IEEE Int'l Conf. Computer Vision and Pattern Recognition*, 1, 886–893 (2005).

17. B. S. Manjunath, W. Y. Ma: Texture features for browsing and retrieval of image data. *IEEE Trans. Pattern Anal. Machine Intell.*, 18(8), 837–842 (1996).

18. T. Randen, J. H. Husoy: Filtering for texture classification: a comparative study. *IEEE Trans. Pattern Anal. Machine Intell.*, 21(4), 291–310 (1999).

19. A. C. Bovik, M. Clark, W. Geisler: Multichannel texture analysis using localized spatial filters. *IEEE Trans. Pattern Anal. Machine Intell.*, 12(1), 55–73 (1990).

20. A. Jain, D. Zongker: Feature selection: evaluation, application, and small sample performance. *IEEE Trans. Pattern Anal. Machine Intell.*, 19(2), 153–158 (1997).

21. I. Guyon, A. Elisseeff: An introduction to variable and feature selection. *Journal of Machine Learning*, 1157–1182 (2003).

22. P. Viola, M. J. Jones: Robust real-time face detection. *Int'l Journal of Computer Vision*, 57(2), 137–154 (2004).

23. R. Quinlan: See5: An Informal Tutorial. http://www.rulequest.com/see5-win.html. (2007).

24. K. Muller, S. Mika, G. Ratsch, K. Tsuda, B. Schólkopf: An introduction to kernel-based learning algorithms. *IEEE Trans. Neural Netork.* 12(2), 181–202 (2001).

25. Robert E. Schapire: The boosting approach to machine learning: an overview. *MSRI Workshop on Nonlinear Estimation and Classification*, (2002).

Index

Printed in the United States
by Baker & Taylor Publisher Services